I0887625

# The Burden of History

*Elizabeth Furniss*

# The Burden of History: Colonialism and the Frontier Myth in a Rural Canadian Community

**UBC**Press / Vancouver

© UBC Press 1999

All rights reserved. No part of this publication may be reproduced, stored in a retrieval system, or transmitted, in any form or by any means, without prior written permission of the publisher, or, in Canada, in the case of photocopying or other reprographic copying, a licence from CANCOPY (Canadian Copyright Licensing Agency), 900 – 6 Adelaide Street East, Toronto, ON M5C 1H6.

Printed in Canada on acid-free paper ∞

ISBN 0-7748-0710-5

---

**Canadian Cataloguing in Publication Data**

Furniss, Elizabeth, 1959-
The burden of history

Includes bibliographical references and index.
ISBN 0-7748-0710-5

1. Williams Lake (B.C.) – Colonial influence. Indians, Treatment of – British Columbia – Williams Lake. 3. Indians of North America – Cultural assimilation – British Columbia – Williams Lake. 4. Williams Lake (B.C.) – Race relations. 5. British Columbia – Colonization. I. Title.

E78.B9F87 1999 971.1'7500497 C99-910160-9

---

This book has been published with a grant from the Social Sciences Federation of Canada, using funds provided by the Social Sciences and Humanities Research Council of Canada.

UBC Press gratefully acknowledges the ongoing support to its publishing program from the Canada Council for the Arts, the British Columbia Arts Council, and the Department of Canadian Heritage of the Government of Canada.

UBC Press
University of British Columbia
6344 Memorial Road
Vancouver, BC V6T 1Z2
(604) 822-5959
Fax: 1-800-668-0821
E-mail: orders@ubcpress.ubc.ca
www.ubcpress.ubc.ca

# Contents

# Preface

This book explores questions that have intrigued me as a result of living in the central interior of British Columbia and working with Secwepemc and Carrier communities over a number of years. I first became interested in Cariboo ethnography and the politics of history in 1985, when, as a graduate student in anthropology, I took a summer job with the Nazko First Nation. Leaders of the Nazko First Nation were in the midst of heated debates with government and nonprofit groups over the development of an ancient Aboriginal trade route recently renamed the Alexander Mackenzie Heritage Trail after the early fur-trade explorer. Band leaders thought that the project not only erased the Carrier history of the trail but also celebrated the colonization of Canada, the taking of Aboriginal lands and resources, and the Carrier people's ultimate subordination to the Canadian state. Over the summer, I carried out research into the history and contemporary significance of the trail to Carrier people and produced a video on the trail's Aboriginal heritage to be shown to local high school audiences. Through the events of that summer, and through the negative reaction that the government funding agency had to the resulting video, I became aware of the strong commitment that many Euro-Canadians have to frontier histories and figures such as Mackenzie and of the intense conflicts that arise when Aboriginal and Euro-Canadian histories intersect.

Since then I have continued to work with Secwepemc and Carrier communities in the Cariboo-Chilcotin on a variety of ethnographic and applied research projects. In the fall of 1985, I carried out ethnographic research for my master's degree in the Secwepemc reserve village of Alkali Lake, tracing the history of the band's sobriety movement, through which community members were working toward a collective recovery from alcohol abuse and related social problems. In 1986, I returned to Williams Lake to take up work with the Cariboo Tribal Council as a land claims coordinator. Over the next four years, I worked with Secwepemc and Carrier First Nations conducting research to support Aboriginal title and specific land claims, training band members in research techniques, and coordinating educational workshops on developments in Aboriginal rights.

The late 1980s was a time of growing politicization as First Nations leaders in the Cariboo-Chilcotin were pressing their demands for public recognition of Aboriginal title, hunting and fishing rights, and self-government. In this period, past students of St. Joseph's Mission, the Roman Catholic residential school near Williams Lake, began to disclose instances of sexual abuse while at the school; these disclosures eventually led to criminal charges against three past employees. Many other past students began openly discussing the devastating consequences of the residential school experience on their own lives and its long-term impact on their families and communities. For a number of area First Nations leaders, the residential school issue served as a focal point for a much broader critical examination of the problems that persist in Aboriginal peoples' relationships with the Canadian state and the institutions, policies, and bodies of legislation that continue to unjustly restrict their lives. In short, this was a period in which virtually all dimensions of Aboriginal relationships with Canadian society were being critically reexamined. Inevitably, conversations would also turn to relations with whites in Williams Lake. As people began to speak openly to me about local, everyday forms of domination, I became interested in tracing more fully what it meant for people to be Indian in the context of a rural, right-wing, Euro-Canadian town.

During this time, I was also a resident of Williams Lake. Like many other young professionals who move to the city, I became involved in a number of local events and activities. I was an active member of the Williams Lake Museum and Historical Society and the local New Democratic Party constituency, taught an evening anthropology course at the local college, and took various night courses in the arts. Through these activities, I became absorbed into various social networks and familiarized with aspects of local, small-town culture. This was not an entirely new experience for me, as I grew up in a middle-class Euro-Canadian home in a small town on central Vancouver Island. I was raised with the same Canadian cultural fare of frontier history and Indian lore as that found in Williams Lake and many rural settings in Canada, and I was familiar with the friendly informality that comes with living in, and being part of, a small community. In my hometown, though, Aboriginal people were a small minority, and, in the 1960s and 1970s, largely invisible in the town's public culture. In contrast, Aboriginal people make up a much more significant proportion of the Cariboo-Chilcotin population. What was also new were the pronounced divisions between the Aboriginal and non-Aboriginal worlds. Friends and acquaintances held various views on Aboriginal people and issues, but I was struck by the negative attitudes toward Indians that prevailed in the city and by the casual ease with which these attitudes were expressed in private and public settings. The divisions between the two populations were also apparent in more subtle ways in the discomfort and silence that often arose when I spoke with Euro-Canadian friends of my work in reserve communities and the awkwardness that was created when, on a couple of occasions, I invited both Aboriginal and Euro-Canadian friends to dinner gatherings.

My association with area Aboriginal communities as well as my involvement in the Euro-Canadian community of Williams Lake have influenced not only the kinds of questions that I have asked but also my analytical approach and methodology. I consider the Williams Lake area as much of a home as anywhere else, having spent almost seven of the last thirteen years living in the region and having developed strong friendships with people in the area and an equally strong appreciation for the beauty of the natural landscape. I have also been influenced by exposure to a particular style of political action among a number of First Nations leaders that emphasizes reconciliation rather than violent confrontation with Euro-Canadian society. These factors, I think, have led me to employ an analytical strategy that envisions Aboriginal and non-Aboriginal people not as isolated cultural enclaves but as members of the same broader community, however ill-functioning; that sees Aboriginal and non-Aboriginal people as being encompassed by the same dominant cultural system; and that requires the study of Aboriginal/non-Aboriginal relations to proceed through ethnographic research with both groups.

This is not a standard approach. Most social scientists studying rural Aboriginal/non-Aboriginal relations in Canada have focused their ethnographic research on either the Aboriginal or the white population. Elias, in his study of Churchill, Manitoba, found that positioning himself within the white middle class of the community alienated him from the Aboriginal people of the region. He concluded: "as other social scientists working in the North have discovered, you are either a student of the whites or a student of the Natives, rarely both."[1] Certainly, fieldwork with both Aboriginal and non-Aboriginal populations can be difficult in settings where local relations are strained. Negotiating permission to conduct research can be especially difficult when one is limited to a short period of fieldwork. To accept this limitation as inevitable, though, is only to reproduce the conventional system of social segregation that many rural Euro-Canadians claim as natural.

This book was also facilitated by my ability to work with relative ease in both Secwepemc and Euro-Canadian circles. My familiarity and friendships with various Secwepemc people have allowed me to explore some of the more sensitive issues, particularly their experiences of interpersonal racism. In contrast, my Euro-Canadian identity has given me immediate access to the cultural world of other Euro-Canadian townspeople, where I have often been drawn into a presumed shared universe of understanding in which both friends and strangers have voiced frank and often negative opinions about Aboriginal people and issues. This ease of movement between Aboriginal and non-Aboriginal contexts was also geographical. For the period of formal research in 1992, 1994, and 1995, while carrying out research in Williams Lake, I stayed some twenty kilometres out of town with friends in their home at the Soda Creek First Nation's reserve at Deep Creek. At times, though, moving between Euro-Canadian and Secwepemc social worlds was very jarring, particularly when moving from informal social gatherings in town in which Indians were the subject of jokes and banter to a reserve home in which the targets of these jokes were friends. Because my fieldwork involved crossing these social boundaries, I have been unable to portray those who engage in harsh discourses or demeaning jokes simply as victims of a dominant culture or an exploitative system of capitalist social relations,[2] a portrayal that would deny both agency and responsibility. I have also been unable to avoid consideration of the consequences of such attitudes for Aboriginal people.

Although this book draws on knowledge and experience gained in years prior, it is based on formal fieldwork carried out over a fourteen-month period between April 1992 and March 1995, just before and during my enrolment in the PhD program in anthropology at the University of British Columbia. I explained to friends, acquaintances, and others I met that I had returned to the city to study the relations between Aboriginal and non-Aboriginal people in the Williams Lake area. I would discuss problems such as racism and socioeconomic disparities and would highlight the different ways in which Aboriginal and non-Aboriginal people understand history, differences that are brought to the forefront in land claims debates. My goal, I emphasized, was to develop a better understanding of these issues so that more positive relationships might be created.

Earlier drafts of this manuscript were circulated among twelve Aboriginal and Euro-Canadian residents (friends, colleagues, and "key informants"), all of whom can be considered community leaders in their respective spheres. The majority provided feedback – some wrote detailed notes – and generally supportive commentary. I recognize, however, that this book may take a more critical perspective of social relations in Williams Lake than some Euro-Canadian residents might prefer. At the same time, it may present a less critical analysis than some Aboriginal people might prefer. This work reflects my attempt to deal honestly with sensitive and controversial issues while walking the thin line between a critically responsible and a morally vacant cultural relativism.

Although many ethnographers who have studied rural communities have used pseudonyms for their research sites, I have chosen to use the real names of the city and the surrounding reserves. I have done so, in part, because the city would be readily identified anyway from my naming of the three Aboriginal nations of the region and of the city's annual festival, for which Williams Lake is internationally known. In addition, most of the local residents who read earlier drafts thought that I should use the name of the city; not to do so would be overly protective. Several readers pointed out the double standard of identifying First Nations but not Williams Lake. I have used pseudonyms (indicated by names in quotation marks) when referring to specific individuals. In some cases, primarily when the identities of the individuals were in the public record, I have used their real names.

The terms "Indian" and "white" are commonly used in public and private discussions in the region. Both Aboriginal and non-Aboriginal people freely use the terms to designate the other. To identify themselves, Aboriginal people use a variety of context-dependent terms. In informal discussions, many prefer the designation of "Native." In more formal political discourse, the terms "First Nations" and "Aboriginal" are now preferred. First Nations leaders occasionally use the term "Indian" in their formal political discussions with non-Aboriginal people. In such contexts, Indian is used as a term of pride and defiance of the negative connotations long conveyed through local usage. I have attempted to stay within local convention by using the more formal term "Aboriginal"; I occasionally use "First Nations" when referring to political leaders and contexts. I use "Indian" to refer specifically to non-Aboriginal perspectives. This term refers less to real Aboriginal people than to the idea of the other as created and perpetuated in the dominant culture and discourse.

"White" remains the most common colloquial term in rural settings to designate non-Aboriginal people in Canada. Alternate terms, though, are emerging. "Non-Native" is occasionally used in both private and public discussions in the Cariboo-Chilcotin by individuals so designated. A more formal variant is "non-Aboriginal," which I have used here. A more precise variant is "Euro-Canadian," rarely heard in popular discourse but now the accepted term in formal academic discourse to refer to the dominant segment of Canadian society. I have chosen to use the term "Euro-Canadian" to specify the dominant population of Williams Lake and the term "non-Aboriginal" to designate the broader range of city residents, which includes a significant number of individuals of East Indian ancestry.

A number of people from the Cariboo-Chilcotin have played an important role over the years in shaping my understanding of Aboriginal/non-Aboriginal relations. I would like to thank in particular Kristy Alphonse, Charlene Belleau, Roy Christopher, Diana French, Joan Gentles, Lynne Gilbert, Rick Gilbert, Agnes Jack, Doreen Johnny, Francis Johnson, Bruce Mack, Reg Michel, Ralph Phillips, Liz Robertson, Nancy Sandy, Bev Sellars,

Alice Vogler, Jean William, and Chris Wycotte. A number of these individuals have read drafts of this book and have provided me with valued feedback. I would also like to thank the members of my dissertation committee, Julie Cruikshank, Martin Silverman, and Michael Kew, and the additional examiners, Michael Blake, Paul Tennant, and Harvey Feit, for their comments on the earlier draft of this book. The research and writing of my PhD dissertation was supported by a doctoral fellowship from the Social Sciences and Humanities Research Council of Canada. I revised the manuscript for publication while I was a Social Sciences and Humanities Research Council post-doctoral fellowship holder at the Centre for Cross-Cultural Research at Australian National University. I am grateful for these forms of support.

One of the central mandates of anthropology is to produce knowledge relevant to addressing the major social issues of our time. In their influential *Anthropology As Cultural Critique,* George Marcus and Michael Fisher charted a course for the future of anthropology. They urged anthropologists to commit themselves to the principles on which modern anthropology was first founded: "to offer worthwhile and interesting critiques of our own society; to enlighten us about other human possibilities, engendering an awareness that we are merely one pattern among many; to make accessible the normally unexamined assumptions by which we operate and through which we encounter members of other cultures."[3] I believe that anthropology has tremendous potential to contribute to the mediation of conflicts between Aboriginal and non-Aboriginal peoples in Canada by making sites of confrontation the subject of analysis and by rendering comprehensible the circumstances in which competing bodies of knowledge emerge and are contested so that a process of building more just relationships can proceed. Such a mediation of social conflict is needed in the heated public debates about Aboriginal issues in British Columbia, debates that centre on competing understandings of the history of British Columbia, the legitimacy of Aboriginal claims, and the place of Aboriginal people in British Columbian society. This process of mediating conflict also requires a reflexive self-awareness among members of the dominant society. Key aspects of Williams Lake's "frontier" culture resonate with commonsense assumptions in rural and urban communities across the province. For myself, through the course of this work I have become much more aware of how this colonial cultural legacy continues to shape my own habits of thought and language. In keeping with the pragmatic potential of this book – so that it may encourage a greater self-awareness and understanding of the roots of current social conflicts – I have attempted to write in a fairly straightforward narrative style accessible to both academic and general readers.

# The Burden of History

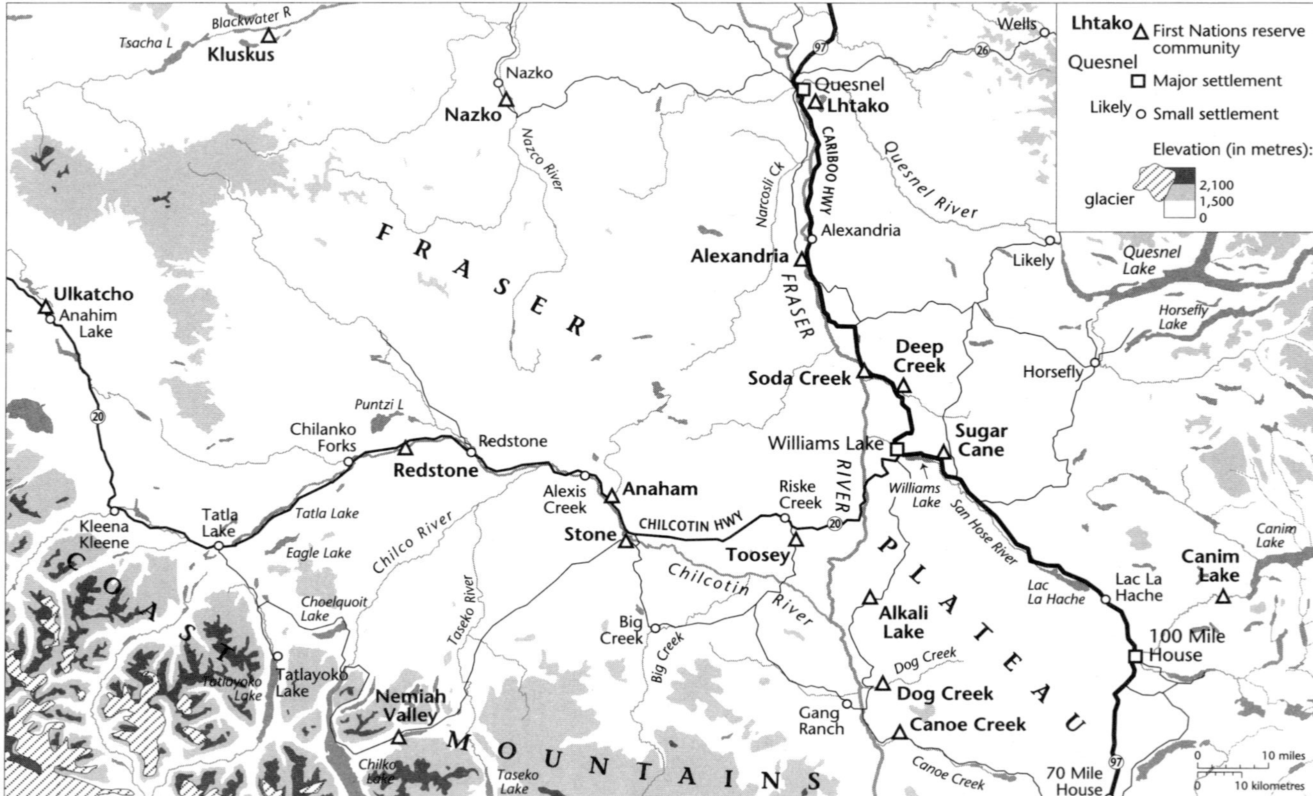


Map of Cariboo-Chilcotin

# 1 Culture and Colonialism in Rural British Columbia

In the summer of 1995, the Gustafsen Lake blockade in the Cariboo region of British Columbia captured nationwide media attention and transfixed the viewing public with images of armed RCMP teams, helicopters, and camouflaged Aboriginal men determined to protect the remote Sun Dance grounds from outside interference. The issues raised during the standoff were complex, and the political alliances and rhetorical positions of those involved shifted on an almost daily basis. However, by the end of the summer, various Aboriginal parties – including men and women behind the lines at Gustafsen Lake, the nearby Canoe Creek First Nation (in whose traditional territory the grounds were situated), and Assembly of First Nations Grand Chief Ovide Mercredi – publicly defined the issue as the inevitable consequence of the failure of successive governments to address the issue of Aboriginal title. The non-Aboriginal public of the Cariboo, encouraged by mounting opposition to the province's new treaty negotiation policy and by the federal Reform Party's anti-land claims platform of "one law for all Canadians," saw the armed occupation of private ranchland as an issue not of unresolved historical injustices but of Aboriginal criminals receiving special treatment from RCMP officers, who refused to storm the site and arrest its occupants.

The polarization of public opinion on the Gustafsen Lake issue was only one indication of the intense conflicts between Aboriginal and non-Aboriginal people in resource-based communities throughout British Columbia. Although it captured much sensationalistic media attention, the Gustafsen Lake crisis was not an isolated incident. Since the 1970s, road blockades and occupations have increasingly been used by Aboriginal peoples throughout the province to protest the clear-cutting of Aboriginal territories, the trespass of public roads through Indian reserve lands, and the failure of the provincial government to acknowledge the persistence of Aboriginal title.[1] Several months before the Gustafsen Lake standoff, blockades at Adams Lake and Douglas Lake in the BC central interior brought a range of unresolved problems regarding Aboriginal lands to public attention and incited equally heated tempers and rhetoric among local residents. In the context of rising economic insecurity over the future of the forest industry, looming job layoffs, and the provincial government's decision to negotiate Aboriginal treaties, the confrontations at Gustafsen Lake, Adams Lake, and Douglas Lake brought to full public view the critical and long-standing problems that many rural communities now face in coming to terms with the legacy of European colonialism; in addressing issues of Aboriginal title, rights, and self-government; and in defining the terms of a new and more equitable coexistence between the local Aboriginal and non-Aboriginal populations.[2]

The Gustafsen Lake standoff was a microcosm of the broader process by which Aboriginal people across the country are attempting to confront the legacy of colonialism and to renegotiate their relationships with the Canadian state and Canadian society. A wealth of anthropological literature is documenting the challenges that Aboriginal peoples face as they attempt to secure greater political and cultural autonomy through changes in Indian Affairs administration and public policy, through challenges to the Canadian justice system, and through treaties and self-government agreements. In contrast, relatively little anthropological attention has focused on how these political processes are occurring in the everyday dynamics of Aboriginal/Euro-Canadian relations in the small cities and towns across rural Canada. Yet it is in these settings that one finds the greatest discrepancies in material wealth, social conditions, health, and education between the Aboriginal and non-Aboriginal populations. One finds the greatest degree of separation of the two populations, a separation reinforced by the openly negative and prejudicial attitudes about Aboriginal people that prevail in these settings. And in BC resource-based towns, one now finds the greatest fear among industry, municipal government, business, and labour leaders that Aboriginal treaties will bring about the shutdown of the forest industry and the destruction of non-Aboriginal lifestyles and communities.

Aboriginal people in rural regions are confronting not only the legal, administrative, economic, and political structures in which they are entangled. Power exists not only in the activities of the state, its agencies and institutions, and their supporting bureaucratic ideologies. It is also deeply embedded in cultural forms and practices that frame commonsense understandings of the world. In their ongoing political activity, Aboriginal people in rural communities are also confronting the very terms of Canadian culture itself: the frontier histories celebrating the early white "discoverers" of British Columbia, the widespread assumption of the historical inevitability – and desirability – of cultural assimilation, the liberal democratic myth of the "self-made man," and the demeaning stereotypes of Aboriginal people that deny their individuality, humanity, and integrity. The politics of decolonization in these rural settings are being fought out not just on legal or bureaucratic grounds but also on the cultural terrain of competing definitions of the nature of history, society, and identity.

This book presents an ethnography of the cultural politics of Aboriginal/ Euro-Canadian relations in a small, interior BC resource city at the height of land claims conflict and tension. I am primarily concerned with tracing the relationship between colonial power – the power that reinforces and maintains the subordinate position of Aboriginal peoples in Canada – and Canadian culture as experienced in the lives of small-town Euro-Canadians. In the following chapters, I explore different facets of the dominant Euro-Canadian culture of this region and show how this culture exists as a set of widespread, common-sense orientations to history and identity, orientations that revolve around the idea and the symbol of the frontier. These beliefs, values, and attitudes are encountered in diverse settings, from casual conversations, popular historical literature, museum displays, and community festivals to political discourse on Aboriginal land claims and treaties. I assess how these assumptions about identity and history enhance relations of inequality between Euro-Canadians and area Secwepemc, Tsilhqot'in, and Carrier peoples.[3] Finally, I show how area Aboriginal people are engaging in plural forms of resistance against this dominant culture, not only as strategies of collective empowerment but also as part of their ongoing efforts to renegotiate their existing relationships with the regional Euro-Canadian society.

## The Setting

Williams Lake is the largest city in the Cariboo region of British Columbia and lies some 500 kilometres north of Vancouver on the main highway to the northern interior of the province. The Cariboo region is often referred to more generally as the Cariboo-Chilcotin, the Chilcotin being the area lying west of the Fraser River and the Cariboo proper being the region lying to the east. The Cariboo-Chilcotin is part of the broad, dry interior plateau, an area of flat to rolling terrain covered by coniferous forests of fir, spruce, and lodgepole pine and, in the wetter regions, deciduous forests of poplar and birch. The forests are interrupted by the grasslands that lie along the terraced benches of the Fraser River and that extend westward through the east Chilcotin. Cariboo-Chilcotin summers are typically short, warm, and dry, punctuated by sudden thunder and lightning storms that blow through the river and creek valleys in a matter of minutes. The first snow often falls in November, and by Christmas there is a permanent blanket covering the ground. The snow usually disappears by late March in what bush workers call "spring breakup," when the ground thaws, turns to mud, and makes logging and hauling from the bush impossible.

Williams Lake is the main industrial, administrative, and commercial centre of the Cariboo-Chilcotin. The economy is dominated by the forest industry, but ranching, mining, tourism, and government employment are also important. As the principal government centre for the Cariboo-Chilcotin, the public service sector has been a stabilizing factor in the city's economy in recent years, when both the forest and mining industries have experienced downturns. The city has about 10,500 residents. Although technically a city, in everyday conversation most residents refer to Williams Lake as a town, reflecting a prevalent attachment to populist imagery of social and community relations. The majority of residents are of European ancestry: British, German, French, and Dutch. There is a significant population with East Indian ancestry, comprising between 7 and 12 percent of residents, and Aboriginal people make up at least 5 to 9 percent of residents.[4]

The actual number of people flowing through the city on any day, though, is higher. Many Cariboo residents place high value on the rural lifestyle that the region affords, and a significant number of those who work in the city live on small acreages or hobby farms. In addition, rural families from as far away as the west Chilcotin regularly travel to the city to buy groceries, clothing, hardware, and livestock supplies and to obtain medical and government services. On Fridays and Saturdays, dust-covered pickup trucks fill the parking lots of the mall and the major grocery stores as people from rural areas make their weekly or monthly purchases. Case-lot sales – bulk sales of huge quantities of canned food items – are a regular event at the city's grocery stores.

The population of the Cariboo-Chilcotin region is estimated at between 40,000 and 60,000, depending on how one draws the region's boundaries. This figure includes individuals living in the expansive region from Horsefly and Likely, some sixty kilometres to the east, to Anahim Lake, over 300 kilometres to the west across the Chilcotin plateau. This broader region includes fifteen Secwepemc, Tsilhqot'in, and Carrier First Nations communities totalling about 6,000 registered band members.[5] Aboriginal people therefore comprise at least 10 to 15 percent of the regional population. Non-Aboriginal settlement in the Chilcotin is sparse, with families typically living on widely dispersed ranches. The Tsilhqot'in reserve community of Anaham, for example, with a population of about 600, is three times more populous than the nearby non-Aboriginal settlement of Alexis Creek. As is characteristic of the curious selective invisibility of Aboriginal people in the geographical landscape, Anaham and other reserve communities often go unmarked on provincial road maps, whereas smaller, non-Aboriginal settlements such as Alexis Creek are highlighted.

Williams Lake shares the same characteristics of many other rural cities and towns, where the regional economies are based on natural resource extraction or agriculture, where the cities are service and commercial centres for satellite reserve communities, and where the proportion of Aboriginal people in the population is relatively high compared with that in urban settings. As in small rural cities and towns in Manitoba, Saskatchewan, and northern Ontario,[6] Aboriginal people in the Cariboo-Chilcotin over the last four decades have been largely excluded from employment as the forest industry and the infrastructure of businesses, services, and government agencies have grown and prospered. Aboriginal workers are largely absent in the mills or in the city's restaurants, retail stores, banks, businesses, or offices. Two First Nations educators are employed in the school district's administration, and, although the district in the past has hired First Nations teachers, at present there are no Aboriginal teachers for mainstream classes in any of the city's schools. In short, as in other rural settings, Aboriginal people in the Cariboo-Chilcotin have been marginalized from the regional society and economy, a position maintained through dependency on welfare provisioning, the legacy of the Indian reserve system, and the restrictive Indian Affairs bureaucratic regulations.[7] This position is only now beginning to shift with the political and economic changes being introduced through pending land claims settlements.

The non-Aboriginal population of Williams Lake, in contrast, has prospered greatly from the expanding resource economy. The dominance of the forest industry in Williams Lake is evident: four major sawmills, one plywood mill, and several secondary manufacturing industries are situated along the Williams Lake valley running through the city. Massive log storage yards and beehive burners are clearly visible from downtown. On any day, one can see a steady flow of loaded logging trucks arriving from the Chilcotin. The logging industry is literally imprinted on the city's landscape in the deep ruts that heavily laden trucks have worn into the paved roads. Many people are employed directly by the local mills as mill workers, truckers, or contract loggers or indirectly by businesses such as machine-repair shops and heavy-equipment suppliers that provide the mills with goods and services.

The logging industry has imprinted itself on the local Euro-Canadian culture as well. The city has the distinct ethos of a "working town," where physical labour in the mills or in the bush, and the entrepreneurialism of associated small businesses, are the most valued forms of work. The emphasis on independence, hard work, and competitiveness captures an essential "frontier spirit" of the city: it is a town where owning a gun and a chainsaw is part of everyday life and where the vehicle of preference is not a BMW or Mercedes but a heavy-duty, usually four-wheel drive, pickup truck. The impact of the forest industry is evident in everyday language, in which phrases such as "beetle kill," "chip trucks," and "annual allowable cut" have meaning to virtually all residents. So symbolically important is the logging industry that it is celebrated in the city's annual Loggers Sports Day. One school, Glendale elementary, recently became the first public school in Canada to abandon the traditional summer vacation period. Now students have April off to coincide with the spring breakup and the annual layoffs of loggers and truck drivers, allowing fathers and children to spend their vacation time together. In short, Williams Lake has accommodated the forest industry in many ways. It is not merely the economic base of the city; it is also seen by local people to comprise a distinct lifestyle that is deeply valued and publicly celebrated.

The frontier spirit of Williams Lake is also heavily influenced by the city's roots in the ranching industry. The Cariboo-Chilcotin region is widely known as "cowboy country," and the city itself is widely known for its annual summer stampede. During the four-day rodeo and festival, the city transforms itself into a mythological Wild West town, with storefronts and interiors decorated with motifs of cowboys, Indians, and cattle. The stampede is the most important ritual celebration of the city's official public identity and frontier history, drawing thousands of visitors and putting the city on the map of international tourism.

There are fifteen First Nations communities in the Cariboo-Chilcotin: six Tsilhqot'in, four Carrier, and five Secwepemc.[8] Ten of the fifteen use Williams Lake as a major commercial centre. The Secwepemc reserve communities are situated east of the Fraser River, whereas the Tsilhqot'in are located to the west and the Carrier to the northwest. The Secwepemc reserve of Sugar Cane, at the south end of the lake, is only twelve kilometres from the city and is clearly visible from the main highway. In contrast, the closest Tsilhqot'in community is Toosey, some fifty kilometres away. The Nemiah band is the most remote, tucked into the extreme southwest Chilcotin, several hours away by rough road. With the exception of the Ulkatcho Carrier at Anahim Lake, Carrier people usually travel to the northern city of Quesnel for supplies and services.

Aboriginal people are a visible presence in the city. On any given day, one can find Aboriginal people having meals in the fast-food outlets, socializing in the food court of the mall, playing bingo at the downtown bingo hall, waiting in bank lineups, or shopping in the grocery stores. At the same time, Aboriginal/non-Aboriginal relations in the city are marked by the same tensions found in many other rural towns.[9] The same tacit, invisible line separates the two populations into relatively distinct social groups.

This social separation, however, is not absolute. Aboriginal and non-Aboriginal people come into informal social contact in a number of settings. One of the most important settings is the public school system. Although many reserve communities now operate their own elementary schools, Aboriginal students make up approximately 15 percent of the secondary school population in the city. Recreational sports teams are another critical venue for informal contact, and ice hockey, ball hockey, soccer, and slow- and fast-pitch softball are popular activities. Although Native-only sports teams and leagues operate throughout the year, many people also participate on integrated teams in the city. During hockey season, the civic arena is often packed with Aboriginal and non-Aboriginal spectators who have come to cheer on relatives and friends.

Aboriginal and non-Aboriginal men and women do intermarry and have been doing so since the first settlers arrived in the Cariboo-Chilcotin some 130 years ago. Over time, these intermarriages have created a significant number of people with both Aboriginal and non-Aboriginal heritage. The ever-present reality of racism has long encouraged those of mixed ancestry to publicly deny their Aboriginal roots and to claim Euro-Canadian identity. Following the federal government's passage of Bill C-31 in 1985, which broadened the terms in which official Indian status is legally recognized, more individuals have publicly claimed Aboriginal status and attempted to reestablish ties to reserve communities. In short, Aboriginals married to non-Aboriginals, and individuals of mixed ancestry, may be embedded in social networks that mediate the two populations. These less visible, and often unspoken, networks belie the conventional model of the absolute separation of the Euro-Canadian townspeople from the Aboriginal reserve communities.

Despite the varied contexts in which Aboriginal and non-Aboriginal people encounter one another and negotiate public definitions of identity, there exists a widespread model of the ideal order of social relations in Williams Lake, an order defined by two essentialized, presumably "natural," and opposing social categories: Indian and white. It is against these prevailing dominant categories that Aboriginal individuals seeking to control their public identities must struggle.

These categories are reinforced in a number of ways. For example, non-Aboriginal newcomers to the city are typically exposed to strong pressures of socialization – such as in the ritual joking about Indians – to accept the absolute difference, constructed in terms of morality and culture, between the Aboriginal and non-Aboriginal populations. These differences are reinforced by a conventional behaviour of avoidance that plays itself out in public spaces. Although Aboriginal and non-Aboriginal people may occupy the same public space (in the mall, on the streets, in the civic arena, in the bars), the two groups do not mix easily and are not often seen talking freely. Spontaneous interchanges between strangers become more guarded as social distance declines. The reluctance of individuals to talk "across the line" is an implicit social convention maintained by many Aboriginal as well as non-Aboriginal people.

The idealized separation between Indian and white is reflected in the identification of some sites in town as "Indian" places. There is the Indian bar near the foot of Oliver Street; there is the housing complex known to some Aboriginal people as "Little Anaham"; there is the Chinese restaurant popular among many Aboriginal patrons. Although Aboriginal people are no longer refused service in the town's restauraunts and hotels, as they were up until the 1960s, implicit tensions as well as voluntary preferences still combine to reinforce these distinctions of place. Such distinctions are also reflected in the isolation of the reserve communities from the non-Aboriginal settlements and towns in the Cariboo-Chilcotin. Whereas Aboriginal people move freely between their reserves and the city, a similar movement among non-Aboriginal people does not occur. Few non-Aboriginal people, it seems, have visited reserve communities, and many seem to be unaware of the names or locations of the different reserves. Many reserves are invisible to non-Aboriginal people except in the abstract: they are imagined as dangerous, foreign, and violent places where whites are not welcome.

The cultural life of reserve communities, and the significant differences that distinguish the Secwepemc, Carrier, and Tsilhqot'in cultures, also remain invisible to many non-Aboriginal people. Although the Secwepemc, Tsilhqot'in, and Carrier communities have existed on the peripheries of the regional economy, their degree of dependency and powerlessness due to absorption into the capitalist socioeconomic system varies. Like other northern Aboriginal groups, Cariboo-Chilcotin First Nations, to differing degrees, may also engage in a "dual economy" in which subsistence hunting and fishing continue independently of the wage-labour and welfare economies.[10] Conventions of reciprocity and sharing of subsistence foods persist within extended family groups and among the elderly of the reserve village. These and other practices strengthen traditional patterns of sociopolitical organization and the bonds of solidarity among extended families and band communities.[11]

Tsilhqot'in continues to be spoken in reserve homes and band offices throughout the Chilcotin region. Carrier is regularly spoken in all southern Carrier communities, particularly the more remote reserves of Nazko, Kluskus, and Ulkatcho, whereas Secwepemc is regularly used in ritual and ceremonial contexts in those communities. Secwepemc, Tsilhqot'in, and Carrier peoples continue to use culturally distinct oral traditions to express their worldviews and cultural identities and to make sense of the current social changes that their communities are undergoing.[12] Many Secwepemc, Tsilhqot'in, and Carrier leaders have a deep commitment to the collective future of their reserve communities. They see themselves as having unique histories and special rights that distinguish them from regional Euro-Canadian society, and they assert distinct identities rooted in their histories and their relationships with the landscape. These convictions fuel their current struggles to secure treaties acknowledging Aboriginal rights to land and self-government.

The social problems, violence, suicide, alcohol abuse, poverty, and substandard living conditions that plague reserve communities across Canada also exist in many Secwepemc, Tsilhqot'in, and Carrier reserves. These problems lend urgency to First Nations leaders' efforts to resolve outstanding issues of Aboriginal title. Treaties, many leaders believe, will provide reserve communities with the resources to address and overcome these social problems. In the past decade, there has been an exponential growth in the political activity of area First Nations and the umbrella political organizations that represent the three nations. The Tsilhqot'in National Government (representing five Tsilhqot'in First Nations), the Carrier Chilcotin Tribal Council (representing four Carrier and one Tsilhqot'in First Nation), and the Cariboo Tribal Council (representing four of the five Secwepemc First Nations) all have large offices in Williams Lake. These organizations are active on a number of political fronts, from lobbying for improved rental housing in the city to developing programs for assuming control of provincial child-welfare services to coordinating strategies for negotiating treaties.

## Theoretical Framework

A fundamental premise of this book is that the power maintaining the political, economic, social, and cultural marginalization of Aboriginal people in Canadian society resides not only in the policies, practices, and ideologies of state institutions and their officials. Nor can the domination and marginalization of Aboriginal people be reduced to an epiphenomenon of class relations created through the imposition of capitalism. In addition, power radiates out from the corporate and administrative centres of urban Canada to infuse the everyday cultural attitudes and practices of "ordinary" rural Euro-Canadians who, knowingly or unwittingly, serve as agents in an ongoing system of colonial domination. To make this theoretical approach clear, two points require elaboration: first, the notion that Canada persists as a colonial (rather than "postcolonial") society whose culture remains deeply imprinted by the legacy of colonialism and, second, the analytical concept of a dominant culture.

The term "postcolonial" is often used to refer to a particular historical period following the end of colonial rule.[13] It is most commonly applied to previously colonized societies that, throughout the 1940s and 1950s and following intensive anticolonial campaigns, underwent a radical decolonization, which saw the withdrawal of colonial governments and the transfer of political authority to indigenous elites. In contrast, as a settler colony eventually granted dominion status, Canada has evolved to an independent state in which settler populations continue to exert authority over a subordinate minority indigenous population. Because decolonization in the form of the removal of non-Aboriginal settlers and governments will not occur in Canada, the political activity now under way reflects the efforts of Aboriginal and non-Aboriginal people to create alternative relationships that presume the continued coexistence of indigenous and immigrant Canadians.

The legacy of colonialism is evident not only in the ongoing structures of political authority and Aboriginal-settler relations in Canada but also in the cultural fabric of Canadian society. Throughout the four centuries of European settlement in Canada, colonial power has been expressed in political, military, and economic exercises and in cultural ideologies, practices, and texts of the settler populations. These cultural forms – the ideas of history, identity, society, and indigenous "difference" that permeate Canadian literature, film, art, and popular culture – are not secondary derivatives of political/economic practices. Instead, these cultural representations and practices are central to the very process of establishing and perpetuating colonial relationships. The cultures of modern Western societies, and settler cultures in particular, continue to be profoundly influenced by the ideological legacy and the ongoing practices of colonialism. In Canada, there has been no radical break with the past: Canadian culture remains resolutely colonial in shape, content, meaning, and practice.[14]

What, then, are the characteristics of a colonial culture? What makes a colonial culture, and colonial cultural practices, distinct subjects for analysis? Most contemporary scholars immediately refer to the works of Edward Said, who, with the publication of *Orientalism* in 1978 and *Culture and Imperialism* in 1994, provided a foundation for the emergence of a distinctive form of cultural theory: the analysis of colonial discourse. Said's principal argument is that most of the representations produced by Western colonizing nations – whether these representations be artistic, scientific, academic, literary, or religious – are united by the interest in marking the difference between "us" (the West) and "them" (the other: i.e., colonized populations or indigenous peoples). The forms of knowledge produced continually represent colonized peoples as inherently different from, and inferior to, the colonizing populations. By their sheer saturation of the landscape of "official" knowledge, these representations come to have a truth value that, in establishing their own criteria for the derivation of "truths" about the colonized and in excluding competing understandings, ultimately serve as strategies of power that not only legitimate but also necessitate the ongoing surveillance, control, and subjugation of colonized peoples. In short, Said provides an initial characterization of a colonial culture: it is marked by a variety of discourses that are fundamentally racist in nature, being centrally concerned with the construction of indigenous difference and inferiority, and that have specific effects of power.

Said's work has been criticized for its overhomogenization of colonial discourses and for its overemphasis on the negative images of the colonized.[15] Recent critics argue that there can be no simplistic characterization of colonial discourses; instead, one must pay attention to the diverse discourses as they are articulated by different colonial agents in particular geographical settings and in distinct historical periods.[16] For example, anthropologist Nicholas Thomas points out that, although at times colonial discourses and narratives encode racist images of indigenous inferiority, at other times they represent difference without any evaluative commentary: differences between Western colonizers and indigenous peoples are inherent yet neutral, equal in worth. This attitude, for example, is evident in the Western curiosity with and fascination for the "exotic." At other times, colonial discourses may highlight indigenous difference in terms of its cultural and moral superiority to Western society. The idea of the noble savage living in a harmonious, egalitarian, nonconsumptive society has long been constructed as a means for expressing disillusionment with modern industrial and urban society. These idealizing tendencies, highlighting the superiority of indigenous spirituality or relations with nature, continue in some streams of the New Age and environmental movements. Such expressions of romantic primitivism convey a sympathy for Aboriginal peoples that is nevertheless framed by equally narrow, illusory definitions of the essential difference of Aboriginal and non-Aboriginal peoples. Aboriginal people are expected to live up to unrealistic ideals that only further deny their individuality, diversity, and contemporaneity. In even other settings, some colonial narratives may be explicitly homogenizing, denying Aboriginal/non-Aboriginal difference. The assimilative projects of Christian missionaries and governments that sought to remake the Aboriginal in the colonizer's own image made use of discourses of both similarity and difference. These assimilative ideologies, reshaped to suit the context of the 1990s, are evident in the Reform Party's opposition to Aboriginal treaties.

In short, what characterizes a colonial culture in Canada, then, is not merely the presence of racist discourses but also the intense energy devoted to contemplating Aboriginal/non-Aboriginal relations either through the assignation of difference – negative, neutral, or positive – or through the denial of difference. These alternating tendencies toward incorporation and exclusion, toward assertion and denial of indigenous difference, are central dynamics within colonial discourses and practices.[17]

As I argue in the following chapters, a colonial culture and colonial cultural practices involve more than the assignation of public identities to colonial and colonized populations. These cultural practices are also framed by a dominant historical epistemology that provides taken-for-granted understandings of the past and rules for constructing knowledge of both the past and the present. A colonial culture rests on a deeply rooted set of understandings about the relationship between the individual, society, and the natural world. The complexity of these cultural beliefs and processes remains virtually unexplored in the ethnographic literature on Aboriginal/non-Aboriginal relations in Canada, yet they are vital to an understanding of the dynamics of domination, subordination, and resistance in rural regions.[18]

The dominant Euro-Canadian culture of Williams Lake is an example of such a modern colonial culture. Canadian culture is neither static nor monolithic; rather, it is multivalent and diverse, shaped by local traditions, historical contingencies, and political and economic contexts. My object here is to explore how a colonial reality is expressed in Canadian culture as it exists in the 1990s in the setting of a small resource city in British Columbia, a region with its own distinct traditions of imagining Aboriginal/Euro-Canadian difference and a region now engaged in intense public debates over the legitimacy of past colonial practices and the future relationships between the Aboriginal and settler populations.

To explore the relationship between culture and power, I draw on the idea of a "dominant culture" as articulated by Marxist literary critic Raymond Williams and anthropologist William Roseberry.[19] Williams states: "In any society, in any particular period, there is a central system of practices, meanings and values, which we can properly call dominant and effective."[20] This dominant culture infuses many domains of everyday life, from family life, schooling, the media, and organized religion to literature and the arts. Its dominance lies, in part, in its ability to saturate everyday life: it is continually affirmed in multiple dimensions of ordinary experience. Williams emphasizes this point: "It is a whole body of practices and expectations; our assignments of energy, our ordinary understanding of the nature of man and of his world. It is a set of meanings and values which as they are experienced as practices appear as reciprocally confirming. It thus constitutes a sense of reality for most people in the society, a sense of absolute because experienced reality beyond which it is very difficult for most members of the society to move, in most arenas of their lives."[21] A dominant culture, in essence, is experienced as a set of commonsense, taken-for-granted truths about the nature of reality and the social world.

Although a dominant culture infuses everyday life, its dominance is not complete. Not all non-Aboriginal residents of the Cariboo-Chilcotin participate in the same way in the dominant culture. Individuals and groups – Euro-Canadians, Indo-Canadians, men, women, upper- and lower-class families, the employed and the unemployed, the young and the old – are variously positioned within these fields of social and political power. The different life experiences of individuals, conditioned not only by their individual biographies but also by their varied positions within structures of inequality and domination, may give rise to different perceptions of reality and lead to challenges to the legitimacy of a dominant culture.[22] A dominant culture, then, is a selective worldview that is continually being challenged by alternative systems of meaning and belief. Its dominance lies in both its ubiquity and its flexibility: its ability to be continually modified in order to deflect or incorporate challenges to its legitimacy.

It is here where unequal access to power becomes critical. Power, in this sense, can be equated with the epistemological power to control the representation of cultural forms, symbols, and meanings. But this power is also material, in that the production of culture is linked to the political and economic forces controlling public school education, publishing, media, tourism, and so on. If a dominant culture is defined as a material social process of the production and representation of meaning, then the question to be asked is: Who is controlling the production of culture, in what contexts, and for what purposes?

Secwepemc, Carrier, and Tsilhqot'in people, too, are positioned within the reaches of the dominant Euro-Canadian culture of the region. Their own worldviews, cultural histories, and traditions, and their subjection to various forms of colonial power (the Indian Act, the Indian Affairs bureaucracy, Roman Catholic residential schools, and everyday racial discrimination), have created collective historical experiences that sharply distinguish them from the regional non-Aboriginal population. At the same time, the "separate universes" model of Aboriginal/Euro-Canadian relations, emphasizing the cultural gulf between and the autonomy of Aboriginal and non-Aboriginal populations, may overemphasize cultural difference at the expense of a more complex understanding of the nature of contemporary cultural and political processes.

In *Weapons for the Weak*, James Scott argues that much of everyday peasant resistance occurs not from outside but from within a hegemonic culture.[23] When groups are engaged in relationships that are partly conflictual and partly collaborative, challenges to the inequalities and injustices within those relationships will be couched in language judged to be relevant and legitimate to the party in power.[24] As a result, much of peasant resistance seeks not to criticize the terms of a dominant culture but to bring about a redistribution of power and resources by making appeals to key values, morals, and normative rules and by illustrating how those in power have failed to live up to certain standards of conduct. Oppositional discourse, Scott argues, is essentially a normative discourse that strategically manipulates the contradictions between ideal and actual behaviour while implicitly affirming key aspects of this dominant culture.

These insights have much applicability to the current political struggles of First Nations in the Cariboo-Chilcotin. In many ways, Aboriginal people living in rural reserve communities are articulated with the regional dominant culture: they speak the English language, they watch TV, they shop in local stores and malls, they attend public schools, and they read popular literature. As Williams argues, the effective incorporation of individuals into a dominant culture is often achieved not through blind socialization but through "a (resigned) recognition of the inevitable and the necessary."[25] In the case of Aboriginal people, this means realization, but not necessarily acceptance, of divergence between Euro-Canadian and Aboriginal experiences and perceptions of reality. Yet more and more frequently, this resigned recognition of the inevitable is transforming into a refusal to accept the terms of the dominant culture: Aboriginal people are challenging the negative identities that they are ascribed, the terms of the frontier histories that erase Aboriginal people from history, and the legitimacy of the Crown's claim to own the lands and resources within their territories.

First Nations are thus raising challenges to key terms of the dominant culture. Yet as much as these challenges are emerging from without – from the divergence between Aboriginal experience and the dominant Euro-Canadian worldview – the *strategies* for seeking recognition and social, political, and economic change are being articulated from within the terms of the dominant culture. To be sure, some resistance may be articulated through distinctively Aboriginal modes of discourse, such as the way in which Aboriginal storytellers use traditional narrative genres to communicate with non-Aboriginal audiences.[26] But increasingly, First Nations people are strategically manipulating some key values, identities, discursive genres, and symbols of power embedded in the dominant Euro-Canadian culture. Aboriginal people, for example, are highlighting the apparent contradictions between egalitarianism and multiculturalism with their historical experience of racial discrimination and federal policies of assimilation in order to bring about changes in their relationships with government, industry, and area Euro-Canadians. This is not to say that these values or modes of discourse may not also be central to Aboriginal cultures. What is significant is that they resonate with those of the dominant culture, and they are being mobilized to secure public support for Aborignal concerns. To understand the current cultural and political processes of domination and resistance within Aboriginal/Euro-Canadian relations, one must first consider the ways in which Aboriginal people are at times reluctant and at times strategic participants in the regional dominant culture.

### The Frontier Cultural Complex

The frontier complex is the thematic framework that I have developed for understanding the dominant culture of Williams Lake. This complex consists of a diverse yet interrelated set of values, beliefs, attitudes, identities, and understandings about society, history, and Aboriginal/non-Aboriginal relations that appear repeatedly in multiple domains of Euro-Canadian everyday life, ranging from casual conversations to public history to political discourse on contentious issues. At heart, the frontier complex consists of a form of historical consciousness – an awareness of history – that is culturally conditioned and deeply influenced by Canada's colonial heritage. This historical consciousness is made manifest as a historical epistemology: a way of knowing about history that provides a certain set of rules and assumptions that guide how "truths" about the past, and by extension the present, are to be created, understood, and conveyed. Many historical epistemologies may coexist in a particular society. As I argue below, the dominant historical epistemology shaping popular understandings of history in the Cariboo-Chilcotin region is a Canadian variant of the myth of the frontier. In developing this argument, I rely on Richard Slotkin's comprehensive study of the frontier myth in American culture and politics, which I describe shortly.[27]

The frontier complex, though, involves more than a dominant historical epistemology. The idea of the frontier is also evident in the way that Euro-Canadians construct a regional identity as a "small town" on the periphery of mainstream society, a town surrounded by a natural wilderness offering an abundance of natural resources that are unowned and "free" for the taking. The idea of the frontier has been carried into Euro-Canadians' conceptualization of their relationship with area Aboriginal people, in which the categories of Indian and white are mutually exclusive and oppositional and in which Euro-Canadian cultural superiority, material privileges, and political authority are taken as unquestioned truths. Frontier imagery is most apparent in the city's annual summer festival, a ritual celebration of the town's imagined Wild West heritage. At its deepest level, the frontier complex provides a set of metaphysical assumptions about the nature of history, individual agency, and one's relationship with the social and natural worlds. In later chapters, I will explore the many ways in which the frontier complex is expressed in public and private contexts in the city.

Richard Slotkin describes the frontier myth as one of the most important cultural myths for understanding the history of European colonization and settlement in the United States.[28] The frontier myth developed in the United States over a period of three centuries and can be identified in a variety of genres ranging from early settlers' narratives to nineteenth-century dime novels and Wild West shows to contemporary Hollywood movies. It contains several standard themes. The story begins with the settlers' journey to the wilderness and their cultural, moral, and material regression to the more "primitive" conditions encountered there. The frontier experience involves a series of encounters with morally opposed forces, the most important being civilization and wilderness, humans and nature, and whites and Indians, although there are many metaphorical variations. The themes of conflict and violence are central to these encounters as the protagonists struggle against the harsh environment and climate and the unknown and potentially hostile Indians. These struggles, taking place on the moral terrain of good and evil, also involve a degree of ambiguity as the protagonists move between these opposing worlds, temporarily mediating these dichotomies. These tensions are ultimately resolved through the settlers' separation from the conditions of the frontier, typically by their establishment of homesteads and settlements and, by implication, their "conquest" of the wilderness and Aboriginal peoples.

Several features distinguish the frontier myth as a distinct historical epistemology. First, history is distilled into the simple narrative structure of a protagonist's conflict with and eventual triumph over opposing forces. Slotkin argues that the theme of "regeneration through violence" – the moral imperative of aggression and violence as a means of achieving progress and civilization – has been fundamental in shaping past and present constructions of American national identity as well as domestic and foreign policy. Second, the complexity of historical processes is further reduced to a series of what anthropologist Raymond Fogelson has called "epitomizing events," dramatic incidents that serve as convenient and easily grasped condensed symbols that represent more gradual and insidious forces of historical change.[29] These epitomizing events typically deal with the heroic actions of individuals whose values, moral standards, characters, motives for action, and internal struggles define the public ideals of both American and Canadian culture: independence, self-sufficiency, freedom, courage, materialism, and advancement through hard work.

The distilling of history into a simple narrative structure of the encounter of opposites renders invisible the complexity of historical interactions and the diversity of social groups encountering one another in colonial settings. For example, the diversity within Aboriginal societies is typically overlooked as Indians are reduced to a homogeneous group, against which the settler's identity is realized. Representations of Indians range between the stereotypes of noble and ignoble savage. At times, Aboriginal people are represented as a hostile force to be subdued; at other times, they are portrayed as helpers of the colonial project or as a child-like people to be patronized and protected. What remains consistent is the inflexibility of the Indian/white dichotomy. What remains overlooked are the multiple identities, the diverse and conflicting interests, and the ambiguities and incompleteness of domination and resistance that characterized the colonial encounter, themes that are now emphasized by anthropological histories and postcolonial studies.[30]

Third, the frontier myth conveys historical truths less through direct argument, polemic debate, or sermon than indirectly through narratives rich in symbolism and metaphor. As Slotkin argues, the "language is metaphorical and suggestive rather than logical or analytical. The movement of a mythic narrative, like that of any story, implies a theory of cause-and-effect and therefore a theory of history (or even of cosmology); but these ideas are offered in a form that disarms critical analysis by its appeal to the structures and traditions of story-telling and the clichés of historical memory."[31] Of particular importance are what Slotkin calls mythic icons: "Through frequent retellings and deployments as a source of interpretive metaphors, the original mythic story is increasingly conventionalized and abstracted until it is reduced to a deeply encoded and resonant set of symbols, 'icons,' 'keywords,' or historical clichés."[32] Each mythic icon, he writes, "is in effect a poetic construction of tremendous economy and compression and a mnemonic device capable of evoking a complex system of historical associations by a single image or phrase."[33] The "pioneer" or the "empty wilderness" are classical examples of mythic icons in Canadian frontier histories.

The frontier myth, although it is an expression of historical consciousness, should not be considered as a form of *false* consciousness – that is, a form of misguided or incorrect belief. Such an assertion not only contradicts the anthropological principle of cultural relativism – that all systems of knowledge are meaningful and reasonable when understood on their own terms and in the particular contexts in which they are experienced – but also reproduces the analytically problematic notion that false systems of knowledge can be juxtaposed with true, objective, rational systems of knowledge, to which the outside observer typically (and arrogantly) claims exclusive access. Instead, the frontier myth represents one of a number of possible frameworks through which historical understandings may be constructed. The ethnographic project is to explore the conditions under which particular visions of history and reality emerge and how these visions become transformed yet maintain their legitimacy among a wide constituency over a lengthy period of time.

In part, the key to the resilience of the frontier myth is that it provides a highly flexible set of images, symbols, metaphors, and narratives that can be used both to affirm and to contest existing structures of power as well as past practices of colonial expansion. Counterhegemonic formulations, for example, often romanticize the noble savage and lament his or her total destruction by the forces of European expansion and settlement. The standard narrative structure, the binary encounter of opposites on the frontier, and the outcome of absolute conquest remain the same; the moral weighting of these agents and outcomes, however, is reversed.

My goal here is to explore the frontier complex as it exists in the Cariboo region and the conditions under which residents draw upon this cultural complex to generate discourses and narratives of the past, of local and national identities, and of Aboriginal/non-Aboriginal relations.[34] Although I am presenting a study of rural Euro-Canadian culture and social relations between the Euro-Canadian and Aboriginal populations, I am primarily interested in tracing the main features of the dominant culture: its core themes, its variations, and its prevalence within public and private settings.

There are two ways in which a dominant culture might be identified: first, through the ubiquity of particular ideas, meanings, discourses, and practices in everyday life and, second, through case studies of particular instances in which aspects of a dominant culture are challenged and how these challenges are deflected or absorbed by the hegemonic culture. There are risks with the former approach in that what is presented as ubiquitous may simply be dismissed as a selective construction by the ethnographer. Furthermore, the widespread appearance of certain ideas, beliefs, and practices could either represent the overwhelming success of a dominant culture – to the extent that opposition is completely suppressed – or simply reflect the fact that everyone agrees; thus, there is no domination. On the other hand, presenting only case studies of multiple domains in which Aboriginal and non-Aboriginal people struggle over public definitions of identity and history, although it would more effectively demonstrate processes of cultural domination, would also move one away from tracing the processes through which residents of Williams Lake are socialized into a particular dominant culture and worldview. I trace some of these processes – informal conversational rituals, public school education, public history – in early chapters. These aspects of Euro-Canadian experience often take place in the absence of Aboriginal people and protests, but they are critical to the creation and maintenance of the dominant culture. Thus, I have chosen to balance my analysis by demonstrating the ubiquity of key aspects of the dominant culture in multiple domains of Euro-Canadian life and, in later chapters, by tracing instances in which these practices are subject to Aboriginal resistance.

As a result, however, I have not explored in detail the diversity and complexity of social relations within the regional Euro-Canadian and non-Aboriginal populations: that is, the way in which these groups are divided according to socioeconomic position, ethnicity, gender, age, and political orientation and the manner in which these sectors are differently situated within, and privileged by, the dominant culture and structures of power and inequality. Given my theoretical approach – that culture exists as a social process of constructing and representing meaning – it is impossible to analytically separate culture from the individuals who create it. In later chapters, I explore how some Euro-Canadian politicians and community leaders draw on aspects of the dominant culture to oppose land claims and to control public definitions of identity and history that further entrench the exclusion of Aboriginal peoples from power and resources. But in order to demonstrate dominance as ubiquitous, at times I have had to overlook the important questions of how more diverse sectors of the non-Aboriginal society – the Indo-Canadian population in the city and the nonelite of loggers, store clerks, single mothers on welfare, teenagers, and others – also actively contribute to or resist these aspects of the dominant culture. I am not denying the agency, responsibility, or heterogeneity of these diverse sectors. But in order to keep this book within reasonable limits, I have had to balance demonstrating the ubiquity of the frontier complex with illustrating how this cultural complex is activated in particular settings and outlining its hegemonic consequences.

To reiterate, I am not presenting the frontier complex as a bounded, static, essentialized culture defined by a list of traits. Instead, I am presenting it as an analytical construct that attempts to freeze and thus make visible a variety of disparate yet thematically integrated cultural practices. In this sense, my goal is similar to that of Edward Said in his analysis of Orientalist discourses: I am attempting to show the resonance between a wide body of cultural discourses and practices that have previously been considered separate or unrelated. My concern with identifying cultural coherence and with highlighting the systemic features of a dominant culture may appear out of step with dominant academic trends that highlight the heterogeneity and multiplicity of cultural processes and perspectives. I have sought to explore this coherence in order to answer one basic question: How can rural Euro-Canadians who voice negative attitudes toward Aboriginal people, who hold that British Columbia's history began with first European settlement, and who strongly oppose Aboriginal treaties, reasonably hold the beliefs, attitudes, and opinions that they do? Rather than simply dismiss their views as mistaken or morally flawed, I have tried to explore how they can be seen as reasonable, at least in an analytical sense, because they are encountered and reinforced in many dimensions of everyday life.

To a degree, therefore, the analytical coherence that I am positing within the frontier complex is a lived coherence. At the same time, I am not arguing that all Euro-Canadians in Williams Lake participate equally in the dominant culture. I do not expect all, or even many, Euro-Canadians to identify with and find themselves equally within all aspects of the culture that I describe. What I hope is that many may recognize as familiar the operation of this particular system of signs, meanings, and practices that various parties engage in and that I describe as constitutive of the dominant culture of the region.

Finally, my choice to undertake a contemporary rather than a historical ethnographic study should not be read as denying an appreciation for the historicity of the frontier cultural complex. I am not arguing that this complex has remained static, nor am I denying the potential for change in the future. The critical question of how colonial discourses – on history, on Aboriginal people, on Aboriginal-settler relations – have become reformulated over the past 150 years of Cariboo-Chilcotin history remains to be addressed. Here I have been concerned with tracing how aspects of the frontier complex are expressed "laterally" and simultaneously in different arenas of contemporary life.

Another acknowledged limitation of this book is the lack of attention to the complexity and diversity of the regional Aboriginal cultures and forms of historical consciousness. In the following chapters, I trace Aboriginal resistance where it relates to my primary interest in following colonial cultural processes. I have not attempted to provide a full, detailed ethnographic study of the regional Secwepemc, Tsilhqot'in, and Carrier cultures.[35] Although a juxtaposition of Aboriginal and Euro-Canadian perspectives on history would enhance my argument of the partiality and subjectivity of Euro-Canadian historical epistemologies,[36] it would draw attention away from my main argument, which traces the systematic way in which a dominant culture appears in many different domains of everyday life. To those who might suggest that the absence of a significant Aboriginal voice here is a flaw, I would argue that a token inclusion of Aboriginal voices is equally problematic if it leaves unanalyzed the way in which relations of power influence processes of cultural or historical representation. Important is not only a postmodern recognition of the multiplicity of historical voices, as literary critic James Clifford suggests in his advocacy of "polyphonic" ethnographies,[37] but also a detailed analysis of the political, economic, social, and cultural mechanisms of power that create and perpetuate these silences. These are the issues that concern me here.

## Outline of Chapters

In the pages that follow, I examine five different contexts in which aspects of the frontier complex appear: (1) in the formal representations of history in public settings; (2) in the political discourses of various individuals and groups opposed to the actions of regional and provincial governments; (3) in the private, casual conversations of Euro-Canadians as they denigrate and joke about Indians; (4) in the political debates surrounding Aboriginal land claims and treaties; and (5) in the ritual celebrations of the town's heritage during the annual stampede festival. In each setting, I investigate the representation of ideas about history and identity and explore the varied ways in which Euro-Canadians imagine their relationships with Aboriginal people through discourses of difference. I also track some of the many ways in which area Aboriginal people are coping with and responding to these forms of cultural domination.

In Chapter 2, I present a brief historical overview of the Aboriginal cultures and the development of Aboriginal-settler relations in the Cariboo-Chilcotin. I highlight the manner in which these relations have been shaped and constrained by economic forces and through the agencies of the Canadian state. I also sketch the economic, political, and social contexts of current cultural struggles.

In subsequent chapters, I examine how colonial power is expressed in the contemporary cultural practices of everyday life in Williams Lake. In Chapter 3, I introduce the frontier myth as a historical epistemology and trace its appearance in public settings in the city. I examine formal representations of history in three settings: high school history textbooks, popular historical literature found on the shelves of city bookstores, and the displays of the city museum. The frontier myth provides a historical framework for constructing a variety of national, regional, and local identities and histories. In contrast to the American master narrative of "regeneration through violence," in the Cariboo region the dominant narrative is one of "conquest through benevolence," a typically Canadian version in which benevolent paternalism defines assertions of Canadian national identity. Aboriginal people appear only in highly circumscribed roles – noble savages, hostile Indians – in these histories celebrating the "conquest" of the frontier. Histories that deviate from or challenge the terms of the frontier myth are exceedingly scarce. The frontier myth thus exists as a dominant mode of history by virtue of its ubiquity in the public domains of the city.

In Chapter 4, I trace the appearance of the frontier myth in Euro-Canadian political discourse. The frontier myth provides more than a framework for explicit representations of the past. It provides a set of images, symbols, and narratives that are part of the fabric of contemporary culture and identity in Williams Lake and that are frequently drawn on by various parties to both rationalize and criticize government actions and public policies. In so doing, individuals construct idealized images of the past that are juxtaposed with the present to become forms of social and political critique.

My methodology for tracing these processes begins with one assumption: much of contemporary political discourse in Canada takes the form of a "politics of embarrassment,"[38] through which individuals and groups attempt to mobilize public support and embarrass their political opponents – and to bring about changes to government policy – by demonstrating how their opponents have deviated from widespread standards of morality and comportment. By definition, then, the currency of political rhetoric will be the public values, ideals, and traditions that speakers deem dominant. The "everyday" normative discourses of resistance that James Scott describes are strategies that are equally pervasive in contemporary Canadian society.

In tracing political discourse in the Cariboo-Chilcotin setting, my first task is to determine the set of dominant values and identities from which a local politics of embarrassment is derived. I do so through interviews that I conducted with Euro-Canadian community leaders during March 1995. These leaders discussed their understandings of the local culture, identity, and prevalent values, understandings that can be consolidated into a form of contemporary, small-town, frontier identity. I then trace two recent controversial events in which these values and identities formed the currency of political debates. Even more important, public values and identities in these two cases were infused with even greater moral power by being historicized and equated with the pioneer traditions of the Cariboo.

The first case involved the government-ordered demolition of a house in Wells, a hamlet northeast of Williams Lake. The second case concerned the response of Cariboo-Chilcotin groups to the provincial government's Commission on Resources and the Environment. In both instances, angry citizens challenged the actions of the government by evoking the symbol of the pioneer and by construing the actions as threats to the sacred pioneer spirit and legacy of the Cariboo-Chilcotin. The symbol of the pioneer is used creatively and flexibly by various groups engaged in political struggle. At the same time, through its use as a symbol of power, each evocation implicitly reproduces a hegemonic historical tradition of imagining the past through the framework of the frontier myth.

In Chapter 5, I examine the dynamics of everyday Aboriginal/Euro-Canadian relations. I trace how one aspect of the frontier complex is manifested in the way that Euro-Canadians construct a collective identity in opposition to area Aboriginal people. The Indian/white dichotomy naturalized through frontier histories is also found in the common-sense racism that characterizes everyday Euro-Canadian conversations. My methodology involved participant observation in informal contexts with Euro-Canadian friends, acquaintances, and strangers as I moved through the Euro-Canadian social world in the city. The ubiquity of these offhand and disparaging remarks about Aboriginal people attests to the taken-for-granted status of racism in the dominant culture of Williams Lake.

I then trace how these forms of everyday racism translate into forms of "status domination"[39] during Aboriginal/non-Aboriginal interactions. The existence of racism, with rare exceptions, is largely excluded from formal public records and newspaper coverage. These experiences, however, comprise a shared reality for area Secwepemc, Tsilhqot'in, and Carrier people. I turn to interviews and conversations that I had with Aboriginal people – particularly Secwepemc people – who described their accumulated experiences of racial discrimination in the city. Finally, both through these interviews and conversations and through my own observations of everyday

Aboriginal life, I discuss the multiple ways in which Aboriginal people are challenging these forms of status domination: through organized public protest, through individual modes of verbal and physical resistance, and through private modes of humour and parody in which stereotypes of Indianness are subverted.

In Chapter 6, I investigate current public debates over Aboriginal treaties and land claims. Here there is a conjunction of several themes that have been discussed in earlier chapters. Racist images of Aboriginal inferiority, the Euro-Canadian national self-image of benevolent paternalism, the self-made man myth, and the prevalent assumption about the desirability of Aboriginal cultural assimilation into mainstream society are aspects of the dominant culture drawn on by those Euro-Canadians who publicly oppose Aboriginal treaties.

I trace these discourses through a narrative account of a public forum on land claims held in Williams Lake in March 1995. The forum was organized by the federal Reform Party to rally public opposition to Aboriginal treaty negotiations. Although the speakers represented one political party, their views resonated with the attitudes and feelings of many other Euro-Canadians in the city. I compare the formal presentations of the speakers with the views in letters to the city newspaper and in interviews that I conducted that month with Euro-Canadian community leaders on current issues facing Williams Lake and the Cariboo-Chilcotin.

At the same time, the Reform public forum offered the opportunity for a dialogue with the many First Nations people who also attended the meeting. At the end of the chapter, I describe the manner in which three Aboriginal speakers responded to the Reform panelists, challenging their views of history, asserting claims to Aboriginal title, and insisting on the importance of treaties. These examples show how Aboriginal people also engage in a politics of embarrassment; they, too, strategically manipulate the terms of the dominant culture, using varied genres of discourse and drawing on dominant symbols of power and authority in order to pursue their own political goals. These examples are testimony to the diversity of interests, identities, and political strategies that exist within the regional Aboriginal communities.

In Chapter 7, I explore the fifth context in which the frontier complex can be traced: the Williams Lake Stampede, the city's annual festival. Within this ritual complex, Aboriginal people are incorporated into public definitions of community as culturally distinct "Indians" in contrast with the collective identity of the non-Aboriginal townspeople. In this chapter, I ask two questions. First, why are Aboriginal people, as Indians, symbolically important to the festival? The answer involves tracing the history of the stampede in general back to its roots in the Wild West performances in the United States in the late 1800s. A core ritual complex has persisted despite the many changes that the festival has undergone over the decades. Second, how do stampede organizers and area First Nations leaders understand the benefits, pitfalls, and meanings that are communicated through "Indian" participation in the festival? Drawing on formal interviews with past and present organizers of the stampede and on informal conversations with stampede volunteers, and on formal interviews with area First Nations leaders who have had some involvement with the festival, I contrast their perspectives on the importance of Aboriginal involvement and their understandings of the reasons for Aboriginal people's reluctance to participate fully. I examine the stampede as a cultural festival in which various groups struggle over the constitution of public identities and over the meanings of performances. Through these interviews, it becomes apparent that stampede organizers and First Nations leaders interpret the significance of performance, and the meaning of symbols of identity, through radically different cultural frameworks. In conversation, Aboriginal leaders discuss their struggles to negotiate their way through issues of authenticity and the hegemony of noble-savage stereotypes and their pragmatic political strategy for using performance not only as a vehicle of resistance against Euro-Canadian stereotypes but also for the cultivation of new, positive identities among Aboriginal peoples themselves.

In Chapter 8, I summarize the major features of the frontier complex, explore some of the ways in which this local complex may relate to cultural traditions across Canada more generally, and discuss the implications for understanding the dynamics of Aboriginal/Euro-Canadian relations and current political debates regarding Aboriginal treaties and self-government in British Columbia.

# 2
# The Burden of History

Aboriginal/non-Aboriginal relations in Williams Lake have been fundamentally shaped by historical events that, for the most part, lie beyond the view of most members of the public. In this chapter, I sketch the early Aboriginal cultures in the region and trace how the influx of European traders, miners, and settlers, the establishment of colonial authority, the handling of the Aboriginal land question, and the expansion of agriculture and forestry have set the context for Aboriginal/non-Aboriginal relations in the present. In its emphasis on the broader political, economic, legislative, and administrative contexts of evolving Aboriginal/Euro-Canadian relations, this history provides an implicit contrast to the popular frontier histories discussed later that draw on a different genre to portray Cariboo-Chilcotin history. This history provides a background for situating current debates about the validity of Aboriginal title and treaties in the Cariboo-Chilcotin and for understanding the efforts of local Secwepemc, Tsilhqot'in, and Carrier leaders to bring these unresolved historical matters to public attention.

Aboriginal peoples – the Secwepemc, Carrier, and Tsilhqot'in and their ancestors – had been established in the Cariboo-Chilcotin for thousands of years before the first European explorers arrived in the late 1700s. The question of when and how Aboriginal people first arrived in the region can be answered in a number of ways. Many Aboriginal people in the Cariboo-Chilcotin assert that their occupation of the region extends back to "time immemorial," time beyond human memory, and that their ancestors came from nowhere else. Aboriginal oral traditions describe not when but how the world was readied for human occupation. Ulkatcho Carrier oral traditions recount how three humanlike beings – Kwakwosat, Yus, and Nowakila – came up the Dean River in the west Chilcotin, transforming the river, introducing salmon to it, and readying the territory for human life.[1] Secwepemc oral traditions tell a similar story through the adventures of the trickster Coyote, who transformed the landscape to make it ready for humans, introduced the first salmon, and created salmon-fishing stations along the riverbanks. Old One, the "chief of the ancient world," taught the Secwepemc the proper techniques for hunting and fishing and instructed them on the appropriate codes of moral behaviour for successful life.[2] These oral traditions, like those of other Interior Salish and northern Athapaskan peoples, highlight the creative powers of mythological beings, the interdependence between humans and animals, and the centrality of the landscape to Aboriginal identity and historical consciousness.[3]

In contrast, many archeologists believe that the first Aboriginal peoples arrived in the BC interior some 12,000 to 11,000 years ago as the last glacial period began to end.[4] According to archeological views, the first people were probably nomadic hunters of large animals that thrived on the open grasslands that quickly spread over the exposed grounds at the higher altitudes. As the climate became warmer and drier, more diverse plant and animal ecosystems developed. In the plateau region of central British Columbia, a diversity of modern ungulates – moose, mountain sheep, elk, deer, and antelope – formed the new basis for Aboriginal subsistence. Between 8,000 and 4,500 years ago, a cooling climate brought an expansion of pine and fir forests onto the open grasslands of the interior plateau.[5] Aboriginal peoples continued to pursue mixed practices of subsistence, hunting large and small animals as well as fishing. Minor runs of salmon had probably become established in the Fraser River as early as 10,000 years ago,[6] but it was not until about 4,000 years ago that salmon became prominent as a food resource. By 4,000 years ago, the interior plateau as it is today had been established. The cultures of the mid-Fraser River area had developed basic patterns of cultural adaptation and subsistence that continued until the early period of European contact.

In the early 1800s, the Secwepemc, Carrier, and Tsilhqot'in peoples had relatively well-established territories. According to ethnographer James Teit, Secwepemc territory ran from the grasslands about fifty kilometres west of the Fraser River across the thick forests of the interior plateau to the Rocky Mountains.[7] (Today this boundary is in dispute, as Tsilhqot'in leaders claim traditional ownership to all land west of the Fraser River.) There were about thirty Secwepemc bands with a total population of about 7,200.[8] Fourteen were in the Cariboo region, controlling the Fraser River area from above Lillooet to Soda Creek. The Tsilhqot'in occupied the central and western portion of the Chilcotin plateau and were divided into three or four bands with a total population of about 1,600.[9] By the late 1890s, six Tsilhqot'in bands were recognized.[10] The Carrier, to the north of the Tsilhqot'in, occupied a broad territory from the Bulkley River in the west to the Rocky Mountains in the east. In the early 1800s, there were approximately eighteen Carrier bands with an estimated total population of 8,500. Five of these bands – the southern Carrier bands – were situated in the Cariboo-Chilcotin, three along the Blackwater River drainage system, one in the vicinity of the Fraser River, and a fifth in the Cariboo Mountains.[11]

At the time of early European contact, the Secwepemc, Carrier, and Tsilhqot'in practised a mobile hunting, fishing, and gathering subsistence that involved regular movements through their territories to harvest seasonally available resources such as deer, elk, caribou, salmon, freshwater fish, hare, grouse, berries, roots, and other plant foods.[12] The round of seasonal activity was similar for all three groups. In the summer, families gathered along the banks of the major salmon rivers – Dean, Chilcotin, Chilko, and Fraser – and harvested salmon with dip nets or large basket traps and fences. In the fall, families dispersed to the mountains to hunt caribou, deer, elk, and marmot before moving to their winter quarters. The Tsilhqot'in and southern Carrier set up small winter camps near lakes, supporting themselves over the winter months by ice-fishing and rabbit-snaring and on stores of dried meat and fish. The Secwepemc, living primarily off their stores of dried salmon, gathered for the winter months in larger, semipermanent pithouse villages along the banks of the lower Chilcotin, the Fraser, and its tributaries. In the spring, with food supplies dwindling, families moved out from their camps and villages to trap fish spawning in the lakes and streams and to gather roots and new plants. In late spring and early summer, groups travelled toward the mountains to hunt game and gather berries before returning for the salmon fishery.

Extended families formed the basic social unit, travelling, hunting, fishing, and camping together throughout the year. A typical family group consisted of several brothers, with their spouses, children, and other relatives, although this group was also very fluid and subject to frequent change.[13] The Secwepemc, Carrier, and Tsilhqot'in were also divided into a number of bands, those families who regularly used a particular region and were known by that geographical referent. For example, the 'Ulkatchot'en were the people of the Gatcho Lake area in the west Chilcotin. The Dog Creek band were the "people of the deep hollow," and the Williams Lake band were the "people of Skola'ten" (Williams Lake).[14] Each Secwepemc band recognized a hereditary chief, who was determined partly by patrilineal descent and partly by his ability to command respect and to demonstrate leadership. Some of the Tsilhqot'in bands recognized hereditary chiefs, and some of the bands, such as Toosey and Anaham, derived their names from their chiefs.[15] The southern Carrier did not recognize formal band chiefs. Instead, temporary leaders were chosen to coordinate particular tasks when needed.

The Secwepemc, positioned as they were along the Fraser and lower Chilcotin up to Farwell Canyon, controlled the most productive salmon fisheries in the Cariboo-Chilcotin region. These bands relied heavily upon salmon, and each summer vast quantities were harvested, dried, and stored in underground pits for winter use. As the early surveyor and ethnographer George Dawson noted, "The right to occupy certain salmon-fishing places, with the annual visit to these of the more remote families and the congregation of large numbers of Indians at specially favoured places, largely influenced the life and customs of the Shuswap. In the same way, the most important news which could be conveyed from place to place, if not that of some warlike incursion, was that of the arrival of the salmon or the success or otherwise of the fishery."[16] The capacity to harvest and store a surplus of salmon enabled the Fraser River bands to profit from a trade in salmon products. As early as 3,300 years ago, trade networks linked the societies of the interior plateau to those in southern British Columbia, the Rocky Mountains, and the northern plains. By 2,500 years ago, mid-Fraser River groups were directly or indirectly linked through trade to Northwest Coast groups.[17] The principal commodities traded by the Secwepemc, by the early 1800s and probably long before, included dried salmon and salmon oil. The Fraser River Secwepemc traded these goods to the Tsilhqot'in, Carrier, and neighbouring Secwepemc groups, and the latter Secwepemc traded salmon products farther east to the Cree.[18]

The four Secwepemc bands occupying the lower Chilcotin River region up to Farwell Canyon controlled the best salmon fisheries in Secwepemc territory. According to ethnographer James Teit, these canyon bands were virtually sedentary: they "gave all their energies to salmon-fishing, the preparation of oil, and trading, and did very little travelling or hunting."[19] Through their production and control of vast quantities of dried salmon and salmon oil, these bands developed a highly specialized role as economic middlemen in the trade between the other Secwepemc bands and the Tsilhqot'in. "Because of their frequent trading and profit-making, the Cañon Indians were a wealthy people, and gave frequent potlatches," and at times they acted as peacemakers between the other Fraser River and Tsilhqot'in bands when hostilities threatened to interrupt trade.[20]

The Tsilhqot'in and southern Carrier traded with other neighbouring groups. A number of Aboriginal trade routes stretched across the interior plateau and down over the Coast Mountains to the Bella Coola valley and the inlets north and south.[21] So well marked and travelled was the Carrier route along the Blackwater River that in 1793 the fur trade explorer Alexander Mackenzie referred to the trail as a "road" and referred to the Blackwater as the "West Road River."[22] The Tsilhqot'in and southern Carrier had close trading relationships with the Nuxalk (Bella Coola), from whom they obtained dried salmon, dentalium shells, oolachen oil, and the first European-manufactured goods.[23]

It was in this context that the land-based European fur trade was introduced in the early 1800s. By this time, the three groups were involved in the maritime fur trade, either directly through the Nuxalk, who had been acting for the last decade as middlemen in the trade with European ships on the Pacific coast, or indirectly through Aboriginal trade networks. The southern Carrier in particular were well engaged in the fur-trade business, bringing beaver, bear, lynx, fox, and marten pelts down to the coast to trade with the Nuxalk.[24]

In the first decade of the 1800s, the North West Company expanded its operations westward into the northern interior of British Columbia with the building of four fur-trade posts: Fort McLeod in Sekani country, and Fort St. James, Fort Fraser, and Fort George in central Carrier territory. To the south, Fort Kamloops was built in southern Secwepemc territory in 1812. These posts drew an indirect trade in furs from the Secwepemc, southern Carrier, and Tsilhqot'in of the Cariboo-Chilcotin region. In 1821, the Hudson's Bay Company (HBC) amalgamated with the North West Company and opened Fort Alexandria near the summer village and salmon fishery of the Lhtakot'en Carrier, initiating a period of direct trade relations with Cariboo-Chilcotin Aboriginal groups.[25] In 1829, an HBC fort was built in Tsilhqot'in territory just above the confluence of the Chilcotin and Chilko Rivers.[26] The Tsilhqot'in generally did not support the post, and it closed in 1844.

Over the following decades, the Secwepemc, Carrier, and to lesser degrees the Tsilhqot'in became directly involved in the trade for furs with the Europeans. Rather than Aboriginal groups becoming incorporated into the European land-based fur trade, the reverse could equally be argued: that the European traders became incorporated into the preexisting Aboriginal trading system. This was most evident in the forts' dependence on local provisions, especially dried salmon, for their annual food supply. In the months between November and July at Fort Alexandria, for example, dried salmon was the staple food; 8,000 dried salmon were consumed in a thirteen-month period between 1827 and 1828.[27] This supply was secured by fort employees by fishing directly from the rivers using Aboriginal techniques and at times Aboriginal labour or by trading with Aboriginal groups and/or other forts. Pack trains were sent out from Fort Alexandria late in the salmon-fishing season to purchase dried salmon from groups stationed along the Fraser and Chilcotin Rivers, at times returning with as many as 11,000 dried salmon.[28] On occasion, particularly when the salmon runs were at the low points of their cycles, the refusal of local Aboriginal groups to provide salmon to the forts led to a crisis that threatened the fort's survival.[29] Aboriginal control over the salmon trade, plus the availability of other trade networks – particularly those linked to the Pacific coast – should Aboriginal trappers not receive the prices that they wished for their furs, gave the Secwepemc, Carrier, and Tsilhqot'in some control over their relations with Europeans.[30]

Historian Robin Fisher has characterized the land-based European fur-trade period in British Columbia – roughly between 1800 and 1850 – as enjoying generally peaceful and reciprocal relations between Aboriginal groups and European traders.[31] More recently, however, geographer Cole Harris has portrayed day-to-day relations between European traders and Aboriginal people as fraught with a "politics of fear."[32] Fur-trade posts were often protected by palisades and guns, and there was a constant surveillance for signs of Aboriginal aggression and attack. Fur traders were quick to respond to signs of danger through public threats, or actual demonstrations, of violence against those challenging the traders' presence and authority.[33] These chronic tensions and fears are clearly evident in the early journals of Fort Alexandria and particularly in the journals of Fort Chilcotin. Despite such problems, relations at Fort Alexandria were well established by the 1840s. Aboriginal involvement in the European fur trade did effect some significant cultural changes. Trapping became much more important in the annual round. There was a new desire for materials such as guns, ammunition, kettles, and blankets only available through the fur trade. Among the Fraser River Secwepemc, extended family groups tried to claim exclusive rights to specific trapping grounds, claims that undermined prior concepts of equal access to lands and resources by all tribal members.[34] Nevertheless, the Secwepemc, Carrier, and Tsilhqot'in maintained control through this period over their cultures and territories; in fact, the success of the fur trade depended on their continued occupation of their lands.

Whereas the European fur trade itself did not profoundly disrupt Aboriginal societies in the Cariboo-Chilcotin, the indirect product of European contact – epidemic disease – was much more devastating. In recent years, scholars have increasingly focused on the antiquity and impact of European diseases in the Northwest Coast and plateau areas.[35] Smallpox epidemics swept the Northwest Coast and plateau regions in the late 1770s and again in 1800-1, with three routes of transmission postulated: from early Spanish exploring ships on the coast, from the Russian colony at Kamchatka to the Tlingit, and/or from the Plains Aboriginal societies to the plateau.[36] By 1802, smallpox may have reduced plateau Aboriginal populations by as much as a devastating 45 percent.[37] For plateau societies, however, documentary evidence is limited to the Kutenai, Colville, Flathead, and Nez Percé; there is no direct evidence that these smallpox epidemics reached the central interior of British Columbia or the Secwepemc, Carrier, or Tsilhqot'in. Smallpox again swept through the northern BC region in 1836-8.[38] The disease spread as far south as Ootsa Lake, where an entire Carrier band succumbed to the epidemic.[39] It is unclear to what extent other southern Carrier, Secwepemc, and Tsilhqot'in bands were affected.

Traders stationed at Fort Alexandria, however, reported a variety of diseases among Aboriginal populations in the Cariboo-Chilcotin in later decades: whooping cough in 1845, measles in 1850, and smallpox in 1855, the last of which they traced to infected blankets that the Secwepemc had acquired from the Thompson River area.[40]

The most destructive epidemic on record was the 1862-3 smallpox outbreak, which ultimately reduced Aboriginal populations in British Columbia by a massive 62 percent.[41] The disease swept up the Pacific coast and travelled inland from Bella Coola and across the Chilcotin plateau to the Tsilhqot'in, Carrier, Secwepemc, and other interior tribes, devastating them in its wake. Passing through Secwepemc country in the winter months, the epidemic completely wiped out the six Secwepemc bands on the west side of the Fraser River (about 850 individuals in all). Two-thirds of the overall Secwepemc population may have died in this epidemic, and, of the fourteen Fraser River bands, only seven survived.[42] If not completely unprecedented, the 1862-3 outbreak must have been devastating to the Secwepemc, Carrier, and Tsilhqot'in peoples, destroying whole villages and communities, shattering well-established networks of trade and commerce, and forcing survivors to form new cooperative social units and continue living as best they could.

The 1860s was a period of critical change in Aboriginal-European relations in the Cariboo-Chilcotin region. The relatively balanced relationships established in the fur-trade era were irrevocably changed by the influx of thousands of miners in what became known as the Cariboo gold rush. By 1858, between 20,000 and 30,000 miners, many lured north from the depleted California goldfields, were working their way up the Fraser River.[43] By the early 1860s, miners had fanned out along the banks of the mid-Fraser, Quesnel, and Horsefly Rivers and their tributaries, and the Cariboo had become the centre of mining activity in the colony. On the heels of the miners came the entrepreneurs – the free traders, the roadhouse operators, the merchants – who provided goods and services to the mining population; the settlers who established farms and ranches to provision the mining towns; and the government officials who sought to establish law and order in the frenzied atmosphere of the mining frontier. The Cariboo gold rush initiated the era in which Aboriginal people were viewed as obstacles to and competitors in the advancement of the economy and the settlement of the colony and in which Aboriginal-European relations were defined by direct competition over control of the lands and resources.

The gold rushes in British Columbia brought with them not only a dramatic increase in the settler population but also an expansion of government activity. In 1858, mainland British Columbia was officially made a British colony. James Douglas, as governor of the new colony as well as that of Vancouver Island, faced the task of implementing new policies to encourage settlement in the colonies, to regulate Aboriginal-settler conflicts, and to address the Indian land question. Previously, as governor of Vancouver Island and following British colonial policy directives, Douglas had set about to free up Aboriginal lands for non-Aboriginal settlement through the signing of treaties. Fourteen treaties were signed with Aboriginal nations on Vancouver Island by 1854. These treaties clearly demonstrate early colonial recognition of Aboriginal title. The handling of the Indian land question in the mainland colony, however, took a different path. The Colonial Office in London refused to provide funds to cover the expense of settling treaties, and Douglas himself was disillusioned with the failure of the Vancouver Island treaties to alleviate the plight of those communities now in close contact with non-Aboriginal settlement.[44] Accordingly, Douglas altered his earlier policy.

By the early 1860s, Douglas believed that the only course for Aboriginal people's survival was through their gradual "civilization" and assimilation into mainstream colonial society through the adoption of Christianity and agriculture. As Paul Tennant has shown, Douglas devised an Indian land policy based not on the relinquishment of Aboriginal title through treaties but on the allotting of reserves throughout the colony to protect the village sites and cultivated fields of Aboriginal groups.[45] He viewed the reserve system as affording temporary protection for Aboriginal communities, allowing them to be economically self-sufficient until such time as Aboriginal people were absorbed into colonial society as individual landowners and farmers. To facilitate this process, he implemented legislation to enable individual Aboriginal people to preempt lands on the same terms as non-Aboriginal people. Whereas Douglas's earlier treaty policy was framed on a direct acknowledgment of Aboriginal title, the reserve system imposed after 1858 simply sidestepped the question. For this reason, the issue of Aboriginal title remains unresolved today.

Gold commissioners were subsequently dispatched to various regions of the colony to record mining claims, enforce colonial law and order, and mediate Indian-settler conflicts by establishing reserves. By this time, the Secwepemc had been heavily affected by the gold rush. The old Aboriginal trail up the east bank of the Fraser River that had connected the winter villages of the Canoe Creek, Dog Creek, Alkali Lake, and Williams Lake Secwepemc was now a major trail to the Cariboo goldfields.[46] Roadhouses and hotels were built close to many of the Secwepemc villages. The Soda Creek Indian village was adjacent to the last leg of the Cariboo Wagon Road, which terminated at the burgeoning settlement of Soda Creek at the southern terminus of steamboat operations up the Fraser River. With this sudden flood of settlers into their territories, the Secwepemc experienced an unprecedented loss of control over their lands, resources, and communities.

The most immediate crisis was over control of agricultural lands and water. Agriculture had been introduced to the Fraser River Secwepemc during the fur trade,[47] and by the 1860s Secwepemc families throughout the region were producing crops of grains and root vegetables. The principal villages of the Fraser River Secwepemc were typically situated on the benchlands above the Fraser or several kilometres up small rivers feeding into the Fraser. Being relatively low in altitude and on good water sources, these lands were among the best agricultural sites in the Cariboo.[48] Such lands were among the most desired by settlers, and conflicts quickly arose at Williams Lake, Soda Creek, and Canoe Creek for control of these lands.[49] To quell these conflicts, gold commissioners apparently allotted reserves for the Alexandria, Soda Creek, Alkali Lake, Dog Creek, and Canoe Creek Indians.[50] Although they did offer some degree of protection from encroachment, the reserves did not ameliorate Aboriginal demands to settle the broader issue of ownership of their territories.

With Douglas's retirement in 1864, Indian policy in British Columbia again shifted. Joseph Trutch, as chief commissioner of lands and works, assumed the authority for implementing Indian policy. In contrast to Douglas, Trutch viewed Aboriginal people as a primitive, savage, and inferior race, with no capacity for advancement and no inherent right to the land.[51] The reserve policy was abandoned, and the existence of Aboriginal title was no longer tacitly ignored but now explicitly denied, a position that sharply deviated from both British colonial policy and the handling of the land question elsewhere in Canada.

Successive land policies over the next decades worked not only to deny Aboriginal land rights but also to deny Aboriginal people an equal measure of the justice extended to settlers. Governments vigorously promoted the interests of settlers, and Aboriginal self-sufficiency in agricultural pursuits was seen as a hindrance to the advancement of the colonial (i.e., the settler) economy. Consequently, in 1866 the Land Ordinance was amended to deny Aboriginal people the right to preempt land without the special written permission of the governor.[52] In contrast, settlers could continue to preempt up to 320 acres of "unoccupied" land in the interior.[53] This move was supported by colonial newspapers, whose editors argued that Indians would make undesirable neighbours and should be isolated on reserves rather than scattered among the settlers.[54]

Aboriginal people found little protection for their rights through appealing to the courts. Colonial land legislation expressly prohibited settlers from preempting Indian village sites, cultivated fields, or burial grounds. Yet settlers in the Williams Lake district were ploughing over Aboriginal burial grounds, taking up Aboriginal hay meadows, and cutting timber from reserves. In some instances, when Aboriginal people sought redress by appealing to justices of the peace, they were turned away.[55] By 1871, when British Columbia joined Confederation, the Douglas reserves across the province had largely been nullified, and the lands, many of which had long been desired by settlers for their rich agricultural potential, were now thrown open to preemption.

The 1870s was a decade of crisis for the Fraser River Secwepemc. Although the Secwepemc were still largely reliant on Fraser River salmon and hunting, the cyclical crashes of the salmon runs, the decline in the trapping industry, and the loss of hunting territories to settlement resulted in agriculture assuming greater importance.[56] Secwepemc families throughout the region were producing crops of grains, hay, and vegetables, constructing irrigation ditches, cutting wild hay meadows, and running herds of horses and cattle.[57] Yet as farming lands and water rights were overtaken by settlers, the agricultural subsistence was also becoming precarious. This was clearly the case with the Canoe Creek band, as described by Oblate father C.J. Grandidier in 1880:

> At Canoe Creek ... the Natives have not more than fifteen or twenty acres of land to support one hundred and fifty Indians. Their cattle are on the mountains; if they come down, they are exposed to trespass, are seized, and not delivered until a fine has been paid. If the Indians need milk for their families, they are obliged to go up the mountain for a mile, [carry] with them their cans, and take the milk down. When they want to cut wild grass for hay, to feed their horses and cattle in winter, the whites step in, and claim the grass as their own. This state of things has lasted for many years.[58]

By 1879, with the failure of the salmon run, the land crisis in the Cariboo region was reaching severe proportions. In desperation and facing a winter of starvation, Chief William of the Williams Lake band dictated a letter eventually published in the Victoria *Daily Colonist* in which he conveyed the plight of his people:

> I am an Indian chief and my people are threatened by starvation. The white men have taken all the land and all the fish. The country was ours. It is all gone. The noise of the threshing machine and the wagon has frightened the deer and the beaver. We have nothing to eat. We cannot live on the air, and we must die. My people are sick. My young men are angry ... I do not know what to say next week when the chiefs are assembled in council. A war with the white man will end in our destruction but death in war is not so bad as death by starvation. The land on which my people lived for five hundred years was taken by a white man; he has piles of wheat and herds of cattle. We have nothing not an acre. Another white man can take three hundred and twenty acres of our land and the Indian

> dare not touch an acre ... Now, what I want to say is this – there will be trouble, sure. The whites have taken all the salmon and all the land and my people will not starve in peace.[59]

William's letter drew a flurry of sympathetic support from the editor of the *Daily Colonist* as well as missionaries and settlers in the Cariboo, who condemned the provincial government for not addressing the land question, for neglecting the desperate situation of the Indians, and ultimately for putting the lives of settlers at risk.[60]

The crisis in the Williams Lake district was brought about by the provincial and federal governments' persistent failure to deal with the Indian land question in British Columbia. Under the terms of the province's union with Canada, the federal government was to assume authority for Indian matters, following a policy "as liberal" as that carried out earlier in British Columbia. In contrast to the rest of Canada, where treaties were being implemented to secure Aboriginal lands for settlement, no formal measure for obtaining a relinquishment of Aboriginal title was pursued in British Columbia. Instead, in the early 1870s, a joint federal-provincial committee was established to address Indian matters in the province by creating reserve lands to be held in trust by the federal government. Yet there were constant arguments between the provincial and federal governments regarding the size of reserves to be allotted: provincial officials insisted on a maximum of ten acres per family, whereas federal officials argued that eighty acres per family should be set aside. This was still much less than the 160 to 640 acres per family that had been allotted in the recent treaties on the Canadian prairies.[61] These debates hinged on the presumed "liberality" of British Columbia's earlier Indian policy, which in reality was much less liberal than the policies followed elsewhere in Canada. At the time of union, federal officials apparently had little knowledge of the province's Indian land policy, and evidence indicates that provincial officials, in having this clause included in the terms of union, sought to mislead federal officials and conceal the true nature of the province's earlier policy.[62]

The ongoing disagreements between federal and provincial officials over reserve allotments, and the provincial officials' deliberate tactics to obstruct the reserve commission's progress, severely impeded the process of dealing with the land question.[63] As a result, land conflicts between Aboriginal people and settlers in the interior of the province were escalating, and rumours of an impending Indian uprising were sweeping through the settler populations. Even the federal Indian superintendent of British Columbia, I.W. Powell, was moved to state that, "if there has not been an Indian War, it is not because there has been no injustice to the Indians, but because the Indians have not been sufficiently united."[64]

The situation of the Williams Lake Secwepemc was a case in point. In the early 1800s, the band numbered 350 and had seven winter villages along the Chimney Creek, Fraser River, Williams Lake, and San José River valleys.[65] Chief William initially attempted to accommodate the first wave of settlement. In 1859, he gave permission to the first settler in the district to build a cabin and cultivate a garden on land at the foot of Williams Lake on which the band had its own cabins, cultivated fields, and burial grounds. The settler, Thomas Davidson, then recorded the land as his own preemption, an act that contradicted the colony's legislation protecting Indian villages, fields, and graveyards. As recounted by Father C.J. Grandidier in 1880, "The chief was offered twenty dollars by Davidson; but he refused to part with his father's land, and rejected the money ... Shortly after the other part of the valley was preempted by other parties, and the Indians were driven away to the top of the hills, where cultivation is out of the question." Their lands in the Chimney Creek valley were also quickly taken up: "They also had a summer resort in a little valley some eight or ten miles from Williams Lake, at Chimney Creek, where they used to fish [for] salmon. All the cultivable land was taken up by the whites in that valley, so that, not only are they without one inch of land, in their own country, but there is no good land left to give them." Grandidier concluded that the Williams Lake Indians "have been most shamefully despoiled of all their lands."[66]

Government officials failed not only to protect Indian lands from preemption but also to address the needs of the Williams Lake band by allotting reserve lands. In the spring of 1861, the gold commissioner to the district, Phillip Henry Nind, requested permission to establish a reserve to secure some cultivatable land for the Williams Lake band. The band was in desperate need of land, because "the greater proportion of available farming land has been preempted and purchased and it is probable that before the summer is over it will all be taken up."[67] Nind was subsequently instructed to set up a reserve of 400 to 500 acres for the band.[68] This reserve, however, was never established. As a result of the government's repeated failure to address the needs of the Williams Lake Secwepemc and to enforce its own legislation and policies, the band was eventually forced to seek refuge on land recently taken up by the Oblates at the newly established Roman Catholic mission just south of Williams Lake.

In 1881, Reserve Commissioner Peter O'Reilly finally visited the Aboriginal groups in the Cariboo to allot the first reserves. By the time of his arrival, much of the land still available was that undesired by settlers: land that was rocky, unproductive, lacking water, and thus ill suited for agriculture. The Quesnel, Alexandria, Soda Creek, Williams Lake, Alkali Lake, Dog Creek, and Canoe Creek bands had small reserves allotted, covering their village sites, cultivated fields, and a number of hay meadows, salmon and freshwater fishing stations, and burial grounds.[69] In the case of the Williams Lake and Soda Creek bands, the dearth of available land forced the reserve commission to establish reserves through the purchase of farmland from area settlers. Even then, it was generally acknowledged by the reserve commissioner, the local Indian agent, missionaries, and settlers alike that the reserves were inadequate to meet these bands' agricultural needs.[70] As the Indian agent to the district stated in 1884, "the proportion of farming land for each Indian in the various reserves is so absurdly small that it may be put down at almost nothing."[71] The allotment of reserves, in short, did little to alleviate the crisis, and Secwepemc leaders continued to bitterly protest the failure of the reserve commission to address their land requirements.

The broader issue of Aboriginal title had not been dealt with by the reserve commission, and the small reserves were just a fraction of the larger territory over which bands held Aboriginal title. When Soda Creek chief Kramousalist demanded in 1881 that O'Reilly grant a reserve covering a larger portion of the band's traditional territory, stretching over some twenty miles, his request was flatly denied.[72] The law prohibiting Indians from preempting land had also severely constrained the Secwepemc's ability to cope with the influx of settlers. The reserves that were finally allotted were much smaller than the lands that Aboriginal people might have secured had they been allowed to preempt land on an equal basis with non-Aboriginal settlers. That the handling of the land question in the Cariboo was guided by a policy of promoting settlers' interests while ignoring the needs of area Indian bands was evident in O'Reilly's report some years later. After allotting several additional hay meadows for the Alkali Lake band, he apologetically reported that the reserves were "not likely to interfere with the progress of the country, as there are no white settlers in the immediate neighborhood."[73]

In contrast, the area west of the Fraser River underwent much less dramatic settlement. Although there was increased non-Aboriginal traffic across the Chilcotin plateau during the gold rush, particularly along the old Aboriginal trails linking Bentinck Arm and Alexandria, the region was thought to have little gold potential. The southeastern region of the Chilcotin plateau, however, particularly the valleys of the lower Chilcotin River and its tributaries, contained natural grasslands ideal for cattle ranching. By 1885, a number of settlers had preempted lands and established farms and ranches. The Tsilhqot'in, since the decimation of the canyon Secwepemc from smallpox, now occupied all the plateau area west of the Fraser River. In 1887, O'Reilly allotted reserves to the Stone, Toosey, and Anaham Tsilhqot'in. These reserves covered agricultural lands already under cultivation, grazing ranges, hay meadows, and a fishing station on the Fraser River. Conflicts over water rights soon arose, particularly among the Toosey and upstream settlers. The Land Act prohibited Indians not only from preempting land but also from recording water rights, whereas settlers enjoyed full rights to record water with their preemptions. The Toosey band, which by the late 1880s had been settled in the village for almost twenty years, now found its agricultural water supply cut off as settlers began to record upstream water rights.[74] Despite these conflicts, the Tsilhqot'in, in contrast to the Secwepemc, remained relatively prosperous in the following years through farming, stock raising, hunting, fishing, and trapping.[75] Southern Carrier territories, although heavily impacted by the gold rush east of the Fraser River, were relatively free from non-Aboriginal settlement in the west, where the southern Carrier bands were able to maintain a relatively autonomous existence with little interference. By 1903, reserves for all the southern Carrier bands had been established.

The land question, however, remained unresolved. In the first two decades of the 1900s, there was a growing political movement among coastal and interior tribes in British Columbia to press the provincial and federal governments to deal with the land question. In 1909, interior chiefs gathered at Spences Bridge and formed the Interior Tribes of British Columbia.[76] In 1910, Secwepemc, Okanagan, and Nlaka'pamux chiefs travelled to Kamloops to present Prime Minister Wilfrid Laurier with a petition asserting their Aboriginal title to traditional lands and demanding that the government recognize that title.[77] Hopes for a prompt resolution of the land question were quashed with the appointment in 1913 of the joint federal-provincial McKenna-McBride Commission. Its mandate was to effect a final resolution of the Indian land question and to resolve persistent federal-provincial disagreements about Indian land matters merely by reviewing and adjusting the sizes of Indian reserves in the province.[78] Despite Aboriginal protests, the commission refused to consider the issue of Aboriginal title.

Intertribal political activity continued. In 1916, Secwepemc, Tsilhqot'in, and Carrier representatives joined thirteen other interior and coastal tribal groups to form the Allied Tribes of British Columbia, whose primary goal, in the face of the governments' unwillingness to negotiate a settlement, was to take the question of Aboriginal title to court. Giving much strength to their case was a 1921 ruling of the Judicial Committee of the Privy Council in London concerning Southern Nigeria; the committee affirmed the existence of Aboriginal title as a preexisting right and found that this right persisted unless it could be proven to have been extinguished.[79] As the Allied Tribes continued lobbying the federal government to strike a special committee to hear Aboriginal claims, as a first step toward bringing the case to the Judicial Committee – the highest court to which Aboriginal people could appeal – federal officials became more resolved to prevent the matter from entering the court system. In 1927, a joint Senate-House of Commons committee heard and rejected outright the claims of the Allied Tribes as "irrelevant issues."[80] Following the joint committee's recommendation, the federal government took the most extreme measure to prevent the issue of Aboriginal title from arising again. In 1927, the Indian Act was amended to make it a crime for any individual to raise money or accept fees for any land claims activity.[81] The law banning land claims activity remained in place until 1951. The issue of Aboriginal title remained dormant but not forgotten among the Secwepemc, Tsilhqot'in, and Carrier, appearing again with the resurgence of the Aboriginal rights movement across Canada in the late 1960s and early 1970s.

The suppression of Aboriginal political activity and land rights was only one aspect of a much broader web of legislation and bureaucracy designed to control Aboriginal populations. Nineteenth-century federal Indian policy was founded on the common presumption that Aboriginal people were an inferior, primitive race whose salvation could only be attained by their abandonment of traditional culture and their assimilation into Euro-Canadian economic, social, and cultural practices. In 1876, existing Indian laws were consolidated into a new body of legislation known as the Indian Act, which gave government officials sweeping powers to control virtually all aspects of Aboriginal lives. By 1880, a separate government bureaucracy, later known as the Department of Indian Affairs, was created to oversee the implementation of the Indian Act and to manage Indian matters.[82]

Departmental officials held wide-ranging powers. For example, the Indian Act determined who could be designated as a status Indian. For over a century, until 1985, Aboriginal women who married non-Indian men, and the children of such a union, lost their official Indian status. Under the terms of the Indian Act, government officials had the power to remove any non-status Indian from a reserve, regardless of his or her affiliations. These provisions directly attacked the traditional structure of Aboriginal families and communities. The 1880 Indian Act gave government officials the authority to disrupt Aboriginal forms of government by imposing elected band councils. These councils exercised only minor decision-making powers typically subject to departmental approval. Government officials could arbitrarily determine the structure of band councils and who could vote in band elections, and they could unilaterally depose chiefs.[83] In 1884, in an attempt to destabilize the political and social structures of Northwest Coast Aboriginal societies, the Indian Act was amended to outlaw potlatches, the formal public feasts in which social rank and chiefly political authority were witnessed and validated by the community.

These, then, were among the powers held by the first Indian agent to the Williams Lake district in 1883, who was responsible for providing assistance and medical care and for enforcing the terms of the Indian Act.

What transpired "on the ground," however, was a more complex negotiation of relations of power. Throughout the 1880s, the Secwepemc bands remained in a precarious state due to the shortage of agricultural lands and other reliable means of subsistence. Indian Agent William Meason occasionally was moved to provide supplies to the sick and destitute. In keeping with the policy of assimilation, he encouraged bands to devote their time to agricultural practices and threatened to withhold relief if they failed to follow his precise instructions.[84] Meason viewed the large gatherings at memorial feasts, to which a family would invite friends and relatives to honour the deceased by erecting a new fence enclosing the grave, as a distraction from "work," leaving the host poorer through generous provisions for the guests. To prevent these gatherings, Meason classified them as potlatches and outlawed them under the terms of the Indian Act.[85]

In other ways, the Indian agents became embroiled in the political factionalism within reserve communities. The Indian agent's coercive powers were tempered on occasion as different sectors of the Aboriginal population used the Indian agent to advance their own political interests. For example, the Quesnel, Soda Creek, and Dog Creek chiefs for many years had attempted to control drunkenness in their villages.[86] With the arrival of the Indian agent in the Williams Lake district, these chiefs drew on new sources of power, collaborating with Meason to punish those caught drinking or supplying Indians with alcohol, both of which were prohibited by the Indian Act. In 1883, a group of Williams Lake community members opposing hereditary Chief William appealed to Meason. Under their guidance, he appointed a second chief, an outspoken opponent of Chief William.[87] A few years later, several Stone Tsilhqot'in, dissatisfied with their own chief, made a similar request of the Indian agent to appoint a new chief.[88]

One of the clearest examples of the coercive powers exercised by the Indian agent involved his support of the Oblate-run residential school for Aboriginal children at St. Joseph's Mission. It was a central premise of both the Indian Affairs department and Christian missionaries that, if assimilation was to succeed, Aboriginal children would have to be removed for a lengthy period from the "destructive" influences of their families and communities. In residential schools, students would be isolated far from their home villages in large, centralized institutions where they would be taught basic academic skills, Christian values and morals, and agriculture, trade, and domestic skills in preparation for their entry into non-Aboriginal society. These schools were seen by both government and religious leaders as the ideal means to bring about this cultural cleansing and social transformation.

Since 1867, with the establishment of the Roman Catholic mission just south of Williams Lake, Secwepemc attitudes toward the church had been complex and varied, ranging at times from enthusiastic support to complete rejection of the missionary program.[89] The missionaries at St. Joseph's were primarily concerned with "saving" Aboriginal souls. Armed with the conviction of the primitiveness and savagery of Aboriginal customs, they instigated a vigorous campaign to prohibit feasting, dancing, shamanism, and other traditional practices and to convert Aboriginal people to the Roman Catholic faith. Yet the missionaries at times assumed a protective role as advocates for Aboriginal interests, and on occasion they were outspoken in their efforts to push governments to address the Indian land crisis in the Cariboo.[90]

The Secwepemc chiefs, as with the Indian agents, manipulated their relationships with the Roman Catholic missionaries to further their own goals. In the 1860s, the Secwepemc chiefs were desperately attempting to assert their authority and to restore social order in their communities, which were still reeling under the impact of non-Aboriginal invasion. In the late 1860s and again in the 1890s, Secwepemc chiefs collaborated with the missionaries to impose a strict church system of hierarchical village administration and social control in which dancing, gambling, drunkenness, and immorality were publicly punished.[91] Secwepemc relationships with the missionaries were thus complex and varied, involving measures of coercion, resistance, and collaboration.

The most coercive, and ultimately destructive, missionary initiative was the creation of the residential school at St. Joseph's Mission. The first group of students arrived in 1891, and for the next six decades increasing numbers of Secwepemc, southern Carrier, and Tsilhqot'in children were sent to the mission to receive formal education and training. Students typically resided at the mission for ten months, during which time they were allowed little or no contact with their families. They were subjected to a strict regime of discipline in which public humiliation, beatings, and physical punishments were used to maintain their submission.[92] Only in the 1960s did Aboriginal children begin to be integrated into the public schools, and by 1981 the mission school had closed.

The local Indian agent fully supported and enforced the continued attendance of children at the residential school. In 1894, the Indian Act was amended to empower Indian agents to remove any school-age child from his or her home to fill the residential schools. Parents and other relatives had no legal recourse to resist the forced removal of children from their homes. Although some parents agreed that residential school education would be of benefit to their children, most were extremely reluctant to hand their children over, succumbing only to the forceful influence of the Indian agent and the missionary. Others attempted to hide their children by disappearing to the hay meadows or hunting grounds to avoid the annual roundup of children.

The coercive nature of the residential school system became fully apparent when complaints began to be raised about the system of education, the regime of discipline, and the care of students at the mission. In the first three decades of the mission's operation, the Department of Indian Affairs conducted three separate investigations into allegations that students were being poorly treated, underfed, and subjected to excessive physical punishment.[93] Children were running away from the institution; when asked why, they complained about being chronically underfed, forced to eat rotten food, and excessively punished and whipped. The investigations exonerated the staff. The government investigators praised the mission school's staff and dismissed complaints, in some cases ignoring clear evidence to the contrary. The investigators insisted that it was simply in the "wild nature" of Indians to resist discipline. Their very acts of resistance were taken not as evidence of problems in the institution but as proof of the need for children to be "civilized" through the residential school program.[94]

One final form of legislative power bearing down on Aboriginal populations concerned the franchise: for many decades, Aboriginal people were denied the right to participate in the political processes of choosing governments in Canada. Aboriginal people were denied full voting rights in British Columbia until the 1949 provincial election, and they only gained full federal voting rights in 1960.[95] Thus, Aboriginal people had little chance to help shape government policy, despite the fact that, in having a separate government department created specifically for their management and in being subjected to the regular scrutiny and control of Indian Affairs officials, Aboriginal people were among the most intensively governed sectors of Canadian society.

In short, after the 1860s, the Secwepemc, Tsilhqot'in, and southern Carrier were subjected to a series of separate laws, regulations, and policies that isolated them on reserves and exposed them to the coercion of Indian agents implementing a policy geared to the eradication of Aboriginal culture and identity. Discriminatory laws prevented Aboriginal people from gaining access to the Canadian democratic process of choosing governments and took away their right to raise and educate their children. Aboriginal people's struggles to have the land question addressed by colonial, provincial, and federal governments were blocked by a range of political and legal mechanisms that barred access to the Canadian (and British) government's system of justice as a venue for resolving such matters of law. Whereas frontier historical accounts highlight the settler's freedom, independence, and unlimited opportunities in a land seen to be unoccupied and rich in resources free for the taking, the story of Euro-Canadian settlement in British Columbia is also one of blatant discrimination, coercive and destructive government policies, and systematic repression of the rights of freedom and equality among the Aboriginal populations.

The exercise of power, however, was never total. It was mediated by the varied and often conflicting agendas of diverse sectors of colonial society as well as by Aboriginal people's own strategies of responding to the colonial presence. Whereas Indian agents encouraged Aboriginal assimilation through agricultural pursuits, provincial officials and legislators, espousing the view that Aboriginal people were incapable of advancement, prevented such a transformation by denying Aboriginal people access to agricultural lands. In some cases, Aboriginal people were able to direct the powers of various colonial agents to advance their own interests. Forms of collaboration – an engagement with Roman Catholicism, a strategic use of colonial laws – were matched by forms of resistance: the persistent commitment to cultural traditions, the hiding of children from the residential school authorities, the continued protests over the land question. In the more remote regions of the Cariboo-Chilcotin, where the Indian agent rarely visited and where non-Aboriginal settlement was sparse, forms of colonial power were only intermittently felt.

These, then, were the political, legislative, and administrative conditions in which non-Aboriginal immigrants were enabled and empowered to take up land, to establish homesteads and ranches, and to form a patchwork settler society across the expanse of the Cariboo-Chilcotin. Non-Aboriginal settlement at Williams Lake itself has a somewhat discontinuous history. In 1859, under circumstances discussed above, Thomas Davidson took up land at the foot of the lake and built a roadhouse and a prosperous farm. Two years later, Gold Commissioner Philip Nind set up a government office there, and soon the new settlement of Williams Lake boasted a number of homes, a courthouse, and a jail. An English immigrant, William Pinchbeck, employed by Nind as a constable, soon built his own stopping house, saloon, and store and eventually came to own much of the Williams Lake valley.[96] This brief period of fluorescence ended with the transfer of government offices to the booming gold town of Richfield.[97] When the Cariboo Wagon Road bypassed Williams Lake, diverting northward from 150 Mile House to reach Soda Creek in 1863, the settlement at the foot of the lake began to decline.

Throughout the latter half of the 1800s, non-Aboriginal settlement in the Williams Lake district consisted of scattered homesteads and ranches. During the gold rush, many immigrants arrived in the Cariboo from Ontario, the United States, England, Ireland, Scotland, Germany, France, and China. Generally speaking, English immigrants often came from wealthy and educated backgrounds, whereas American immigrants arrived with little and hoped to make their fortunes through the gold rush.[98] A number of non-Aboriginal men, while establishing farms and ranches, formed relationships and had families with Aboriginal women. What resulted was a significant population with mixed ancestry; indeed, many of the currently identified pioneer families in the Cariboo-Chilcotin have had Aboriginal ancestors.

By 1901, the Williams Lake district census, one of five census divisions in the Cariboo region, recorded approximately 350 non-Aboriginal people in the region.[99] Most had been born in Canada, although a significant number had recently immigrated from China and the United States. The census, displaying a race consciousness typical of the era, despite the existence of many individuals with mixed racial backgrounds, listed not only the "colour" of each individual (white, yellow, red) but also the "racial or tribal origin" of the population. The dominant ethnic groups were Chinese, English, Irish, Scottish, French, and German. The Chinese constituted about 20 percent of the settler population. Many made a living by trapping, gold mining, and working as labourers on ranches and as cooks and waiters in hotels along the wagon road. The Secwepemc people in the Williams Lake region, despite devastation by diseases and loss of land, constituted the majority of the area population at about 500.[100]

The railway boom of the first and second decades of the 1900s drew many new residents to the Cariboo. Men found work in the construction of roads and bridges and in the laying of the rail lines, merchants set up stores to cater to the needs of labourers, and a new wave of settlers arrived to take up land and establish small farms or ranches. With the arrival of the Pacific Great Eastern (PGE) railway at the foot of the lake in 1919, Williams Lake was reborn. By the following year, a village – complete with homes, hotels, restaurants, bars, a post office, a livery stable and feed store, a dance hall, a pool hall, and two banks – had grown up around the train station.[101] At the end of the 1920s, churches, government offices, a police station, and a courthouse had been established, and the village of Williams Lake became incorporated officially as a municipality.[102] The town was destined to become a principal nexus for transportation in the region. Cattle from ranches across the Cariboo and Chilcotin were now driven to Williams Lake, instead of to the previous railhead at Ashcroft on the transcontinental Canadian Pacific Railway line, to be sold and shipped via rail to markets in the south.

From the 1860s to the 1940s, the settler economy focused on ranching, farming, mining, transportation, and small-scale logging and sawmilling. Agriculture, though, became the backbone of the Cariboo-Chilcotin economy. In the early years of settlement, prospective ranchers could apply to preempt 320 acres of land. No individual, however, could hold more than one preemption certificate, although he could purchase additional lands from other owners. This restriction limited the ability of Cariboo-Chilcotin ranchers to establish large operations.[103] Instead, ranchers wishing to build up their herds, and requiring more grazing land than their preemptions provided, practised a system of open-range stock raising, allowing their cattle to run freely over "unoccupied Crown land" and rounding them up periodically for branding and for fall sales.[104] Aboriginal ranchers ignored the restrictions imposed by the reserve system and grazed their horses and cattle freely on land that they considered theirs by traditional right.

At the end of the First World War, with more settlers arriving in the Cariboo-Chilcotin, and with the majority of ranchers depending on access to Crown grazing land, competition and conflict over the use of grazing lands intensified. In response to growing conflicts, the provincial government instituted a lease/permit system to regulate access to these lands. In the 1960s, about 60 percent of ranches in the Cariboo-Chilcotin relied on grazing leases, which were competitively sought.[105] In particular, leases and permits were critical to the survival of ranches in the Chilcotin, where the ratio of leased to privately owned land was three to one.

The 1950s also witnessed the emergence of the competing interests of the agriculture and forest industries for the use of Crown lands. The forest industry began to expand rapidly in the central interior, and small logging and sawmilling operations sprang up throughout the Cariboo-Chilcotin. Whereas the earlier logging and sawmilling operations had provided materials for local use only, now lumber was exported for sale to regional and international markets. The majority of the small sawmills in the region were portable units set up at the logging sites, and they remained on the sites until the local timber supply was depleted. The sawed lumber was shipped out from the bush mills by truck to the nearest point on the PGE rail line.

In a number of ways, ranching and forestry were incompatible. Ranchers complained that the bush mills and logging practices destroyed fences, irrigation ditches, and roads. Roads were being built and portable mills were being set up in the middle of long-established grazing areas. The noise of the mills and the logging activities were not only destroying forage but also disturbing cattle, causing them to scatter into the bush and resulting in a loss of weight and consequently of value.[106] In other ways, the advance of logging into previously isolated regions meant that new Crown grazing lands were opened up for lease/permit holders.[107]

The growing conflicts between different Crown land users, and the concern that the interior forests were being overharvested, led to a change in provincial Crown land management policies and an increase in government regulations. In the late 1940s and 1950s, the province introduced its new sustained-yield forest-management program.[108] The Forest Branch determined the sustainable annual allowable cut within the administrative unit and then assigned each mill operating in the Cariboo-Chilcotin a relative percentage, or quota, of that cut, dependent on the mill's previous output. The quota system was ostensibly created as a means whereby the provincial government could increase its regulation of the forest industry as well as mitigate conflicts between competing land users. In practice, this system favoured established forest companies with the greatest productivity and made it difficult for new companies to secure timber licences.[109]

Technological improvements in logging and milling operations between the 1950s and the 1970s exponentially increased the productivity of large companies that could afford the highly capital-intensive equipment. The smaller companies, having poorer productivity and smaller annual allowable cuts, were squeezed out of the industry. Larger forest companies bought out the smaller bush mills, acquiring their harvesting rights at the same time. Finally, as sawmilling became more automated and technologically sophisticated, it became more feasible for the larger companies to build large and highly automated sawmills in central locations and to truck raw logs to the mills for processing.

The end result was the concentration of timber rights in the hands of a few interior forest companies, the rapid disappearance of small bush mills, and the establishment of major sawmills in the three major Cariboo settlements of Quesnel, Williams Lake, and 100 Mile House. Overall, the number of sawmills operating in the interior was reduced from 2,000 in the 1950s to only 330 in 1978.[110] The majority of lumber milled in the Cariboo-Chilcotin now is sold to markets in the United States, making the region's forest economy largely dependent on market factors beyond local control.

This period also saw increased utilization of Cariboo-Chilcotin forests for harvesting. New licences were granted to companies to harvest what two decades earlier would have been considered unmerchantable timber. In the late 1980s, two pulpwood harvesting licences were granted that assigned potential harvesting rights to timber too small to be utilized by sawmills. The inevitable disappearance of forests is poignantly evident in the shift in vocabulary among forest industry spokespeople, who now speak of ensuring continued access not to "trees" or "wood" but to "fibre flow."

The expansion of the forest industry not only brought an intensification of conflict between competing Crown land users – forest companies, independent ranchers, and Aboriginal hunters and trappers – but also introduced a new population of wage workers who have greatly benefited from industrial expansion. The influx of workers and cash into the local economy brought greater prosperity to the local merchants. A steady stream of businesspeople arrived in the Cariboo. Accompanying them were a new population of young professionals, including doctors, accountants, and teachers, who provided an infrastructure of services to the rapidly growing population. In 1941, Williams Lake had a population of 540; two decades later, it had quadrupled to 2,120.[111] By the 1970s, Williams Lake had become a government administrative centre for the Cariboo-Chilcotin region, and civil servants added to the social mix. A large influx of Indo-Canadians in the 1970s, mainly from the Punjab region of India, added a new ethnic component to the local population. Between 1961 and 1981, the population once again quadrupled to 8,362, and it rose again by 1991 to 10,385, now outnumbering Quesnel's population of 8,179.[112]

In contrast to the economic prosperity enjoyed by non-Aboriginal residents in the Cariboo-Chilcotin, the period between 1940 and the present has been a time of diminishing opportunities for the Secwepemc, Tsilhqot'in, and Carrier. In the earlier decades, they managed to arrive at a tenuous equilibrium in their relations with non-Aboriginal society. Most families supported themselves primarily by hunting, fishing, trapping, and, where possible, gardening. Many families were involved in stock raising, running herds of horses and cattle and cutting cultivated and wild hay meadows to provide winter feed. The annual round of activity involved regular movements between the reserve village and the hunting grounds, traplines, fishing stations, and summer gardens and hay meadows. Trapping, seasonal employment in packing, freighting, guiding, domestic service, and farm and ranch labour, and the sale of buckskin handiwork provided Secwepemc, Carrier, and Tsilhqot'in families with extra cash income.

The expansion of clear-cut logging practices into hunting and trapping territories began to undermine the Aboriginal subsistence economy, particularly among the Carrier and the Tsilhqot'in, whose territories had been the least influenced by settlement and industrial expansion. Opportunities for seasonal wage work on farms and ranches – one of the main sources of cash income for Aboriginal people in the region – also declined with the increasing mechanization.[113] Many Aboriginal families in the Cariboo-Chilcotin operated their own small farms and ranches, typically running no more than twenty head of cattle.[114] As non-Aboriginal ranching operations expanded, becoming more capital intensive and highly mechanized, competition over control of grazing lands increased. Some new sources of employment were created with the expansion of logging, and a number of Aboriginal people found work in the bush mills set up in the more remote regions of the Cariboo-Chilcotin. By the 1970s, the bush mills had been replaced by larger mills in the regional centres. As work in the mills became more competitively sought, Aboriginal people were gradually excluded from the workforce.

The introduction of a system of government transfer payments also brought changes to the Aboriginal economy. In the 1950s and 1960s, government assistance programs, including old age pensions, family allowances, disability pensions, and social assistance, became more fully available to Aboriginal people.[115] Although these sources of income augmented rather than replaced hunting and trapping activities, they also undermined the bonds of mutual assistance and cooperation that had knit the communities together. With hunting, trapping, and agriculture becoming increasingly difficult, many families gradually became dependent on welfare and the cash economy. Trips to the nearby towns of Williams Lake and Quesnel became more frequent. Many Aboriginal students were emerging from the residential school indoctrinated with a sense of their inferiority and marginality in the dominant society and with no opportunity to find employment or acceptance within that society. Alcohol use became more prevalent after legislation prohibiting Indians from drinking in public establishments and from possessing alcohol was lifted in the 1950s and 1960s. By the 1960s, the social fabric of many of the reserve communities was unravelling, with frequent incidents of alcohol abuse, violence, family breakdown, and child neglect and abuse.

The 1970s witnessed a new era of political activity among Aboriginal people across British Columbia and Canada. At the reserve level, this growing politicization was reflected in the emergence of a number of young, articulate, and educated leaders who took over the leadership of their bands, through the Indian Act's system of elected, fixed-term band councils, from the older, lifetime chiefs. As part of the Department of Indian and Northern Affairs policy to devolve centralized administration and bureaucratic responsibility to band offices, these leaders administered and managed a number of band programs previously handled by department employees.

As well as assuming control of economic and government powers, a number of First Nations began to address some of the social ills of their communities. The success of the Alkali Lake Secwepemc in dealing with alcohol abuse received much publicity,[116] and many individuals in other reserve communities also began the process of "sobering up" and rebuilding their families and communities. Alcoholics Anonymous groups formed in many Secwepemc reserves, and people expressed a renewed interest in Aboriginal culture and spirituality through sweat lodge ceremonies, pipe ceremonies, and powwow drumming and dancing. Aboriginal leaders were publicly asserting their political identity as Indians. By the 1980s, the land issue – the problem of unrelinquished Aboriginal title – was once again raised as First Nations leaders openly challenged the Crown's presumption that it owned provincial lands. In the 1990s, road blockades were set up on various Chilcotin roads to protest unresolved Aboriginal title claims, the clear-cutting of traditional territories, and the Canadian military's occupation of the Toosey First Nation's traditional lands. These blockades interrupted logging traffic and drew much, largely unsympathetic, public attention.

Struggles over Aboriginal rights in the Cariboo-Chilcotin have gained much support from recent Canadian court decisions and changes to federal policy. In the early 1970s, following the Supreme Court of Canada's ruling in the Nisga'a case over Aboriginal title,[117] the federal government revised its earlier policy and agreed to negotiate outstanding claims of Aboriginal title in areas of Canada where treaties had not been implemented. In 1982, the new constitution, in section 35(1), recognized and affirmed the existing Aboriginal and treaty rights of Aboriginal peoples in Canada. In 1993, the BC Court of Appeal in the *Delgamuukw* (Gitksan-Wet'suwet'en) case ruled that Aboriginal rights were never extinguished by colonial, provincial, or federal laws in British Columbia, and that they persist today.[118] In 1997, the Supreme Court of Canada, ruling on the appeal of the *Delgamuukw* decision, further liberalized and broadened the legal definition of Aboriginal rights. It ruled that Aboriginal title is a right not just to carry out specific sustenance practices, but to "exclusive use and occupation" of the land itself.[119] Because they are protected by the Constitution, Aboriginal title and rights cannot be unilaterally extinguished by any government in the future. The Supreme Court further concluded that Aboriginal title is a burden on the Crown's activity, and that the government must consult with, and, in some cases, secure the full consent of, Aboriginal communities before enacting policies regarding the management of Crown lands.[120] The cumulative weight of court decisions has made it necessary, after over 100 years, for the provincial government to not only negotiate settlements with First Nations in the province, but prepare itself for a future in which First Nations will be full and equal participants in the control and management of lands throughout the province.

The increasing political strength of the Aboriginal rights lobby in the Cariboo-Chilcotin is occurring in a time of intensifying public fears over the future of the forest industry and forestry-based resource communities. Forest industry workers, both in the mills and in the bush, are struggling to hold on to their jobs as more and more positions are lost to mechanization. The impact of technological advance is so great that a 33 percent increase in the volume of timber harvested in the Cariboo Forest Region between 1979 and 1993 resulted in no net job growth.[121] With continuing modernization in the industry, job loss is inevitable. Coupled with an area unemployment rate of 18.5 percent in 1992, and a near doubling between 1981 and 1992 of the percentage of employable people in Williams Lake collecting unemployment insurance, some observers predict a looming crisis in the regional economy.[122] These economic conditions are by no means unique to the Cariboo-Chilcotin. They are experienced by virtually all hinterland resource communities dependent on an economy controlled by foreign markets and capital.

In this climate of economic insecurity, the affluent lifestyle that non-Aboriginal people have enjoyed over the last three to four decades is waning. Forestry workers and town merchants alike recognize their dependence on the forest industry and fear the potential impact of any further restriction of forest companies' access to timber resources. With the assertion of Aboriginal title and the perceived threat of forest companies' loss of access to timber resources in Aboriginal territories, tensions between Aboriginal and non-Aboriginal people in the Cariboo-Chilcotin are high.

The burden of history is now confronting both Aboriginal and non-Aboriginal people in the Cariboo-Chilcotin. In bringing unresolved historical matters to public attention, and in attempting to chart a course for social relations in the future, Aboriginal people in the region are challenging the basic structure of their legal, political, and economic relations with Canadian society. But even more, in their discussions with non-Aboriginal people in public meetings, in conference rooms and courtrooms, in the media and on roadblocks, they are calling into question some of the fundamental tenets of the culture and worldview of Euro-Canadian society: the basic beliefs, assumptions, and understandings that have legitimated the denial of Aboriginal title and the imposition of government control over Aboriginal people. These processes are bringing into full view the cultural legacy of colonialism as reflected in the taken-for-granted assumptions that prevail in rural Euro-Canadian society.

# 3
# The Landscape of Public History: Pioneers, Progress, and the Myth of the Frontier

Historical images infuse the public landscape of Williams Lake. Downtown streets are named after early settlers and politicians who were prominent in village life in the 1920s. Images of cattle, cowboys, and the Cariboo gold rush adorn the walls of the city hall council chamber, the public library, and downtown businesses. Tourism brochures promote the Cariboo-Chilcotin as the last vestige of the Canadian Wild West, a frontier rich in historical traditions and where the wilderness remains "untamed" and "untouched." History – Euro-Canadian history – is highlighted in the summer newspaper supplements featuring the region's pioneer families and even in restaurant placemats that pay tribute to the "settlers who came to Canada's West [and] made this magnificent land their own." Although the average resident of Williams Lake may profess a lack of interest in history, his or her everyday world is permeated by the values and identities of a selective historical tradition that celebrates European expansion, settlement, and industry.

Similar constructions of history can be found in virtually any small city and town across Canada. Histories commemorating the arrival of early explorers, settlers, missionaries, and industries in the remote regions of Canada constitute the master narratives of Canadian nationalism. These narratives comprise what Raymond Williams calls a society's "selective tradition," a partial vision of history that provides the official story of that society's past, a story produced and communicated in the most significant of public domains, ranging from public schools and national museums to ceremonies of the state, and a story that plays a vital role in rationalizing past and present social institutions and structures of political authority.[1] Historians Eric Hobsbawm and Terence Ranger have shown how these selective historical traditions were "invented" by colonial governments to promote nationalism and to legitimize the process of colonization and the subjugation of indigenous peoples.[2] The real power of a selective tradition, however, occurs when it becomes transformed into a set of unquestioned historical "truths" that define conventional historical understandings for members of a society. In Canada, these frontier histories are produced by agents of the state and saturate the everyday world of non-Aboriginal Canadians, who encounter (and reproduce) these narratives in the arts and entertainment industries, in the media, in local museums, in small-town festivals, and in popular literature of pioneer life. In short, the ubiquity of frontier histories reflects how certain colonial traditions of imagining history and constructing knowledge have come to dominate common-sense understandings of Canada's past.

In this chapter, I explore the contours of one of the most pervasive and influential selective historical traditions evident in British Columbia today: the myth of the frontier. The frontier myth is a historical epistemology consisting of a set of narratives, themes, metaphors, and symbols that has emerged within the context of North American colonization, that continues to define the dominant modes of historical consciousness among the general public, and that various individuals draw upon to construct understandings of the past and the present, of contemporary identities, and of relationships with Aboriginal peoples.

In the following pages, I explore how the frontier myth appears in those domains of public history in Williams Lake that are among the most authoritative and influential sites of historical knowledge and that play an important role in socializing townspeople into particular understandings of the past.[3] I examine three settings: public school curriculum, popular historical literature available in local bookstores, and the city museum. Among the vast array of events that occurred in the past of the Cariboo-Chilcotin, and among the vast range of historical experiences of different sectors of the population (men and women; European, Chinese, and South Asian immigrants; Aboriginal peoples; wealthy and working-class people), which histories are selected as relevant? How do these histories compare with the academic history presented in the previous chapter? What aspects of history are absent, collectively forgotten? Who controls the representation of history?

On the one hand, the political, economic, and ideological forces shaping the histories produced in each of these settings are quite different. Each site focuses on a different level of history: national, regional, local, or personal. However, there is a remarkable similarity in the histories that *are* produced. Euro-Canadians regularly draw on the frontier myth when they write about history, when they construct museum displays, when they reflect on their lives, and when they discuss contentious historical events and issues. By virtue of their ubiquity, these frontier histories constitute a dominant historical discourse in the city, a discourse that bears down to influence and constrain how local residents understand the past, the present, and their relationships with one another. The exercise of power relies on knowledge, and these habitual modes of knowing about the past, in both what they say and what they do not say, have significant implications for the continued material and ideological domination of Aboriginal peoples of the Cariboo-Chilcotin.

The frontier myth exists as a highly flexible set of metaphors, images, symbols, and narratives through which a variety of historical perspectives and experiences can be voiced. As I show here, it is more appropriate to speak of frontier histories in the plural. In the city is an array of frontier histories: national histories, local histories, and histories written by men and by women, by professional writers and by first-time, self-published authors, by urban residents and by rural pioneers. Many are variations on the frontier myth, each celebrating in its own way the "discovery" of the "empty" land, the arrival of the settlers, and the establishment of colonial society.

Frontier narratives may be put forth both to affirm and to criticize existing structures of power and past practices of colonial expansion. Counterhegemonic formulations, for example, may romanticize the noble savage, either expressing regret over the destruction and disappearance of Aboriginal peoples and cultures or celebrating their resistance and survival and downplaying colonialism's impact. The standard narrative structure, the binary encounter of opposites on the frontier, and the outcome of absolute conquest (or absolute resistance), remains the same; the moral weighting of these agents and outcomes, however, is reversed. It is precisely this flexibility – the ability of the frontier myth to serve a variety of purposes and interests, both hegemonic and counterhegemonic – that has enabled it to survive as a dominant historical mode into the present.

Buried within the bulk of public history in Williams Lake are a few alternative histories. Some of the counterhegemonic histories produced by First Nations and Euro-Canadian writers are also put forth within the symbolic language and themes of the frontier myth. They seek to challenge the legitimacy of colonization by retaining the narrative structure of history as contact, conflict, and conquest but providing a critique of colonialism by inverting the moral weighting of the historical agents and the ultimate outcomes. Others attempt to step outside the framework of the frontier myth, challenging the notions of discovery and conquest and the binary narrative structure of the frontier experience and attempting to highlight the coexistence of multiple histories and experiences. Finally, there are the life histories and oral traditions of First Nations people – exceedingly scarce in the public domain – in which the past is conveyed through historical narratives emerging from Aboriginal epistemologies and traditions.

My intent here, however, is not to trace instances of conflict over public history but to survey the most important and authoritative domains of public history in order to sketch the dominant themes and variations of frontier histories as they appear in the context of a small city in rural

Canada in the 1990s. I present a quick inventory of the histories encountered in these settings and comment on the potential implications of such selective historical accounts for naturalizing relations of power and inequality between Aboriginal and non-Aboriginal peoples.

### High School History Textbooks

The public school curriculum in British Columbia is controlled by the provincial government. As institutions of the state, public schools play a powerful role in the socialization of young people into the dominant beliefs, values, and identities of Canadian society and in the inculcation of selective understandings of history that promote Canadian nationalism. At the same time, public schools are also sites of resistance and struggle over the structure of the educational system, teaching methods, and the content of the curriculum. In the last two decades, an important focus of debate has been the teaching of Canadian history.

Standard textbooks have long portrayed Canadian history through the actions of the two founding nations, the British and the French.[4] Their account of Canada's past has highlighted the heroic actions of white male elites while ignoring the different historical experiences of other groups – women, working classes, immigrant minorities – and the roles played by capitalist expansion, class conflicts, and Aboriginal-state struggles. In general, history textbooks have celebrated the processes of European expansion while rendering Aboriginal peoples invisible or grossly caricatured in either romantic or demeaning stereotypes.[5]

With the official adoption of multiculturalism in the 1970s, the rise in public interest in Aboriginal issues, and the growing political strength of First Nations, politicians and educators have acknowledged the need to revise public school curricula to reflect the perspectives and values of diverse cultural groups in Canada.[6] The two Canadian history textbooks now standard in BC schools were written in this context, the grade 9 textbook in 1979, the grade 10 textbook in 1987. These textbooks are official, state-sanctioned accounts of Canadian history that have been designed specifically to shape how Canadian children understand the history of the nation, the process of colonization, and the relationship between non-Aboriginal society and Aboriginal peoples. In the following pages, I examine these texts and ask a number of questions. How is the past remembered? How are Aboriginal people portrayed? How is Canadian national identity constructed? By paying attention to the narrative structures and metaphors, we can determine to what extent the authors have drawn on the frontier myth to structure their accounts.

A common criticism of Canadian historiography concerns the lack of attention to Aboriginal people's roles in shaping Canadian history. Bruce Trigger suggests that "Canadian historical studies as a whole have suffered from the chronic failure of historians and anthropologists to regard native peoples as an integral part of Canadian society."[7] This marginalization of Aboriginal people has been practised and reinforced not only by early writers of British and French Canadian historical literature but also by the developing academic disciplines of archeology and anthropology in the nineteenth and early twentieth centuries.[8] Images of Aboriginal people have shifted according to changes in the climate of Aboriginal-settler relations and the dominant intellectual approaches to understanding the diversity of human populations and societies. But several themes have continued to appear.

Aboriginal cultures are often presented as static, as lacking history prior to European contact. Colonial and Aboriginal societies continue to be treated as separate spheres, and the role of Aboriginal peoples in facilitating, shaping, and/or hindering the course of colonial expansion has been ignored. When incorporated into Canadian histories, Aboriginal people are shown to respond passively to forces of change, to be secondary and largely irrelevant to the course of history, and to have lost their culture following European expansion.

In various ways, such portrayals have affirmed the colonial assumption of Aboriginal people's inherent inferiority and legitimated European expansion and domination. Yet the hegemonic potential of these histories is a product not just of the way that Aboriginal people are portrayed but also of the more general type of colonial history in which these images are embedded. The narrative structures, the metaphors, and the symbolic images of these histories are firmly rooted in the frontier myth. Furthermore, these national histories are framed by a series of epitomizing events captured through the heroic deeds of courageous men. History is told through the individual experiences of the explorers, such as Champlain and Cartier, who "discovered" Canada; of the missionaries, such as Brébeuf and Lalemant, who were martyred in their struggle to bring Christianity to Aboriginal peoples; and in the accomplishments of colonial officials, such as James Douglas and Matthew Baillie Begbie in British Columbia, who brought "civilized" society, law, and order to the wilderness. These individuals are portrayed as heroes, as symbols of national pride and identity, as the founding ancestors of the contemporary nation.

These themes are central in the two secondary textbooks assigned to BC classrooms in the mid-1990s. These texts are explicitly nationalistic and celebrate European colonization. This fact is evident in the titles alone: *Exploration Canada*[9] and *Our Land: Building the West.*[10] The first text covers a period from first human arrival in the New World to 1812. The second text begins with the British conquest of New France and ends with comprehensive chapters on the contemporary industrial economies of Canada and British Columbia.

Both textbooks use value-laden adjectives to describe European colonization as a heroic triumph over adversity. In the first, the arctic environment is described as "hostile." Missionaries eagerly accepted the "dangerous, difficult, and uncomfortable life of the wilderness."[11] Settlers are recognized for their "courage" in leaving their homelands.[12] The Ohio Valley had "scarcely been touched," a place where Indians "had lived quietly in its forests and its streams."[13]

The second textbook describes the "triumph" of the Hudson's Bay Company. In British Columbia, colonial governor James Douglas is described as "a stout, powerful, active man of good conduct and respectable abilities."[14] The building of the Cariboo Wagon Road through the Fraser Canyon was the Royal Engineers' "greatest accomplishment."[15] All of these images directly evoke the frontier myth, in which nature is feared and endured, in which (white) man encounters and eventually conquers the wilderness, in which the territory is unoccupied, "untouched," and thus free for the taking, and in which Indians live a "quiet" life as noble savages.[16]

Aboriginal people remain a marginal presence in both books, although in the grade 9 text there is some attempt to recognize the Aboriginal presence in several introductory chapters. The first five of its thirty-two chapters describe the cultures of Aboriginal Canadians (Inuit, Haida, Blackfoot, Iroquois, Beothuk, and Micmac). One chapter presents a contemporary Inuit woman's reminiscences about Inuit culture. These chapters, however, use the past tense timelessly; Aboriginal history is denied. After brief discussions, the Aboriginal presence soon fades. History is then presented in chapters describing the first Europeans to arrive in the New World, the development of the fur trade, and the struggles between the British and the French for control of much of North America.

The portrayal of Aboriginal people in the grade 10 text is often starkly negative. For example, a discussion of the extinction of the Great Plains buffalo herds refers to the "stone-age" Aboriginal cultures and reinforces the widespread and erroneous notion of the "primitiveness" of Aboriginal cultures. Once Europeans introduced horses and guns to the Aboriginal tribes, however, bison hunting intensified, and Aboriginal overhunting led to the "near extinction of the bison."[17] There is no discussion of the widespread slaughter of buffalo by white sport hunters and hide collectors or of the deliberate American slaughter of buffalo herds to destroy the base of subsistence of the Plains nations in order to bring about their subjugation.[18]

Inordinate attention is given to the relationship between Aboriginal people and alcohol. Under the first major heading mentioning Aboriginal people – "The Fur Trade and Native People" – the book suggests that the fur trade brought about the destruction of Aboriginal cultures.[19] Aboriginal people became "dependent on the brandy or rum forced upon them by traders." Weakened by alcohol and dependent on trade goods, they then succumbed to European diseases and often died, "even though the sickness was not fatal to Europeans."[20]

The most vitriolic treatment of the Indian-alcohol relationship is the section headed "The Whiskey Trade." There the reader is told that, "for bottles of cheap rotgut," Aboriginal people were trading "valuable buffalo robes, furs, horses, food, and some even their wives and daughters."[21] "Many deaths and murders had followed drinking sessions in the Native camps."[22] Again, disease and malnutrition are presented not as the results of dislocation from traditional territories but as the effects of "alcoholism," which "interfered with traditional Native hunting and food-gathering activities."[23] The North West Mounted Police formed in an effort to curb the whisky trade, heroically marching 2,000 kilometres in the hot summer sun to the western prairies to impose law and order on the Canadian frontier.[24]

These writers engage in a prevalent myth of colonization: Aboriginal peoples were inherently weak and incapable of controlling their impulsive thirst for alcohol. Alcohol is treated as the cause of the decline of Aboriginal societies rather than as a symptom of more complex forces, among them territorial dispossession and the disappearance of the base of subsistence brought about by European expansion. The actions of colonial society are excluded from the explanation.

In neither text is there much mention of Aboriginal land claims, treaties, or the need for colonizers to acquire Aboriginal lands through formal processes. The second text states that Aboriginal people had no concept of individual land ownership and did not fix boundaries to their territories.[25] "The idea of buying or selling land was totally foreign to these Native hunters. The land was theirs – but they did not own it."[26] Canadian Aboriginal people, the book states, willingly signed the treaties offered by the Canadian government. In so doing, they acknowledged and benefited from the benevolent paternalism of government officials, enjoying a relationship not available to their Aboriginal "brothers" in the American West, who were the targets of "warfare" launched by settlers and the US army. This brief mention apart, the text is resoundingly silent about Aboriginal/Euro-Canadian land conflicts.

Both textbooks provide official views of the history of Canada in which images of heroic courage and benevolent paternalism define Canadian colonial practices. Nationalist histories present what could be called the "big man" theory of history, in which history is made by the heroic actions of elite European men. These figures then become condensed symbols of national identity; in their actions are embedded the ideal values of contemporary Canadian society. Aboriginal peoples are slotted into these dramas as supporting characters in a larger historical script through which (Euro-Canadian) national identities are constructed. Pluralism, alternative identities, contrasting values, and competing historical perspectives – issues hinted at in the grade 9 text – are suppressed in the more overtly nationalistic history of the grade 10 text.

This celebratory view of colonial history both omits some of the more brutal aspects of Canada's past treatment of Aboriginal peoples and evokes this brutality in the racist stereotypes of Aboriginal people. The stereotypes of the drunk Indian, the Indian squaw, and the lazy, irresponsible, and immoral Indian resonate not only with prevailing attitudes heard in Williams Lake and in many other small cities and towns in rural Canada[27] but also with literary traditions in Canada more generally.[28] These images are all the more surprising given the grade 10 text's recent publication. That these images persist in state-sanctioned histories is testimony to the widespread and purportedly uncontroversial nature of anti-Aboriginal racism in Canada.

The limitations imposed by the genre of frontier history are evident in the strategies that have arisen since the 1970s to accommodate multicultural and antiracist critiques. James Walker, in his review of popular and academic histories produced during the 1970s, found this strategy to be largely one of silence: of erasing Indians from history. Walker illustrates how historians have responded to a growing awareness of the inadequacies of earlier works by simply removing any mention of Aboriginal peoples. "Measured in column inches of print, histories written in the 1970s pay less attention to Indians than ever before."[29] This is only one manifestation of the hegemonic power of the "invisible Indian" stereotype, through which writers render Aboriginal people invisible from their historical accounts, thus avoiding rather than confronting the politics of representation. The strategy of adding preliminary chapters on Aboriginal cultures presented in ahistorical contexts gives the appearance of pluralism while retaining the central narrative themes of heroic individualism, discovery, and conquest. To what extent histories produced in the 1980s and 1990s have moved away from these trends remains to be explored.

These official histories of Canada, funded, produced, and sanctioned by the state, provide comfortable, noncontroversial accounts of the past and encourage students to accept the legitimacy of state authority, the myths of conquest, and the theories of Aboriginal inferiority that rationalize colonialism. Yet these textbook histories contrast sharply with other state discourses and practices, among them the initiatives, under way for the last two decades, to negotiate outstanding claims of Aboriginal title. Official historical discourses of the Canadian state are themselves diverse and plural.

For example, in 1995 the BC government created a provincewide elective course for grade 12 students: BC First Nations studies. One of the stated objectives is "To provide students with an alternative to the ethnocentric histories traditionally taught. Students require a more balanced perspective of the history of relations between colonizing powers or incoming settlers and B.C. First Nations. The resistance and resilience of First Nations people in response to imperialism and colonialism should be affirmed."[30]

That such a course was deemed necessary for British Columbia is undoubtedly a reflection of the growing prominence of First Nations issues in the media and in the courts and of the rising tensions between Aboriginal and non-Aboriginal peoples over impending treaty settlements. The recommended resources include a variety of recent scholarly publications on Aboriginal history and culture in the province. To what extent these histories are being interpreted and implemented in classrooms in ways that step beyond the terms of the frontier myth or in ways that only reverse the morality of the colonial process, highlight Aboriginal resistance, and offer comfortable accounts of Aboriginal/Euro-Canadian relations in the present remains an open question. It is significant, though, that such challenges to the dominant nationalist histories are being introduced on the fringes of the educational system: in a supplementary curriculum rather than in official textbooks and in elective courses rather than in required courses. High school textbooks remain the most conservative and archaic of the official nationalist histories in the public domain.

## Popular Historical Literature

The shelves of the two major bookstores in Williams Lake are filled with popular histories of the romantic past of British Columbia. Within the last decade, growing public interest in heritage issues and heritage tourism has resulted in an exponential increase in the number of regional and local histories available to the public. These books are bought not only by summer tourists but also by local residents interested in the region's past and searching for gifts for distant relatives and friends. Such popular histories become standard historical reference books and are emblems of all that is considered unique about the Cariboo-Chilcotin.

A different set of political and economic forces influences which books are available to the general public and consequently whose histories are aired in these settings. Publishing houses cater to a presumed market for historical information and entertainment; the histories that they publish are shaped by their assessment of what will sell to the public. Whereas large national publishing houses have a competitive edge in producing and marketing books, a variety of provincial and regional publishers have taken the lead in producing popular histories with a local focus. This opening up of the industry is linked in part to the technological advances in desktop publishing, through which small publishing houses, First Nations organizations, school districts, and even self-publishing authors have been able to produce and sell their works. These books make their way onto the shelves of local bookstores, their owners and buyers alternately turning away books judged to be controversial or enthusiastically supporting those written by local authors or describing local histories and Aboriginal cultures.

Well over fifty regional and local histories are now available in city stores, and overwhelmingly they are written within the same romantic frontier tradition. Regional histories, written by both nonlocal and local authors, recount key events in the advance of non-Aboriginal settlement and focus heavily on the "discovery" of gold and on the Cariboo gold rush. Local histories, often written by Cariboo-Chilcotin residents themselves, typically relate the achievements of early settlers and pioneer families. The vast majority of regional and local works are written by non-Aboriginal people; history is presented as a series of positive events, as a linear process of development.

In contrast to the nationalist textbooks, popular pioneer autobiographies are written not from a position of scholarly distance but through the authority of personal experience, giving voice to the experiences of "ordinary" men and women overlooked by the elitist focus of national histories. Yet popular histories are fully compatible with the histories in high school textbooks. These histories are equally enmeshed in the imagery, symbols, and narrative forms of the frontier myth. They are equally engaged in a commemoration of European colonization, now writ small in the lives of individual men and women on the Cariboo-Chilcotin frontier.

## Regional Histories

Among the most prolific publishers of popular history is Heritage House, a small BC company that specializes in slim, inexpensive paperbacks. Its regional history collection is contained in the Western Canadiana bookracks that are prominently displayed in stores across the province. A main focus in this collection is police history; that is, the bringing of law and order to the Western Canadian frontier. Among the titles are a three-volume set of *Outlaws and Lawmen of Western Canada*,[31] *Off Patrol: Memories of BC Provincial Policemen*,[32] *B.C. Provincial Police Stories* in three volumes,[33] and *March of the Mounties*, by Sir Cecil E. Denny,[34] which describes the formation of the North West Mounted Police. Its front cover reads: "Despite their impressive red coats and white gauntlets, virtually all of the new policemen were inexperienced ... Despite these handicaps, their Commanding Officer reported that they 'performed one of the most extraordinary marches on record.'" The heroic individualism of regional histories is no longer centred on missionaries, explorers, and colonial officials but on figures of law and order: the Mountie, the BC provincial policeman. Here the Canadian version of the frontier myth takes on a distinctive narrative theme that distinguishes it from the American version.

Richard Slotkin argues that the quintessential feature of the American frontier myth is the master narrative of "regeneration through violence," in which the moral imperative of violence as a means of achieving progress and civilization has been fundamental in shaping past and present constructions of American national identity. Just as the hero of many American frontier histories is the Indian fighter, and just as regeneration through violence is a central narrative theme of many American versions of the frontier myth, in Canada a dominant heroic figure is the Mountie, and a dominant narrative theme is what could be called "conquest through benevolence." Canadian heroes do not inflict violence; instead, they impose peace, order, and good government on Aboriginal and non-Aboriginal people alike. Yet the Mounties, too, encounter forces of opposition and engage in conflict. These forces of opposition are not hostile Indian tribes but renegade criminals, both Aboriginal and non-Aboriginal. These criminals play key roles in these historical dramas: they are the dark forces of lawlessness and immorality against which the protagonists must struggle for the advance of "civilization" and "progress."

This theme of conquest through benevolence – the definition of the Canadian spirit and of the Canadian national identity through the continual assertion of history as a narrative of paternal domination of Aboriginal peoples – weaves in and out of Canadian literature and popular history. As noted, the conviction that in Canada "we have treated our Aboriginal people well" is central to high school history textbooks. Pierre Berton, Canada's foremost popular historian, has characterized the Canadian frontier as a series of benevolent and paternal extensions of British authority.[35] The North West Mounted Police were really "civil servants and social workers."[36] "The Indians called [the Mountie] 'father' to his face, but it was not only the Indians who appreciated his paternalistic qualities."[37] Berton celebrates the absence of violence on the Canadian frontier: "The Indian fighter is as foreign to our experience as the fighting Indian."[38]

BC scholars have also noted how early historians emphasized the contrast between the peaceful and law-abiding settlements in British Columbia and the settlements on the American frontier.[39] Bruce Trigger notes that the idea of Canadian benevolence existed among nineteenth-century historians, who "relished comparing the brutal treatment of native people by the Americans with the 'generous' treatment they had received from Euro-Canadians."[40] Such writers construct an oppositional national identity in the shadow of American cultural and economic imperialism. Although the particular political and economic conditions in which the myth of Canadian benevolence has arisen and been reformulated over time have yet to be explored, a long-term implication is one of silence regarding the realities of Canada's own repression of Aboriginal people and a cloaking of forms of domination and power as paternalistic expressions of goodwill.

In a number of regional histories, Aboriginal people do emerge as the central symbolic counterpart to settlers and the advancement of Euro-Canadian "civilization." Aboriginal people at times are portrayed as bloodthirsty, violent, and irrational savages. One example is in McKelvie's *Tales of Conflict: Indian-White Murders and Massacres in Pioneer British Columbia,*[41] which announces on its cover: "The Indians were an extremely proud people, fierce warriors quick to avenge a real or imagined wrong. Indian justice did not require that retaliation be made upon the persons who committed the wrong, only that blood be spilled. This form of justice resulted in the murder of settlers and the massacre of crews on several sailing ships." Likewise, Rothenberger's *The Chilcotin War* describes the conflict that arose when a crew of Euro-Canadian surveyors was murdered in the course of building a road through Tsilhqot'in territory in 1864.[42] The book depicts on its cover an attack by Aboriginal people on a camp of sleeping whites. The cover claims that the book is about "the true story of a defiant chief's fight to save his land from white civilization." Their defeat, it is implied, is inevitable.

These accounts reduce the complexity of Aboriginal-settler conflicts to simple narrative structures in which the imagined savagery of Aboriginal people justifies the use of violence as a natural and inevitable process in the expansion of "civilized" European societies. Rothenberger's story of the Chilcotin War, in fact, has become the subject of intense public criticisms by Tsilhqot'in political leaders. Although no published written history yet provides Tsilhqot'in perspectives on these events,[43] the subject is occasionally debated in letters to the editor of the Williams Lake city newspaper, and the public hanging of the Tsilhqot'in men, in the name of colonial justice, is a source of great bitterness among many Tsilhqot'in people today.[44]

Books on the discovery of gold in the Cariboo are popular and numerous. These books play upon the romance of riches to be found in the "untouched wilderness," luring destitute men into the region with the hope of prosperity and redemption. Such books, emphasizing the abundance of valuable natural resources essentially free for the taking, are another version of the frontier myth. *Cariboo Gold Rush,*[45] for example, notes: "In 1858 some 30,000 Gold seekers stampeded to the Fraser River. Scores drowned in the tumultuous rapids or were killed by Indians. But survivors pressed upstream. In a land called Cariboo they found nuggets by the ton, their discovery resulted in today's province of British Columbia." The gold rush is a story of conflict between the principal oppositional elements of the frontier myth: man versus nature, whites versus Indians. Those with the courage to attempt the challenge and the luck to survive it found their fortunes in the abundant nuggets that were free for the taking. The province of British Columbia, it is claimed, was built on such individual initiatives.

The epitomizing events in such histories are the "discoveries" of untapped riches by heroic individuals. These protagonists embody the cultural ideals of Canadian society: individualism, courage, the quest for material wealth, and the ability to prosper through hard work, determination, and ingenuity. As Julie Cruikshank notes about Klondike gold rush narratives, this theme of discovery condenses what in reality was a slow historical process of the emerging knowledge of gold among non-Aboriginal immigrants.[46]

The discovery of gold in British Columbia was equally slow and sporadic. In 1852, there was a brief gold rush to the Queen Charlotte Islands; in the face of Haida resistance, both miners and Hudson's Bay Company officials abandoned their quest.[47] Throughout the 1850s, colonial officials in Victoria received reports of gold discoveries in the interior of the mainland, and in 1858 construction of an HBC post began at the forks of the Thompson and Fraser Rivers for the purpose of trading for gold from Aboriginal miners.[48] HBC officers had sought to protect their trading monopoly with Aboriginal peoples by containing the knowledge of gold strikes, yet rumours of gold eventually spread beyond the colony, drawing thousands of prospectors from the depleted California goldfields. In 1858, the lower Fraser River gold rush was at full height. Aboriginal peoples along the Fraser continued to assert ownership of the gold resources, and that year there were violent confrontations as Aboriginal people sought to fend off the flood of non-Aboriginal prospectors entering Aboriginal territories.[49] As the gold of the lower Fraser became depleted, miners again moved north to the upper reaches of the Fraser, and by the early 1860s the Cariboo gold rush was at its height.

From an academic perspective, the Cariboo gold rush was only one incident in a broader scenario of advancing European industry, colonial authority, and settlement. In contrast, popular histories mark the onset of the Cariboo gold rush with a specific event: the "discovery" by a group of American prospectors, assisted by an Aboriginal guide, of gold on the Horsefly River. Aboriginal people are portrayed as helping in the process of colonial economic expansion and settlement; Aboriginal perspectives on these events remain inaudible and unavailable to the general public.

### Local Histories: Pioneer Stories

Pioneer stories of the Cariboo-Chilcotin region have always been popular with wider Canadian audiences.[50] The past five years have seen a tremendous growth in the number of books discussing Cariboo and Chilcotin pioneer history. Many of them have been written by contemporary Cariboo-Chilcotin residents, including Irene Stangoe, Diana French, Branwen Patenaude, Todd and Eldon Lee, and Chilco Choate. Several of these authors are now writing their second or third books. These books, recounting the experiences of early ranchers, schoolteachers, road builders, cowboys, big-game guides, ministers, and roadhouse operators, provide a glimpse of the diversity of historical experiences among the many individuals who arrived in the Cariboo-Chilcotin over the past 100 years.

In contrast to this new array of books, the best-known stories of the Cariboo-Chilcotin, and, as I was told by one bookstore manager, the books that continue to be the most frequently purchased, are two autobiographical books first published in the 1950s: Eric Collier's *Three against the Wilderness*, and Rich Hobson's *Grass beyond the Mountains*.[51] They were published by major publishing companies and are still promoted by local bookstores as the classic stories of the Cariboo-Chilcotin. Collier's book, an international best-seller, has been condensed in a Reader's Digest version and is described on the cover of the 1991 edition as "the classic Canadian wilderness tale." These two books, one by a British immigrant and the other by an American immigrant, draw on essentially the same frontier myth to narrate a story of arrival and establishment in the Cariboo-Chilcotin. They also reflect the ways in which the frontier narrative is differently formulated by writers.

Eric Collier, the son of a wealthy English businessman, emigrated to Canada in the 1920s. He and his "quarter-breed" wife established a homestead in the Meldrum Creek area in the northeastern Chilcotin plateau. For the next thirty years, they raised a family and made a living by trapping and hunting. The Collier family's achievement is indeed remarkable. Collier tells of felling trees and building a log cabin by hand, of fencing acres of meadowland, of surviving long and bitterly cold Chilcotin winters, and of reseeding beaver into Meldrum Creek to eventually establish thriving beaver colonies all along the creek. What makes this the story of a Euro-Canadian settler, rather than of an Aboriginal family, many of whom were living successfully under similar conditions, is the way that Collier frames his experience.

Collier's book is the story of conflict with and struggle against dark forces. These forces are conceptualized in terms of both the elements ("summer's searing heat and winter's penetrating hostility") and nature ("our only neighbours [were] the moose, bears, timber wolves and other wild life of the muskegs and forest; some of whom seemed ever ready to dispute our right to be there at all").[52] Nature is to be feared and respected, something against which to be constantly vigilant. Collier, in fact, summarizes this heroic struggle in the book's title, *Three against the Wilderness*.

Margaret Atwood has identified this chronic fear of nature as a defining feature of Canadian literature.[53] Whereas Aboriginal people have played a central oppositional role in literary depictions of American history, Atwood suggests that in Canadian literature the wilderness is the dark force against which settlers continually struggle. Whereas in American literature these frontier struggles are eventually resolved through conquest, in Canadian literature the battle with nature is ongoing, domination is only partial and transitory, and the struggle for survival is never ending. Her generalizations capture some of the central themes of Collier's story.

Aboriginal people enter Collier's account, but only to provide a colourful, exotic, and at times threatening presence that adds to his heroism. Aboriginal people are rarely presented as individuals with their own personalities; rather, their Indianness is emphasized, often in negative terms. "Redstone Johnny had often dropped in at our cabin to share a meal or a cup of tea with us, and tell of his woes – as Indians ever will if they can strike a sympathetic audience."[54] Paradoxically, a labourer whom he hires is described as a man "sparing of words as so many primitive Indians are."[55]

Conflict over possession of the land is a central tension in the book. Collier arrived in the region on the wave of postwar immigrants seeking to preempt land and homestead in the Chilcotin region. Their search for "free land" was enabled by the apparatus of colonial authority and bureaucracy that, by this time, had been in place for sixty years. Nevertheless, non-Aboriginal settlement was still minimal in the Chilcotin, and Tsilhqot'in people continued to hunt, fish, and trap in their original territories with relatively little interference. Aboriginal title became a subject of conflict only in the intermittent encounters with settlers, encounters that intensified as postwar settlement increased. These broader contexts enabling Collier's immigration to the region, however, are not part of his story. Collier presumes that the land he preempted is his and that the Tsilhqot'in people have no legitimate claim to it.

The theme of conquest through benevolence is also highlighted. Collier "expected trouble from our Indian neighbours" and worried constantly that they would "poach" on his trapline.[56] When he did find a group of Aboriginal people trapping on the land that he now claimed as his, he could not become angry with them, "any more than I would hold a grudge against a little child who climbs up on a stool and helps himself to the cookies."[57] Instead, he reprimanded them in a stern, paternal fashion and taught them a lesson in the importance of managing the beaver populations, during which the Indians stared at the ground. Grateful for his benevolence, the Indians became his friends.[58] In short, the inevitable land conflicts and encounters with Aboriginal people become part of the romance and the natural danger of his homesteading experience. These tensions are resolved through paternal domination; the morality of Euro-Canadian settlement and the superiority of Euro-Canadian civilization are affirmed.

A similar set of themes and images, with some variations, is found in *Grass beyond the Mountains*. The book describes how New York City real estate salesman Rich Hobson decided to abandon city life after the stock market crash of 1929 and move west to pursue his childhood dream of becoming a cowboy. While working on a Wyoming ranch, he met fellow cowpuncher Pan Phillips. Phillips planted seeds in Hobson's imagination of a vast grassland lying beyond the mountains in the northern Chilcotin plateau. "Yeah – that's my gold mine. Grass! Free grass reachin' north into unknown country. Land – lots of it – untouched – just waitin' for hungry cows, and some buckaroos that can ride and have guts enough to put her over," Pan reportedly said.[59] The two immediately decided to tackle the unknown country and headed to the Chilcotin.

There they found "a new frontier – a frontier as tough, as wild and as remote as the West of the early days. This unconquered barrier stands out, unique in this day and age, for it is the last great cattle frontier on the North American continent."[60] There Hobson also "discovered" Carrier Indians: "Back in its jackpine forests there are Indians who have never seen a white man."[61] A few became his friends, whom he refers to by name and who become characters in his adventures; others resented his intrusion into their territories. In scenes replete with six-shooters and ominous Indian "tom tom" drums, Hobson describes how he had to physically fight an Aboriginal protagonist and win in order to earn his respect.[62] In the end, Hobson and Phillips succeeded in setting up a string of ranches and homesteads in the Blackwater River area and in becoming renowned as the region's first, and perhaps most colourful, non-Aboriginal settlers.

This book contains all of the central ingredients of the frontier myth: the promise of abundant resources free for the taking, the challenge of the heroic trek into uncharted and untouched wilderness, the thrill and danger of discovering Indians who had never seen a white person. With its images of six-shooters, tom-tom drums, and hand-to-hand combat with a fierce Indian around a blazing campfire, and in its narrative of conquest through violence, the book reflects a typically American expression of the frontier myth. The settling of the Chilcotin by non-Aboriginals is reduced to a cliché of the American Wild West.

Once again, conflict over the land is naturalized and is an essential ingredient in Hobson's heroic adventure. There are notable silences. Hobson, like Collier, assumes that the land is free for the taking and that the Carrier have no legitimate right to it. The reader does not learn that the territory was "discovered" thousands of years earlier by Aboriginal peoples. Furthermore, for several decades, Carrier families had been running herds of cattle, fencing off meadows, putting up large amounts of hay for winter feed, and building roads through the country to take their cattle to market, all in the vicinity of the territory that Hobson portrays as unused and unoccupied.[63] Technically, the range was "free" because of the government's failure to address Aboriginal title and because Aboriginal people were legally prohibited from preempting land.[64]

The image of the Indian who had never seen a white man was also a figment of Hobson's literary imagination. When Hobson arrived in the Chilcotin in 1934, the Carrier along the Blackwater River area had been in contact with Europeans since the opening of Fort Alexandria some 113 years earlier, and one group, the Ulkatcho Carrier, were about to receive their first resident anthropologist. Irving Goldman's ethnography paints a dramatically different picture of Carrier life than that presented by Hobson.[65]

These are characteristic silences of frontier histories. The hegemonic potential of these histories lies not only in the facts that are excluded, and not only in the way that Aboriginal-settler conflict is naturalized, but also in the way that Aboriginal and settler identities are constructed. The subtle images of the paternal benevolence of the colonizers and settlers, and those of the savage primitiveness or childishness of Aboriginal people, implicitly affirm the legitimacy of European expansion and settlement. Although the facts of history may be debated, these understandings of colonial and Aboriginal identities persist at the level of taken-for-granted convictions about the morality of the colonial process.

These narratives persist in many of the more recent popular histories on the shelves of Williams Lake bookstores. Their authors engage in a form of salvage history: they seek to record the experiences and contributions of the early pioneers before their voices are lost to the public record. The most recent and comprehensive book is the 432-page *Chilcotin: Preserving Pioneer Memories*.[66] The book, written by the granddaughters of one of the Chilcotin pioneer families, recounts the array of settlers who have arrived in Chilcotin country over the last two centuries. Its introduction encapsulates the motive behind this recent crop of books: "There is a vast storehouse of romantic history connected with the opening and settlement of the Chilcotin country of British Columbia. Yet much will be lost if it is not preserved in writing ... This new book is dedicated to preserving the memory of the early pioneers whose courage and spirit of adventure brought them into this country. With these writings, we hope to bring some of these hardy characters to life to share with the reader the unique magic of the Chilcotin we love."[67]

In contrast to the elitism of nationalist histories, local pioneer stories have an egalitarian orientation. They celebrate the lives of ordinary men and women and highlight their contributions to the building of the Canadian nation. These stories recover silences in the historical record that complement rather than challenge nationalist constructions of the past. The pioneer thus becomes a local and popular symbol of national pride and identity. The success of the colonial endeavour, it is suggested, was due to the courage, determination, and drive of the pioneers, whereas the broader political and economic contexts that enabled their success, and that functioned to suppress Aboriginal resistance to settlers' appropriation of Aboriginal lands, go unmentioned. Instead, we have the narrative structure of contact, conflict, and conquest as relayed through the settler's encounters with the frontier.

Aboriginal people remain secondary to the narrative of settlement. Although the virulently negative images of forty years ago are encountered less often, at times the savage Indian still appears. In *Chilcotin: Preserving Pioneer Memories*, Aboriginal people continue to be portrayed as "wild," "hostile," and "war-like"[68] or as colourful characters who accept white encroachment on their lands meekly and who are "loyal" and "faithful" to their new neighbours.[69] That settlement is a worthy moral project is ultimately affirmed by the "loyalty" of the Aboriginal peoples whose territories the settlers take. Aboriginal admiration for the new settlers is but a reflection of the settlers' own self-image, of the deeply ingrained assumption of superiority that characterizes colonial attitudes and that has been continually reinforced by nationalist identities heralding paternal benevolence as a Canadian tradition.

It is important to look beyond these stereotypes to the underlying narrative genre in which they are embedded. Although my analysis of these three books may seem harshly critical, I am not singling out their authors for personal criticism or implying that they are misinformed about the "real" nature of history. Instead, I am suggesting that the manner in which such writers express history is culturally patterned. Their portrayals of the Cariboo-Chilcotin past are expressed through a conventional narrative genre that has certain plot lines and specific roles assigned to Aboriginal people, and this genre itself emerges from a pervasive historical worldview.

Some writers of popular history in the Cariboo-Chilcotin are concerned with the problems of negative stereotyping and are highly critical of the derogatory portraits of Aboriginal people in earlier pioneer stories. The problem remains, though, of how to incorporate Aboriginal historical perspectives into stories that ultimately celebrate Euro-Canadian settlement of the region. There is no easy solution. At a much more general level, this very issue underlies the efforts of Aboriginal and non-Aboriginal Canadians across the country to address Aboriginal land claims, treaty rights, and self-government and to arrive at a common understanding of who and what constitute the Canadian nation. One local writer whom I spoke with addressed the dilemma of representation by largely excluding mention of Aboriginal people, stating: "I didn't feel I had the right to tell that story." This strategy, although respecting recent criticisms from Aboriginal writers over the traditional power of non-Aboriginal writers to depict (and, some would say, misrepresent) Aboriginal realities, may only reproduce the problems of earlier frontier histories. Erasing Aboriginal people from the historical landscape while presenting history as a story of discovery, settlement, and progress only perpetuates the long-standing silences of official histories.

**Local Histories: Alternative Perspectives**

Local histories that deviate from the celebratory themes of the frontier myth are scarce, although their number is growing.[70] Although the title of Vancouver journalist Terry Glavin's *Nemiah: The Unconquered Country* is explicitly counterhegemonic, morally inverting the terms of the frontier myth, the book weaves within its narrative the historical reminiscences of Tsilhqot'in elders. Jean Speare's *The Days of Augusta*, compiled by a local Euro-Canadian resident and wife of an ex-Cariboo Social Credit MLA, presents the narratives of an elderly Secwepemc woman reflecting upon her life. The book is a remarkable precursor of experimental ethnographies that take a poetic textual approach to Native American discourse as verbal art. These stories reflect the Secwepemc tradition of recounting history through the genre of personal narrative.

Within this category are a few recent publications by area First Nations, produced through grants provided by government agencies or from the curriculum development division of the local school district. In directly challenging the images of Aboriginal people and the celebration of European conquest contained in frontier histories, these books are the only available histories that directly confront the terms of the frontier myth.

A good example is *Ulkatcho: Stories of the Grease Trail*.[71] The non-Aboriginal author presents his own narrative juxtaposed with stories told to him by Ulkatcho elders. The author aims to provide "a native point of view" of that trail's significance in the culture and history of the Carrier people. By presenting the stories and reminiscences of Carrier elders, he attempts to recover the silences created through the trail's official history, which celebrates Alexander Mackenzie's heroic voyage down the trail to arrive at the Pacific Ocean. The author explicitly challenges the invisibility and irrelevance of Aboriginal people in dominant histories and the assumption that "somehow [Aboriginal people] weren't really there until [Europeans] came along and found [them]. Or if [Aboriginal people] were there, what [they] were doing beforehand simply didn't matter very much." The book challenges pioneer histories by arguing that "a story can be told from many points of view."[72]

The few recent publications on local Aboriginal culture and history that explicitly challenge the objectivity of frontier histories, and that present Aboriginal voices to readers, remain exceptions to the historical accounts available to the general reader on the bookstore shelves. Although restrictions of space have caused me to limit my discussion to only a few of the historical books now on sale to the public – and, it could be argued, to oversimplify what is in fact a much more diverse set of popular historical narratives – I hope that the starkness of the frontier myth in each example, each of which is prominently displayed and widely promoted as representative of the Cariboo-Chilcotin, indicates the pervasiveness of the frontier genre in popular writing.

Overall, the dominant historical discourse remains relentlessly that of the European settlers and nationalists. There is a smooth fit between the nationally produced books on Canadian history used in the public school system, the Western Canadiana books produced by the small, provincially based publishing house, and the histories written by regional pioneers. These books are united by their common situation within the frontier myth. They focus almost exclusively on the challenges and triumphs of pioneers and colonial systems. Aboriginal people are either invisible in these histories or scripted as supporting characters who are quaint, childlike, or passive. These books, by their sheer volume, constitute a dominant historical discourse that cannot but pervade the consciousness of the general population.

## The City Museum

The city museum is an important site for the representation of local history. Small-town museums are controlled neither by the state nor by more general corporate or business interests. Rather, they are typically operated by a local historical society, a nonprofit volunteer association that controls which history is to be represented. In Williams Lake, the city museum presents a regional history that ostensibly is produced by "the community" and that is reflected back for community consumption. The city museum occupies a privileged space in public history: it is the only institution devoted exclusively to the collection, representation, and celebration of the region's past.

Despite its democratic appearance, the museum presents an image of regional history that is partial. An organized historical society has been in existence in Williams Lake since the 1950s, but the current Museum and Historical Society has been operating only since 1988. Although a makeshift museum was created in 1967 as a centennial project, it deteriorated over the years through lack of interest and attention. The current city museum opened in 1991 under the leadership of the new society. Although theoretically open to any interested individuals, the society's active members do not reflect a diversity of regional residents. The museum is run entirely on volunteer labour, and its most active members are retired, middle-class, Euro-Canadian women. The museum's construction of regional history has been influenced by the specific interests and perspectives of this sector of the community.

The museum is firmly entrenched in the social structure of the city. It relies heavily on local donations from industries and small businesses, and it depends on the political support of the municipal government, which owns the museum building. The museum directors work to maintain positive relationships with these groups, at times expressing frustration that the importance of their facility is not recognized or appreciated by all community leaders. The degree to which these delicate political and economic relationships shape the manner in which history is represented varies with the particular individuals creating the displays.

On the one hand, it is implicitly expected that the city museum should promote a positive image of the region to enhance the city's potential for business and industrial investment, to attract new residents, and to impress passing tourists. As is true of local histories generally,[73] the treatment of the past is expected to be celebratory rather than critical, and the themes of collective harmony and history-as-progress are expected to be highlighted. On the other hand, the individuals involved in the creation of the museum's displays and interpretive texts do not feel coerced by civic or corporate sponsors. Rather, the general themes to be displayed in the museum were decided upon in the society's early stages of planning, and the final shape of the displays and interpretive texts emerged largely under the influence of the museum's volunteer curator. The curator arrived in the region in the 1950s and is a talented storyteller, keenly interested in the people and history of the Cariboo-Chilcotin.

The museum now highlights two themes: the region's ranching heritage, and the Williams Lake Stampede. These themes were chosen in part to tap into the city's international image as the "stampede capital" – a strategy that reflects the constraining power of selective traditions – and in part to distinguish the museum from other regional museums. Community museums across the province compete with one another to capture tourist interest, and many do so by specializing in one aspect of history, whether mining, forestry, ranching, the gold rush, and so forth. The specialized focus of the city museum is a product of these competitive interests.

Displays on the Williams Lake Stampede are prominently positioned. Walking up the steps to the main floor of the museum, the visitor faces a series of large photographs of the stampede in the 1920s. The scenes depict cowboys on horseback, a gathering of Aboriginal people watching and laughing while leaning on a fence, and the stampede grounds with the many white canvas tents. A striking photograph is of the Roman Race, in which men, each standing astride two horses, race against each other. The caption reads: "Alkali Lake contestants: Joe Dick, Patrick Chelsea, and Pierre Squinahan."

The displays include old trophies, an old stampede queen's crown, and a replica of the infamous Squaw Hall, built in the 1950s as an Indian dance hall but eventually also frequented by non-Aboriginal people. To the latter, it was known as "a place to let down your hair, drink your refreshments and do almost anything that your morals will permit you to do." The stampede collection includes a photograph showing several Aboriginal men and women in headdresses, with a man kneeling and playing a hand drum. The picture is captioned "Sugar Cane residents at Williams Lake Stampede in the 1920s" and includes the names of the individuals.

The rest of the museum is an eclectic display of artifacts and themes. There is a small section of Aboriginal artifacts, with no interpretive commentary, followed by a section on modes of communication: an old switchboard, an old printing press. The side wall of the room is devoted to the story of the BC provincial police. The display includes a mannequin in police uniform, a photograph of William Pinchbeck, who was "appointed Justice of the Peace at the first settlement of Williams Lake in 1860 and maintained Law and Order in the Valley," and a photographic display and brief biographies of the thirteen local policemen who served in the area between 1910 and 1950.

Off the main room are several side rooms reconstructed as a bedroom, parlour, kitchen, blacksmith's shop, Chinese store, and trapping display. A set of cast iron frying pans hangs on the wall: "Frying pans and grill used by the Tom Mikkelsen family while travelling from Ashcroft to Horsefly in 1910. Donated by Jean Mikkelsen." One of the side rooms portrays the history of Williams Lake, with photographs of the town in the 1920s and important local personalities of the time, including one prominent woman, Jessie Pidgeon: "While legend has it that the Cariboo was the land where 'men are men' and the women were proud of it, women have been prominent on many fronts." Small displays on ranching equipment, the Williams Lake stockyards, and cattle brands follow, along with photographs and brief stories about many of the well-known settler families in the Cariboo-Chilcotin.

As in most community museums, the displays have been determined to an extent by the artifacts on hand; that is, stories have been built up around whatever assortment of antiques and relics have been donated. Yet here the eclectic displays are tied together by a central theme. The curator admits to being more interested in people than in objects, and she has used the historical artifacts as vehicles to tell stories about the lives of the people in whose homes the objects originated. In short, despite its ranching and stampede focus, the history presented in the displays is that of the "ordinary people" of the Cariboo-Chilcotin.

For example, a pair of scruffy riding boots are mounted as a display and are used to tell the life story of the woman who owned them, Josephine Robson. Above the boots is a picture of Josephine, a smiling young woman with a child on her back. The boots themselves are captioned: "Josephine Robson's boots were burned in a campfire. She resoled them herself." In the interpretive text, her life story is summarized: "Josephine was born 'under a jackpine in the Itcha Mountains' says her stepson, George Robson ... Her parents were Rosalie Sandyman and Antone Capoose; they only came out of the mountains twice a year." The story goes on to tell of Josephine's life as a rancher, hunter, and trapper and of how she continued this lifestyle well into her elderly years.

The curator has structured the exhibits to make them relevant to the local public. In representing ordinary people, she has drawn extensively on her knowledge of many of the Cariboo-Chilcotin pioneers and on her familiarity and friendships with members of the regional Secwepemc, Tsilhqot'in, and Carrier communities. Rather than presented as anonymous images of noble savages, the Aboriginal people featured in the museum are named. They are presented as individuals.

At the same time, there are silences that reverse the typical features of Euro-Canadian representations of Aboriginal people. In many of these displays, the Indianness of these individuals goes unmentioned. For example, the three Alkali Lake racers were Secwepemc Indians. Josephine Grambush, who married one of the founders of the Williams Lake Stampede in the 1920s, and whose children became prominent in the local rodeo circuit, was Tsilhqot'in. Josephine Robson was a Carrier, a fact hinted at only at the end of her biography: "Josephine never knew what a welfare cheque was. She made her living trapping and tanning hides. She also pitied people who drank liquor, saying it makes people poor and sick."

With Aboriginal people not explicitly identified as such, the museum displays present histories that, in significant ways, diverge from the dominant frontier discourse. The displays honour both Aboriginal and non-Aboriginal people as having an equally important place in the history of Cariboo-Chilcotin settlement. The displays provide one avenue for area Aboriginal people – not as Indians but as humans with all their individuality and diversity – to become visible to the local community and to tourists. At the same time, these displays do not directly challenge the conceptual opposition of Indian and white that is central to frontier conceptions of history. Furthermore, the visitor may leave the museum without realizing that some of the individuals honoured were Aboriginal.

All histories are selective accounts, highlighting certain events and actors while relegating others to the background. The history presented through the city museum is no exception. For example, there is no presentation of the long Aboriginal history prior to European arrival. There is no mention of the more general political context of colonial settlement that enabled pioneers to arrive or of the forms of political and economic domination of Aboriginal populations that worked to suppress their resistance. Stories could have been told of the changing roles of women in the stampede and of their gradual exclusion from rodeo events, changes that might be linked to shifts in the political-economic structure of gender relations in Canadian society.

The focus on ordinary people recovers voices that are often left out of regional histories. Yet these individuals are presented as having existed outside any political-economic context. As Tony Bennett notes in his critique of populist museums, pioneers, early settlers, and Aboriginal people are presented as "a people without politics."[74] Although these histories may honour the lives of individuals and may celebrate their courage, determination, and independence, they also assimilate the values and experiences of diverse subordinate classes and groups – experiences that included conflict, inequality, and struggle against forms of domination – into middle-class notions of the past.

This is not to say that early pioneers and settlers should not be publicly honoured. Nor am I attempting to mute the diversity of historical voices by insisting on the substitution of one dominant historical discourse for an equally narrow history that focuses exclusively on the injustices of colonialism and Aboriginal-settler relations. But I am suggesting that silences have a cumulative effect. In not discussing certain major themes in the region's past, the history presented by the city museum may have hegemonic implications that are only amplified by the lack of competing historical perspectives in the public domain.

In conclusion, the histories encountered in public places in Williams Lake reflect the dominance of the frontier myth as a framework for the telling of history. Frontier histories render irrelevant Aboriginal histories, Aboriginal communities, and the complex relationships between Aboriginal and settler societies. Instead, frontier histories highlight the courageous actions of individual Europeans and assimilate history into a conventional narrative structure of the contact of opposites, the heroic struggle for domination, and the eventual triumph of European colonialists. In these narratives, Aboriginal people are assigned secondary roles that reflect and enhance the identities of the colonizers as paternal benefactors while commemorating colonization as the progress of Western civilization.

At the same time, the frontier myth is capable of accommodating a variety of both voices and histories, ranging from the national histories sanctioned by the state to the individual autobiographies of Cariboo-Chilcotin pioneers. The remarkable degree to which this selective historical tradition has been adopted by local pioneers, settlers, and ordinary people to organize their experiences, to frame their life stories, to account for their collective past indicates the depth to which this tradition operates in the realm of lived experience. Thus, the distinction between the officially sanctioned histories of the state and the popular memory of the "ordinary people," a distinction prevalent in current studies of the exercise of power in colonial and postcolonial settings,[75] is not immediately relevant here.

Rather, pioneer stories and national histories operate within the same mythic framework and are fully compatible with celebrations of European colonization.

Some comment is required about the social effects of these histories. Admittedly, my analysis of high school texts, popular histories, and museum displays is limited by its focus on textual analysis rather than on analysis of how texts are interpreted in contexts of social interaction. For this reason, I have argued for their hegemonic implications or potential rather than their actual hegemonic consequences. My goal in this chapter has been to identify the frontier myth as a narrative genre, to illustrate how this myth encodes certain understandings of history, society, and individual agency, and how it allows certain spaces for Aboriginal peoples. For this goal, textual analysis, I think, is sufficient. In later chapters, I demonstrate how these histories reinforce unequal relations by following how these histories are produced and made meaningful in specific social and political contexts of interaction. With regard to public histories, one might ask how high school history textbooks are being used in classrooms, given that schoolteachers can replace assigned texts with equivalent supplementary texts. In the case of the city museum, it would be important to trace how visitors respond to the displays. Although the displays remain silent on critical issues in the history of the Cariboo-Chilcotin, they may work in other ways to overcome the anti-Aboriginal racism that pervades social relations in the city. For example, the fact that Aboriginal men and women are named in the displays may have a great effect on Euro-Canadian schoolchildren in developing positive images of Aboriginal people, particularly when it is pointed out that the individuals being honoured are indeed Aboriginal. It is in the application of displays and texts that the force of frontier histories becomes apparent.

Nevertheless, the accumulated silences of the frontier myth do have implications for the shaping of public consciousness. The frontier genre, as expressed in Cariboo-Chilcotin popular histories, encodes a systematic forgetting of contentious issues of the past that has significant implications for Aboriginal/Euro-Canadian relations. Aboriginal title to the lands of Canada, the obligation of colonial governments to acquire lands by due process, and the failure of governments to sign treaties or otherwise acknowledge Aboriginal title in British Columbia go unmentioned. The Indian reserve system, the Indian Affairs bureaucracy, and the residential school system, all of which have had a profound impact on a large proportion of the regional population, are not discussed. The very existence of diverse Aboriginal communities with organized social structures, complex modes of subsistence, distinct metaphysical beliefs, and independent historical traditions is not mentioned. Apart from their highly stylized appearances in frontier accounts, Aboriginal peoples and communities are rendered invisible. In their struggles to untangle themselves from the various threads of colonial domination, Secwepemc, Carrier, and Tsilhqot'in people in the Cariboo-Chilcotin today come face to face with a dominant historical tradition that has virtually erased them and their history from the public landscape.

The hegemonic potential of frontier histories – their use in affirming the current structure of relationships between Aboriginal peoples and Canadian society and its institutions – lies not only in what is omitted but also in *how* history is presented. History, we are told, is the product of individual actions: the themes of heroic individualism, survival of the fittest, and the "self-made man" define a particular understanding of history, society, and the individual. Frontier histories provide Euro-Canadians with a sense of collective identity – paternal benevolence and natural superiority – constructed in opposition to Aboriginal peoples. These frontier histories tell us that colonization has been in the best interests of Aboriginal people, who have been treated well by Canadians. These histories constitute a public apparatus for shaping and defining Euro-Canadian historical consciousness, and it is from within this selective historical worldview that non-Aboriginal resistance to Aboriginal treaties and self-government is articulated. Given how deeply embedded cultural myths are in the dominant worldview of a society, it would be simplistic to suggest that the solution to this situation is to abandon the frontier genre or to censor or criticize those who choose to express the past in this format. Important, rather, is a reflexive awareness of the pervasiveness of the frontier myth and of the way in which frontier narratives convey implicit values, assumptions, and beliefs that reflect the legacy of Canada's colonial past. In the following chapters, I show how these implicit themes not only define some of the dominant elements of historical consciousness among Euro-Canadians but also are engaged to render invalid Aboriginal challenges to the status quo of Aboriginal/Euro-Canadian relations.

# 4

# Mobilizing History: Regional Identities, Pioneer Traditions, and the Frontier Myth in Political Discourse

"Cariboo-Chilcotin has long had the reputation of being one of the last frontiers," proclaimed newly elected Reform MP Phillip Mayfield in his inaugural speech to the House of Commons in 1993. Championing the pioneer spirit of independence, hard work, and stubborn resistance to government regulations for which Cariboo-Chilcotin residents are renowned, Mayfield portrayed his riding as one of the last vestiges of the mythic Canadian Wild West. "The entire riding remembers our pioneers and celebrates the way of life these pioneers left for us to continue," he announced. "Today the lumber industry has taken the economic lead. However the independent attitude, self-reliance and earthy frankness which characterize relations among Cariboo-Chilcotin people still continue and may it always be so."[1]

The frontier myth exerts a powerful cultural force in shaping popular conceptions of both the past and the present. As the above quotation suggests, its influence is not limited to the popular histories, textbooks, and museum displays that communicate official histories to the public of Williams Lake. Instead, its force is much more pervasive: it provides a historical epistemology and a set of cultural symbols that individuals in the Cariboo-Chilcotin continually draw upon to construct collective identities, to affirm public values, and to promote certain political interests.

In this chapter, I explore how Euro-Canadians use the language of the frontier myth in political discourse: how they resort to ideas such as pioneer values and frontier traditions when promoting political agendas and criticizing the actions of politicians and governments. Mayfield's strategy, of course, was to use the idea of the Cariboo-Chilcotin pioneer spirit as a convenient point from which to launch his own Reform Party critique of the federal government's excessive taxation, irresponsible spending policies, and intrusive legislation. In the previous chapter, I emphasized the conservative role of the frontier myth in shaping formal representations of the past. Here I emphasize how individuals use the frontier myth in a creative and dynamic fashion to metaphorically render current events and practices congruent with an imagined frontier past. Although this process involves the conservative use of a set of well-established cultural categories to render new circumstances comprehensible, with each metaphorical association a new past is created in juxtaposition with the present. In each case, conventional symbols such as the "pioneer" and the "frontier" take on new dimensions of significance and meaning.

The frontier myth's images and symbols are imbued with such sacredness and moral power that they become an ideal currency for claiming legitimacy for varied political interests. Much of the oppositional political discourse in Western liberal democratic societies aligns along the contradictions between public morality and actual social and political practices. Groups engaged in political opposition attempt to promote their agendas by making appeals to widespread public values such as democracy, individualism, equality, and multiculturalism and by demonstrating how government officials, agencies, corporations, or other groups have failed to adhere to these ideal standards. In launching these attacks, subordinate groups attempt to blemish the public standing and morality of their opponents and to generate sufficient public sympathy to embarrass governments or corporations into changing their policies and practices.

Aboriginal peoples in Canada and other Fourth World settings have become adept at using this "politics of embarrassment" to rally public support for their political struggles against governments. This political strategy is used not just by Aboriginal peoples but also by virtually all groups engaged in forms of political opposition and struggle, whether they be ethnic minorities, feminist organizations, gay rights activists, or environmental groups. The politics of embarrassment is also a central feature of reporting in the news media.[2] The news media assume the role of society's "moral watchdog,"[3] scrutinizing the activities of politicians and governments and creating "news" when their actions appear to deviate from public norms.[4]

In tracing how the frontier myth infuses political discourse, the first task is to identify the terrain of public values and morals in the Cariboo-Chilcotin upon which the local politics of embarrassment is based. I begin by exploring how Williams Lake community leaders define the prevalent public values and identities of the Cariboo-Chilcotin. I draw on interviews that I conducted with Euro-Canadian community leaders representing local and regional governments, the forest industry, the local media, and small business. As community leaders, these individuals are especially active in promoting Williams Lake as a positive place for new residents and for industrial and business investment. They market images of the Cariboo-Chilcotin on a daily basis and have an important influence in the public forums in which regional values and identities are represented.

Community leaders are not a homogeneous group. There is no consensus among them regarding public values, political philosophies, or the best strategies for addressing current social and economic crises facing their region. Nevertheless, there are striking similarities – key themes and emphases – that appeared repeatedly in my discussions with many of them. In particular, many of the community leaders interviewed come from the small-business sector. Their vision of Williams Lake and the Cariboo-Chilcotin reflects a right-of-centre, free-enterprise philosophy that, although not shared by all community leaders, is highly influential in regional politics. These individuals present a clear statement of some of the most important public values and identities that appear in political discourse in other contexts.

I then examine how various individuals and groups use these public identities and values as a symbolic currency in their struggles against government policies and practices. More significantly, in some contexts these political actors historicize contemporary values and identities by associating them with pioneer legacies and frontier traditions of the Cariboo-Chilcotin. The mapping of present values onto past traditions greatly enhances the moral and symbolic power of oppositional political rhetoric. No longer are politicians and governments merely violating public values; they are now also violating the very spirit and tradition of the pioneers. It is at this juncture that the conservative and the creative potential of the frontier myth becomes apparent.

## Regional Identities and Small-Town Values

The public face of Williams Lake has undergone some significant changes over the last decade. The regional economy is prospering. Land prices have risen dramatically in the past five years, and there has been an explosion of condominiums, townhouses, and new subdivisions. The area population is growing, enhanced by the arrival of many individuals and families from the Lower Mainland disillusioned with city life and seeking a quieter, rural lifestyle.

The urban influence is also evident in the impact of urban culture and consumer habits. Although the first indoor mall in Williams Lake was built some twenty years ago, urban cultural trends have only recently appeared in the downtown core. Several cappuccino shops (one established in 1994 was called the Vancouver Café) and restaurants offering vegetarian meals have sprung up. Stores such as the Shaman Shop selling Third World tribal arts and clothing, a healing centre, and the Earth Right store providing environmentally safe products, Birkenstock sandals, and self-help psychology books have appeared. Appealing to middle-class, left-wing consumers interested in environmentalism, New Age spiritualism, and romantic primitivism, these stores add a cultural dimension that clashes with the more conventional features of working-class, resource-town culture epitomized by dusty pickup trucks, cowboy hats, anti-Aboriginal racism, and right-wing politics.

Concepts of regional culture and identity, and understandings of the relationship between Williams Lake and the urban metropolis of Vancouver-Victoria, are in flux. Many people describe the city as "half urban, half rural."[5] As one person commented, "We have the best of both worlds. Vancouver is only a tankful of gas away, but in half an hour we can be out in the wilderness." In the last twenty years, improved transportation links and the creeping urban influence have brought about a shift northward of the conceptual line marking the beginning of northern British Columbia. Whereas twenty years ago locals considered Williams Lake to be a northern town, today there is no consensus. Although a three-hour drive to the University of Northern British Columbia, the Cariboo-Chilcotin is formally considered to be in the central interior of the province.

Despite this dynamic context and the diversity of the area's inhabitants, a distinctive set of themes appears repeatedly in public discussions about Cariboo-Chilcotin identities and values. In interviews, community leaders describe Williams Lake as a "small town" whose culture and social relations are defined by friendliness, hospitality, social harmony, egalitarianism, informality, and a commitment to family. These values are reflected in tourism brochures that promise a "hearty Cariboo welcome" to visitors. Many other residents echo the views of community leaders, identifying neighbourliness, cooperation, and mutual trust as primary characteristics of the Cariboo-Chilcotin lifestyle.[6] Community leaders root the friendly informality and trusting attitude in the closeness of social relations: the Cariboo-Chilcotin is a place where "everyone knows everyone" and where "people watch out for one another."

One member of a pioneer family, for example, described this cooperative, trusting spirit as reflective of the "small-town attitude": "I had a guy come up from Kamloops on Tuesday morning, and his car broke down just outside of 100 Mile House. So he thought, what do I do? So he decided to put his thumb out, and the first person who came along picked him up. And he thought 'Wow.' That was the last thing he would have expected ... We trust people. Because we know them. And in the city we don't trust them, because we don't know them." Another community leader, who lives in a prestigious subdivision, stated with some pride that he never locks the doors to his house. The values of helpfulness and trust that bind the local community are contrasted to the anomie of big-city life, in which individuals are isolated from one another, moving through their daily routines without talking to their neighbours or acknowledging one another's presence.

These values are not unique to the Cariboo-Chilcotin; they resonate with the images of small-town life that prevail in rural cities and towns elsewhere in North America,[7] that are reproduced in romantic Canadian travel literature,[8] and that are ritually portrayed in small-town festivals celebrating egalitarianism, social harmony, and community togetherness.[9] In short, the "myth of the moral superiority of the small town"[10] is widespread and continues to shape public constructions of small-town identity in powerful ways.

Many community leaders draw upon rural-urban distinctions to characterize the culture of Williams Lake. One dimension of difference is lifestyle: the laid-back lifestyle of the Cariboo-Chilcotin is contrasted with the rushed, stress-ridden lives of urban residents. One man referred to the relaxed attitude toward punctuality as being on "Cariboo time." Another man born and raised in the area referred to Williams Lake as the home of the ninety-second minute: "What I value the most, the fact that it is a rural lifestyle, the fact that ... the pressures, perceived or otherwise, aren't there. It can be summed up by saying that Williams Lake has minutes that are ninety seconds long ... the slower pace of life."

Rural communities have long been portrayed as existing out of time, as frozen in history, as epitomizing the traditional, harmonious cultures of the past from which contemporary urban societies have long since evolved. Such portraits are prevalent in Canadian travel writing,[11] in centuries of British literature,[12] and in anthropological studies of British rural communities.[13] Agricultural towns in rural areas are especially prone to being relegated to a preindustrial past. Thus, both rural communities and indigenous peoples are subjected to what Johannes Fabian has called a "denial of coevalness" with respect to modern society;[14] both are the subjects of "imperialist nostalgia"[15] in which the destruction of their traditional cultures is lamented as the regrettable but inevitable result of Western progress and civilization.

In contrast, community leaders see Williams Lake, although having a slower pace of life, as being a fully modern, progressive resource city on the leading edge of industrial development and expansion in Canada. Community leaders, especially those of the small-business class, have a particular understanding of the nature of progress that is captured in the image of the self-made man, which they draw upon to distinguish small-town values and ethics from those in urban centres. The idea of progress and the myth of the self-made man are prominent not only in small-town settings but also in rural and urban regions of Canada, and they comprise key elements of the dominant Canadian ideology.[16]

This ideology, or "conventional wisdom," is framed by a series of assumptions about the relationship between the individual, society, and the economy. Canadian society is ideally seen as continually progressing along a path of increasing prosperity. The motor of progress is believed to be the free-market economy, an autonomous and self-regulating system operating according to its own logic. All individuals are seen to have equal opportunities for advancement in society, competing with one another in the marketplace and achieving status and wealth in proportion to their ambition and inherent talent. In this system, government, democratically elected as the voice of "the people," is responsible for overseeing the smooth functioning of society and its institutions, intervening in the economy only to ensure the principles of fairness and equal access.

Central to this ideal vision of society are the values of individualism, equality, democracy, and freedom and the belief that material progress and prosperity can be achieved through an individual's determination, hard work, and self-sacrifice. This vision of society resonates with the frontier histories that celebrate heroic individualism as the driving force in the development of the Canadian nation. Historical consciousness and understandings of the relationship between the individual and society are closely intertwined and mutually informing.

The myth of the self-made man takes on particular significance when transposed to the setting of a resource-industry city in the Canadian hinterland. The self-made man is not necessarily a millionaire or a mill owner. Rather, he is the individual who succeeds on the local scale of values. The anti-intellectualism, the value of manual over mental labour, and the general suspicion of and hostility toward academics, bureaucrats, and professionals that Thomas Dunk describes among working-class men in a northern Ontario resource town[17] are threads that weave in and out of the dominant culture in Williams Lake. Dunk's working-class cultural values are championed by many of the civic leaders with whom I spoke.

In their view, the self-made man is the individual who takes entrepreneurial risks to establish his own business or works long hours as a labourer in the mining or forest industry. He may run a logging contracting firm, operate a well-established small business, or have a well-paying job in the sawmill. The self-made man in certain contexts may be the single mother who has managed to pull herself off welfare by opening her own day-care business. These people are "doing something," taking risks, and working hard, and they are actively contributing to the capitalist economy.

Civic leaders identify the commitment to a strong work ethic, whether as a self-employed entrepreneur or as a wage worker, as one of the defining features of the "small-town attitude." This ethic is one of the main features distinguishing rural communities from urban centres:

> Anyone who wants to get out and grasp an opportunity ... perhaps they're not as plentiful as they were in ... [the 1950s and 1960s], but the opportunities are still there if you can change with the times ... People sitting in an urban centre would say "The world owes me a living, why don't you

> give me a job?" That's one of the unique things about Williams Lake or the Cariboo, that I know now. I'm sure most small rural towns are much the same ... that people are far more independent, [and have] much more self-esteem that gives them the initiative to get out and create their own job.

One young community leader celebrated the values of individualism and self-sufficiency through the symbol of the redneck: "I'm proud to say that I'm a redneck. A redneck to me is a person whose neck has become red because he's put in long hours out in the field, in the bush, mining, building roads, making infrastructure that makes this country great. And that's to me what a redneck is."

The values of independence, self-sufficiency, personal responsibility, and materialism take their meaning from the context of a late-twentieth-century resource city. These values are defined by the ability of individuals to create their own small businesses, in which they enjoy the freedom of self-employment and accept the responsibility for success or failure. These values are realized by the ability of workers to find employment in the forest industry and its related businesses, in which they can earn high salaries and spend their income as they choose. These values are not created in, nor are they dependent on, a specific set of objective economic conditions.[18] As E. Wight Bakke has shown in his study of unemployed workers during the Depression in the United States, individuals show a remarkable ability to redefine the practical meaning of independence and self-sufficiency, and to maintain a commitment to the ideal of the self-made man, despite long-term unemployment.[19] In Williams Lake, these ideals are upheld as fundamental public values. At the same time, individuals struggle to modify the practical meaning of these ideals in accordance with their changing socioeconomic circumstances.

Finally, community leaders' sense of regional identity is strongly influenced by a sense of geographical and political marginalization from the mainstream of Canadian society. In the local idiom, Williams Lake is "up here" as opposed to "down there" in the urbanized Lower Mainland. As in the northern Ontario resource towns studied by David Stymeist and Thomas Dunk, in Williams Lake there is a strong and widespread feeling of resentment toward urban governments and politicians, who are often seen as outside intruders on local affairs. Many civic leaders complain that local concerns are frequently overlooked and ignored by the provincial government, which arbitrarily imposes decisions informed by urban values. Many feel strongly that rural communities receive a disproportionately small percentage of government services and programs. One community leader proclaimed that the adage "There's no hope beyond Hope" circulated frequently among her colleagues. This saying referred to the futility of expecting fair, equitable treatment from the government to extend beyond the town of Hope on the fringe of the Lower Mainland.

This sense of political marginalization is parallelled by a strong sense of existing on a geographic periphery, a frontier, of settlement. People describe their city as being surrounded by an unoccupied wilderness. The closeness of the wilderness, in fact, draws new residents and tourists to the region. More importantly, this unoccupied wilderness is seen as being rich in natural resources – timber, minerals, and even tourism opportunities – that are free for the taking and that have yet to be fully exploited. "It's a thriving community ... [We have] huge tracts of land with resources all around us, to the east, to the west, and we're right in the centre of it!" Another leader commented: "The ranching, mining, forest industry, tourism ... each industry is holding its own if not growing. We've got so much land here that's not even being used. Like the Lower Mainland, it's just nooks and crannies. Where[as] Williams Lake has a bright future, because there's so much land that's not being utilized." These references to the Cariboo-Chilcotin as a vast region of empty land with resources free for the taking are striking examples of the pervasiveness of the frontier myth. The empty-land image clearly contradicts the vociferous Aboriginal claims put forth by Cariboo-Chilcotin First Nations leaders, themselves significant inhabitants of this presumed empty land.

Although community leaders do not always use the term "frontier" to describe their city, their understandings of regional culture and identity, and their orientations to both the urban world and the surrounding wilderness, can be considered expressions of a contemporary frontier identity. The central features include the values of individualism and self-sufficiency, the idea of the self-made man, the sense of existing on the periphery of urban society and being surrounded by a wilderness rich in resources free for the taking, and a resistance to outside (urban) controls and regulations. The city's official motto, "Prosperity, Courage, and Opportunity," encapsulates the public myth of Williams Lake: it is a modern resource city perpetuating the legacy of the pioneers in its friendly, small-town ambience, in the courageous, competitive spirit of the men and women labouring in the resource industries and small businesses, and in the material wealth that awaits individuals with sufficient drive to succeed.

These expressions of collective identity are themselves historically contingent: they emerge from within a specific climate of mounting economic insecurity, unemployment, and land-use conflicts. They arise within a context of increasing provincial government efforts to regulate the Cariboo-Chilcotin forest industry to ensure long-term sustainability, efforts that are translated as moves to reduce timber harvesting allocations and that are premised on the assumption of a dwindling resource supply. In celebrating small-town culture, in proclaiming the abundance of the region's natural resources, and in denouncing urban life, community leaders are also resisting what they see as the threat of political and cultural domination of the city and region by urban values and provincial governments.[20]

### Public Values as Symbolic Currency: Evoking the Symbol of the Pioneer

Individualism, self-sufficiency, freedom from external constraints: these values appear repeatedly in political discourse as defining characteristics of Cariboo-Chilcotin culture. On occasion, these public values and identities are mapped onto a historical terrain, becoming associated with the traditions of Cariboo-Chilcotin pioneers. In so doing, various groups mobilize the frontier myth to create idealized images of the past, to defend their particular interests in the present, and to criticize the actions of politicians and governments. In these various debates, the symbol of the pioneer takes its moral power from the unquestioned legitimacy of the frontier historical tradition. At the same time, the symbol of the pioneer takes on different meanings through its creative application to a variety of contexts of conflict.

Two recent controversies will demonstrate these processes. The first is a rather bizarre case of a government-ordered bulldozing of the home of a retired Wells resident, Rick Mooney. The second is the bitter conflict that arose surrounding the creation of a regional land-use plan by the provincial government's Commission on Resources and the Environment (CORE) and the struggle of proindustry interests in the Cariboo-Chilcotin to oppose the province's efforts to restrict industry access to forest lands.

### The Demolition of Rick Mooney's House

In 1989, Rick Mooney, a resident of the hamlet of Wells, some eighty kilometres east of Quesnel, built a new house that was to be the retirement home for him and his wife. In the spirit of past generations of Cariboo residents, the retired mill and construction worker built his home in his own fashion, ignoring the building code standards that had recently been put in place by the Cariboo Regional District (CRD). Regional districts are a relatively recent form of government in the province, being created in the late 1960s to regulate zoning and activities in the rural regions beyond municipal boundaries. With the creation of the Cariboo Regional District, the many remote regions of the Cariboo-Chilcotin with a long tradition of independence suddenly became subject to government scrutiny and regulation. One aspect of this regulation was the creation of building code bylaws.

In 1990, a CRD building inspector discovered that Mooney's house was in violation of the building code: its foundation and floors were structurally deficient, it was built with untreated lumber, and it had an unsafe chimney and woodstove. For the next two years, the regional district posted stop-work orders on the house, sent letters to Mooney demanding his compliance, and finally took the issue to court. At times, Mooney agreed to comply; at other times, he ignored the demands. In 1991, the regional district took the matter to the Supreme Court of British Columbia, which authorized the house's demolition.

"On the night of November 30, 1991, Big Brother came from Williams Lake with his hired goons, and crunched to kindling a $60,000 new home and took it to the dump."[21] So wrote Rick Mooney to the Williams Lake *Tribune*, echoing the widespread public condemnation that followed the bulldozing of his home. Even before the bulldozing, he had garnered a groundswell of public support. Local residents, contractors, and tradespeople had formed a volunteer group to go in and upgrade the house. The regional district, unable to find a local bulldozer operator to take on the job of destroying Mooney's house, was forced to hire outside the region. On hearing of the house's imminent destruction, Wells contractors vowed to blockade the path of any bulldozer that came near the home. With a provincial election upcoming in October, all four candidates running for the Cariboo North riding pledged their support for Mooney. When NDP candidate Frank Garden was elected, he intervened and attempted to negotiate a resolution with the regional district, later accusing the regional district of bulldozing the house "in the dark to avoid press coverage."[22]

Protests continued over the following months. Angry residents from Wells, Quesnel, and Williams Lake confronted CRD directors at a January board meeting, demanding a complete investigation into the Mooney affair. The group circulated petitions in support of Mooney, a war veteran, in Royal Canadian Legion branches across the province. Mooney, described in more than one media report as "cantankerous," carried on his battle for over three years. He sued the regional district for damages and later built a replica of his house on the same site. Faced with another embarrassing political situation – Mooney had once again refused to comply with building codes – the regional district resolved the crisis in 1995 by excluding the district of Wells from CRD building code bylaws and inspection services.

Rick Mooney's letter to the *Tribune* reflected the standard frame used by local letter writers to condemn the regional district's actions. The event was portrayed as a classic David and Goliath encounter between the "little guy" and the "state." In so doing, Mooney and his supporters engaged in a powerful form of symbolic politics that could be called the "politics of victimization," in which discrepancies of power are symbolically highlighted and the political, economic, or cultural powerlessness of particular groups is transformed into moral power.

Robert Paine traces similar processes among Saami Aboriginal peoples of Norway and describes how Saami political activists staged "ethnodramas," public protests that took the form of staged displays of the cultural domination and victimization of small Aboriginal minorities by state governments and bureaucracies.[23] Similar political rhetoric, however, can be found not only in Canadian Aboriginal politics[24] but also in the United States and Great Britain in the struggles of rural settler communities against the intrusion of urban governments and/or the expansion of resource industries.[25] I show later how rural-urban dichotomies and David versus Goliath symbolic rhetoric are central to the politics of victimization engaged in by resource communities protesting the imposition of provincial authority (and protecting the privileges of forest companies) in rural regions. In this political rhetoric, powerlessness and vulnerability are equated with virtuosity, and the struggle between the powerless and the powerful is presented as a heroic crusade.

The politics of victimization were central to the public defence of Rick Mooney. Various criticisms were voiced in the opinion columns and letters in the Williams Lake *Tribune* and Quesnel *Cariboo Observer*. Letter writers condemned the regional district for overreacting to the problem, for misusing its bureaucratic power, for wasting taxpayers' money, and for not considering more reasonable means for resolving the problem. Many letter writers called for the resignation of the CRD board and administrator. The Vancouver media picked up the story, running sympathetic coverage of Mooney and his plight and causing intense embarrassment to CRD officials. Both urban and local media coverage of the Mooney affair celebrated Mooney as the "little guy" confronting a big and impersonal bureaucracy.

In local debates, though, the public values appealed to in defence of Mooney – the values of individualism, democracy, and freedom – were not just articulated in the abstract. In some instances, they were also associated with place, with a contemporary regional identity, and with a local historical tradition of settlement. For example, Paul St. Pierre, a regular *Tribune* columnist and a well-known writer of Cariboo-Chilcotin fiction, portrayed the event as a warning to all citizens concerned with protecting individual rights and freedoms: "By now most of us who remember freedom and Lord State Almighty will have heard about Rick Mooney and his fight to prevent his government from wrecking his house. The case is not clear cut. Cases usually aren't. But whatever the details, most who read it feel somebody walking on their grave."[26] He applauded Mooney's independence and stubbornness in refusing to conform to mindless government regulations as emblematic of Cariboo values and identity: "Conforming is just not what Cariboo people are good at." To St. Pierre, who has made a living creating bizarre and humorous stories of the region's fictional inhabitants,[27] the Mooney affair was simply another example of the odd characters who populate the Cariboo-Chilcotin.

In contrast, an older woman, a member of a prominent pioneer family and an author of a recently published popular history, saw the affair in a deeper historical context. She viewed the matter as a violation not only of contemporary Cariboo-Chilcotin values but also, more importantly, of the pioneer tradition of Canada. She denounced the destruction of Mooney's home, writing: "It was a cruel and un-Canadian thing to do. The pioneers of this country always tried to help people instead of hurting them."[28] She concluded, "Years ago I read a story, fiction, in a magazine about a family's home in a far off country like Russia, that was demolished because it didn't comply with government regulations somehow. I thought, how terrible, nothing like that could ever happen in Canada. But it could and did. How times are changing."

A Quesnel man wrote a stinging letter to the *Cariboo Observer*, condemning the "spiteful and dastardly deed by governmental big shots who took such a vicious and heartless attitude" against an impoverished, "courageous, elderly ... pensioner."[29] He demanded the firing of the CRD administrator and cited the regional district's actions as a gross violation of democratic principles. This letter writer, too, drew on historical narratives and metaphors to further support his opinions: "This is Canada – the country built by pioneers who had to live with what they had available and could afford. There were no C.R.D.'s and little or no regulations – only the rule of God and the belief in, and the will, to build this beautiful country for the betterment of future generations. I am sure this type of action by governmental employees and C.R.D. bosses is not what our pioneers had in mind."

Both letter writers weave myths of frontier history and heroic individualism with contemporary public values and identities. The symbol of the pioneer is metaphorically extended to frame Rick Mooney. These writers see in his actions the pioneer's qualities of independence, courage, self-sufficiency, thrift, and personal responsibility. His struggles against government bureaucracy are equated with the determination of pioneers to stand up for the principles of individualism, democracy, and freedom. In embodying the spirit of the pioneers who "built" the Canadian nation, Mooney is transformed into a symbol of national pride and identity. With Mooney shrouded in these sacred symbols, the regional district's actions become tantamount to a public burning of the Canadian flag.[30]

The pioneer is what Richard Slotkin refers to as a "mythic icon," a symbol of "tremendous economy and compression and a mnemonic device capable of evoking a complex system of historical associations by a single image or phrase."[31] In these letters, the symbol of the pioneer evokes a particular historical scenario that highlights the heroic characteristics and actions of unnamed individuals rather than of complex economic and political forces. It suggests that colonialism itself has been less a political and economic project than a moral campaign – even more, a sacred Christian endeavour sanctified by the "rule of God."

At the same time, these letter writers evoke a particular narrative of frontier history that deviates somewhat from those discussed in the previous chapter. Here the frontier encounter is not between whites and Indians or between humans and nature but between settlers and governments. Settlers attempt to escape the shackles of metropolitan government regulations that would constrain their behaviour and destroy their spirit, their independence, and their commitment to personal liberty. The evil force to be opposed and conquered on the frontier is that of the metropolitan government committed not to the principles of democracy and freedom but to the regulation of the human body and spirit. The birth of the Canadian nation, it is suggested, depended precisely on the triumph of the settler over totalitarian government control.

Populist versions of the frontier myth, pitting the small, virtuous pioneer against the dark, menacing powers of urban government, have been one of the major vehicles of social criticism in twentieth-century America. Slotkin identifies two opposing ideological versions of the frontier myth that have dominated the popular culture and entertainment industries. "Progressivist" versions celebrate American history in terms of the continual development of industrial capitalism, the expansion of corporate monopolies, and the development of centralized national political institutions. In contrast, "populist" versions envision twentieth-century industrial and corporate expansion as leading to a breakdown in democracy and an increase in political and material inequalities, processes that have led American society away from the social relations of equality idealized in the agrarian past.[32] The central heroes of populist myths are the "social bandits" – the Western outlaw, the outlaw-detective – who have stood at the margins of society to fight industrial development, the expansion of the railroads, the large ranching conglomerates, and the big-city financiers and banks. In this way, the producers of dime novels and popular westerns employed the frontier myth as forms of "lower-class resistance"[33] – at least as imagined and expressed by the publishing industries.

In a similar way, these Cariboo-Chilcotin letter writers engage populist versions of the frontier myth to construct a historically contingent and selective vision of the past that they use to oppose and criticize the actions of contemporary governments. The writers suggest that certain lessons learned from the past need to be heeded today: the importance of protecting the individual's rights to autonomy and freedom from regulation, the very qualities that enabled the Canadian nation to grow and prosper. Implicitly, they suggest that the present course of history is deviating from this ideal past, and they attempt to realign social practices and values in conformity with idealized past traditions.

In mobilizing the images of the pioneer and the frontier legacy, these Euro-Canadians creatively reformulate the past to suit their political interests in the present. The symbol of the pioneer is often used to evoke a variety of imagined pasts, all variations of the frontier myth. Yet in so doing, Euro-Canadians affirm not only the veracity of the frontier myth as a historical epistemology but also the morality of the colonial endeavour itself. It is simply assumed that an association with early pioneers is positive, that the acts of the pioneers, and of European colonization, are to be celebrated. It is this balance – the ability of the frontier myth to serve as a language of diverse (and sometimes competing) political interests while reinforcing a highly selective historical vision – that enables it to persist as a hegemonic cultural complex. It is this selective historical tradition that justifies the very social arrangements that Aboriginal people are attempting to challenge in quite different domains of political conflict.

The particular version of the past put forth by these letter writers equates the "pioneer" with "freedom." The meaning of freedom is relational rather than absolute: it refers to the relative freedom that pioneers had to build their own homes as they chose, a right denied to Rick Mooney. In their selective association of pioneers with freedom, these writers construct an idealized image of the past designed to suit their agenda of critiquing the actions of the regional district as the unreasonable intrusions of government into the present lives of ordinary residents. Yet this association of pioneers and freedom detracts attention from a more complex historical scenario in which government forms of power, domination, and regulation were central to the course of history.

The pioneers' success did not simply depend on the absence of government regulation. Rather, their ability to take up land, to farm, and to fend off attempts of area Aboriginal people to protest their settlement on Aboriginal lands depended on an apparatus of colonial authority that included missionaries, Indian agents and the Indian Affairs bureaucracy, federal and provincial legislation, justices of the peace, and colonial courts. In different ways, each of these colonial groups sought to control the Aboriginal populations and to make the Cariboo-Chilcotin safe for settlement. Although the early settlers may have enjoyed comparative freedom, they did not live in the absence of government regulations. On the contrary, Cariboo-Chilcotin settlers made extensive use of the colonial court system to resolve interpersonal conflicts and business disputes.[34] Furthermore, the establishment of homesteads, farms, and ranches was supported by an expanding capitalist economy encouraged by the colonial governments, an economy that created a market for local products – furs, minerals, agricultural products, beef cattle, and later lumber – and that eventually transformed the Cariboo-Chilcotin into a resource hinterland of metropolitan Canada, Great Britain, and the United States.[35] To celebrate the pioneer as the builder of Canada renders invisible these overarching structures of colonial power and erases from history the coercion and the oppression of Aboriginal peoples that were central to the settlement of Canada.

These letter writers creatively extend the symbol of the pioneer to embrace Rick Mooney and his actions. The term "pioneer" is frequently used in the Cariboo-Chilcotin in a number of contexts. According to the *Gage Canadian Dictionary,* a pioneer is "a person who settles in a region that has not been settled before; a person who goes first or does something first and so prepares a way for others." This is often, but not always, the sense in which this term is used in local discourse in the Cariboo-Chilcotin.

For example, the term is frequently found in tourism brochures, in popular histories, and in newspaper stories. A brochure advertising the Museum of the Cariboo Chilcotin advises the tourist that "Gold lured settlers to the Cariboo – the green grass meadows kept them here. The Museum of the Cariboo Chilcotin tells the story of these early pioneers who found a way of life, if not their fortunes, in cattle ranching." A pamphlet advertising guest ranches in British Columbia announced: "Since the days of the pioneers, the lure of the West has held an irresistible attraction for anyone with a longing for adventure and wide open spaces." A pioneer is thus someone who arrived from somewhere else, braved the unknown to eventually settle and put down roots in a new land, and succeeded in creating a new life and a new society.

The term "pioneer" is not restricted to these early settlers. In use, it is honorary, the equivalent of the Aboriginal term "elder." It refers more generally to any person who is a respected member of the community, who can demonstrate at least some length of residence in the area, and who is recognized to have contributed in some significant way to the development of the community. At times, there may be debates about the length of time required for a person to be designated a pioneer. In one instance, an individual who arrived in the Cariboo-Chilcotin in the 1950s was honoured as a pioneer, but not without private discussions about the validity of this designation. In 1996, the term was extended to honour an elderly Tsilhqot'in woman who was chosen as Pioneer of the Year at the annual Pioneer Days celebration held in the small Chilcotin town of Alexis Creek. The term can generate a great degree of creative extension and play; the degree to which these processes of metaphorical extension succeed depends on public response.

In the case of Rick Mooney, there was no public challenge to his pioneer status, despite the fact that he had lived in the Cariboo-Chilcotin only since 1978.[36] To these letter writers, however, Mooney embodied the spirit of Canadian pioneers from all parts of the country, those individuals celebrated in frontier histories for risking their lives to venture into the wilderness and carve out homesteads, endure poverty and hardship, and help one another in times of crisis.

It is important to trace not only *how* Euro-Canadians use the term "pioneer" but also the many contexts in which it does not enter the language of political debate. There are many instances in which individual efforts to resist government intrusion are *not* publicly defended by championing frontier histories and the pioneers' right to autonomy. The efforts of Aboriginal people to be independent and self-sufficient, as their ancestors were, by hunting and fishing on Crown land, by cutting firewood and house timbers on Crown land, or by building homes or cabins on Crown land are not publicly defended by Euro-Canadians but subject to intense public criticism. The equally extensive intrusions of governments into the lives of Aboriginal people has proceeded with virtually no public commentary.

There is here a selective application of the concept of freedom and the illegitimacy of government regulation that exclusively favours forms of Euro-Canadian resistance. The symbol of the pioneer is not extended to defend Aboriginal people's resistance to colonial intrusion; rather, Aboriginal people are positioned on the opposite side of the symbolic divide in the frontier myth's narrative structure of history. Instead, their submission to colonial authorities is seen as a necessary component of the triumph of the settlers and the building of the Canadian nation.

**The CORE Protest**

Frontier legacies and pioneer traditions are evoked not only to construct nationalist identities and to defend the rights of individuals struggling against unyielding, domineering bureaucracies. There are also instances in which this imagery is drawn upon to construct homogeneous regional identities that *distinguish* the Cariboo-Chilcotin from the surrounding national society and is used by local interest groups to resist the intrusive policies and practices of the state. A clear example is found in the debates that arose surrounding the Cariboo-Chilcotin CORE land-use process.

In 1992, the provincial NDP government created the Commission on Resources and the Environment (CORE) in a political climate of increasing conflicts between environmental groups, forestry and mining companies, and First Nations regarding ownership and control of the province's resources. The commission's mandate was to create regional land-use plans that would mediate the demands of environmental protection and continued access to timber resources and employment by industry, labour groups, and resource-based municipalities. The issue of Aboriginal claims was addressed in a separate policy shift, in which the provincial government resolved to negotiate outstanding claims of Aboriginal title with First Nations.

The CORE process began in four regions of high land-use conflict: Cariboo-Chilcotin, Vancouver Island, West Kootenay-Boundary, and East Kootenay. In an attempt to devolve centralized decision making to regional communities, in each region negotiating tables were established consisting of local residents representing the various "stakeholders" in regional Crown lands, including the forest and mining industries, labour, local government, business, agriculture, recreation, tourism, and environmental groups. First Nations groups were also invited to participate. Not surprisingly, many boycotted the CORE process, arguing that claims of Aboriginal title had to be resolved before any long-term decisions could be made over the use of Crown lands by secondary groups. Through the CORE process, 12 percent of each region was to be protected to preserve the region's wildlife and ecological diversity. Each table was expected to collectively designate these protected areas and create a regional zoning system to balance the use of Crown lands by industry, agriculture, tourism, and recreation.

Forestry-dependent communities throughout the province immediately began to voice opposition to CORE. Many proindustry sectors interpreted the CORE process, with its strategy of creating "protected areas" and its explicit goal of ensuring the sustainability of the forest industry, to foreshadow a significant reduction in forest companies' access to timber resources. Intense conflicts began to arise between proindustry and proenvironment sectors. These struggles were nowhere as apparent as at the Cariboo-Chilcotin CORE table.

Conflicts between environmental and industry-labour groups in the Cariboo-Chilcotin were already raging when the CORE table was struck. By the early 1990s, a coalition of local, provincial, and national environmental groups had formed under the banner of the Cariboo Mountains Wilderness Coalition to protect the watersheds and wetlands of the eastern Cariboo. Forestry workers and their supporters in Williams Lake had formed the Save Our Jobs Committee and the Share the Cariboo-Chilcotin Resources Committee, and they were lobbying for public support to protect the industry's long-term access to timber resources. At the CORE table, individuals representing these different sectors faced the daunting task of negotiating a mutually acceptable solution to these and other land-use crises.

The CORE process began in the Cariboo-Chilcotin in the summer of 1992. After a series of public meetings, various individuals and organizations formed into sectors, each represented by two individuals who sat at the CORE negotiating table. By March 1993, twenty-four sectors were participating, representing agriculture, mining, forestry, recreation, local government, tourism, labour, small business, and conservation groups. After over a year of negotiations, though, the Cariboo-Chilcotin CORE table collapsed over the failure of the different parties, now polarized as "browns" and "greens," to reach consensus on the lands to be designated as protected areas.

The failure of the CORE process sparked one of the most intense public controversies in the recent history of the Cariboo-Chilcotin. Various sectors accused one another of negotiating in bad faith and lacking a commitment to a regional, consensual planning process. From the start, a coalition of forest company, labour, and business interests had expressed opposition to the CORE process, perceiving it as a threat to the status quo of forest companies' privileged control over timber resources and thus to the employment base and survival of small interior communities. Williams Lake resident and International Woodworkers of America vice president Harvey Arcand later boasted how the coalition of prologging interests had deliberately sabotaged the CORE process by manipulating procedural rules, by stacking the table with proindustry sectors, and by refusing to move from its original position during the fifteen months of negotiations.[37]

Bitter debates went on for months about the legitimacy of the CORE process and about the appropriateness of the conduct of key individuals at the table. In letters to the city newspaper, these debates degenerated into personal attacks and criticisms of the representatives of the environmental and proindustry movements, including the city's mayor, who played a lead role as anti-CORE spokesperson after the CORE failure.

These debates intensified after CORE commissioner Stephen Owen, in the absence of a regional consensus, released his own recommendations for a Cariboo-Chilcotin land-use plan in July 1994. By this time, two groups in the Cariboo-Chilcotin had formed to represent the competing environmental and industry interests in the region; both had created their own regional land-use plans and were lobbying for government acceptance of their recommendations.

Environmental interests were represented by the Cariboo-Chilcotin Conservation Council, headed by a west Chilcotin conservationist. Proindustry interests were represented by the Cariboo Communities Coalition, an alliance of fourteen of the twenty-four original sectors at the CORE table and including forestry and mining companies, agriculture, backcountry tourism, chambers of commerce, local government, and labour. With its headquarters in city hall and the mayor as its spokesperson, the coalition became the voice of the most powerful sectors of the regional society.

Both the Cariboo-Chilcotin Conservation Council and the Cariboo Communities Coalition sought public support for their platforms by demonstrating that their solutions were in the best interests of the regional community. Both groups used a political rhetoric of victimization and appealed to the need to protect the region's natural resources for future generations. Yet their political rhetoric differed radically in the use of symbols of history, of identity, and of public values.

From the outset, public opposition to CORE by forest industries and resource communities was rhetorically framed by images of honest, hardworking, small-town people struggling to resist the intrusive and oppressive actions of urban government forces and environmental activists. At a massive demonstration on the grounds of the provincial legislature in March, the mayor of Port McNeill roused the crowd by proclaiming that "Loggers, farmers and miners ... carry this country on their backs." He condemned the CORE report as the creation of "academics and backroom boys who have never had rain in their lunch buckets and who don't have to live with the consequences of their theory."[38] International Woodworkers of America representative Jack Munroe was widely quoted in the media in his condemnation of "cappuccino-sucking, concrete condo-dwelling, granola-eating city slickers" attempting to impose urban environmental ethics on and interfering in the lives and livelihoods of rural resource communities.[39]

In portraying resource communities as the David against the Goliath of urban governments, speakers engaged a set of powerful cultural symbols and identities to rouse public support. The celebration of the small-town work ethic and of physical labour, the dismissal of intellectual and bureaucratic knowledge, and the antagonism toward urban society and government resonated not only with the perceptions of civic leaders of Williams Lake but also with the widespread attitudes in northern resource communities across Canada. Speakers demanded recognition for the vital role of resource industries in the national economy and insisted that resource industry workers had a moral right to have their jobs and lifestyles protected. Resource industries and their workers were transformed into symbols of nationalism deserving special reverence and protection.

This oppositional rhetoric underwent some important modifications in the Cariboo-Chilcotin. Once again, a politics of embarrassment was undertaken and took its shape from considerations of place, regional identities, and historical traditions.

The Cariboo Communities Coalition hired a Vancouver public relations consultant and launched an extensive local and provincial radio, newspaper, and television advertising campaign in which it claimed to speak for "the people" of the Cariboo-Chilcotin. A distinct regional identity was put forth and used as a vehicle for claiming the right of the people, not urban governments, to control regional lands and resources. This regional identity was a populist one with a heavy emphasis on families and family values. Typical phrases included "Please ... Listen to the people!"; typical images showed "ordinary" mill workers, ranchers, and tourism operators with their families.[40]

In the politics of victimization, hardworking families and their values were pitted against the might of urban government: "CORE has put our families, our workers, our communities at risk," "We need to protect families," "We believe that we need to protect the social and economic well-being of our families." This populist construction, appealing to the central public values that define Cariboo-Chilcotin people, culture, and lifestyle, rendered invisible the very diversity of regional groups and interests that had prevented the success of the CORE process.

The Cariboo-Chilcotin regional identity was also defined by the length of (settler) occupation and activity and by the special attachment that residents felt to the land. A newsletter stated: "Many of us have lived here for generations, working the land as ranchers, farmers, miners, foresters, loggers, guides, outfitters and contractors." It continued: "Our forefathers developed the Cariboo-Chilcotin. They – and we – have helped strengthen the social and economic fabric of the province. And we're proud of that." The coalition argued that Cariboo-Chilcotin people, by virtue of their residence in the area, had political and moral rights to control the region's destiny and that the "local voice" had been denied in the CORE process. "We need a Made in the Cariboo solution!" and "We deserve a say in our destiny" were typical slogans.

These demands were backed by notions of the superiority of practical knowledge of local residents over theoretical knowledge of outside academics and bureaucrats: "This kind of balance [between social, environmental, and economic interests] can only truly be recognized by people who live, work, and play in the area – people who are IN the Cariboo-Chilcotin – people who know the Cariboo-Chilcotin." Finally, the right of local people to direct future land-use practices was also a moral one, stemming from their commitment to future generations and to stewardship of the land. "We feel we have a right and an obligation to have a direct say in the future development of our area – for the sake [of] our children and grandchildren."

These assertions of quasi-indigenous local identities – identities rooted in the unique relationship that rural settlers have to the land – are not unique to the Cariboo-Chilcotin or even to Canada but have been described in other settler colonies, such as New Zealand[41] and Australia,[42] as well as in rural regions of Great Britain.[43] Many rural areas of settler colonies have now been occupied by four, five, or more generations of European settlers: farmers, pastoralists, and ranchers. Over time, these groups have developed distinct cultural traditions and identities centred on their relationship to the landscape. As processes of decolonization proceed – to the extent that outstanding Aboriginal land claims are negotiated – rural settler communities are faced with parallel claims to territories by Aboriginal peoples also asserting indigenous identities. Non-Aboriginal settlers are also faced with the increasing efforts of state governments and transnational corporations to control and exploit the resources of rural areas. In these contexts, rural peoples are creating local identities as vehicles for the assertion of political rights to self-determination and regional autonomy.

Rural constructions of identity are highly influenced by the political context and the tenuous balance of power in which rural settlers, Aboriginal peoples, and state governments are enmeshed. This becomes apparent when contrasting the processes of identity construction in the Cariboo-Chilcotin with that among high-country sheep farmers in New Zealand as studied by Michele Dominy.[44] In both cases, rural settler communities are parties to competing claims to lands and resources (whether the competitors are other rural non-Aboriginal people or Aboriginal groups), claims to be mediated by national or provincial government agents. In both cases, groups are making claims to political autonomy on the grounds of the many generations of residency in the area and of their commitment to local political control, to families and future generations, and to responsible stewardship of the land.

Yet in the New Zealand case, settler families in the South Island high country were struggling against competing claims put forth by the Maori to lands assigned to them through the 1840 Treaty of Waitangi. At the Waitangi Tribunal hearings, high-country families asserted their rights to these pastoral lands by virtue of their distinct cultural identity stemming from their close relationship with the land, the significance of the land to their way of life, their many generations of occupancy of the region, and their commitment to act as custodians of the land. In asserting the importance of the land to their identity and lifestyle, high-country farmers explicitly claimed indigenous status. They claimed to be "like" Maori, and thus their claims should have equal validity.[45]

In the context of a tribunal that eventually proved highly sympathetic to Maori claims, settlers were forced into a defensive stance. Although Dominy argues that high-country farmers did not make political claims based on "an appropriation of Ngai Tahu symbology,"[46] her evidence suggests that at minimum they made claims based on explicit efforts to make features of their cultural identity *analogous* to that of the Maori claimants in a political climate that ultimately favoured Maori interests.

In contrast, the Cariboo-Chilcotin cultural identity put forth by the coalition was not framed by claims of indigenous status similar to that of Aboriginal peoples. In fact, First Nations and the question of Aboriginal title – issues at the forefront of provincial politics – were invisible throughout much of the local CORE debate. The political struggle was not against Aboriginal peoples but against local environmentalists and provincial governments. In this context, the indigenous status that the coalition claimed emerged from the traditions and legacy of Cariboo-Chilcotin pioneers. References to these pioneers, and to Cariboo-Chilcotin values and identities, were scattered throughout the publicity materials:

> The Cariboo-Chilcotin and this province were founded on the entrepreneurial spirit and self-reliance. Our forefathers worked hard to eke out an existence from the land, and we continue to do so – at the same time ensuring that we protect the land from being wasted.
>
> We believe that we have a lot to be proud of in the Cariboo-Chilcotin – of how our forefathers established the area – of how our ranchers have managed the range – of how our small businesses and tourism industry took major entrepreneurial risks to build our local service economy.
>
> The Cariboo-Chilcotin pioneer spirit of self-sufficiency and looking after our neighbours has remained a key value in the area ... We believe that we have the strength, the commitment, the experience, and the heart to continue to preserve the values of the Cariboo-Chilcotin.
>
> BC should never ignore the fact that the foundation of this province was built on the families who immigrated to the province from other parts of the world. This is what made our province prosperous.

Once again, collective identities were forged through populist expressions of the frontier myth of history. The pioneer is no longer the individual heroically battling the wilderness on his own but the *families* of the Cariboo-Chilcotin who, through their hard work and determination, have helped to build the province of British Columbia. The concept of the pioneer is metaphorically extended further to the small businesses and tourism ventures that have taken "major entrepreneurial risks" to "build" the economy. Cariboo-Chilcotin families, the values of independence, self-sufficiency, neighbourliness, and entrepreneurialism, and the resource industries themselves are thus historicized as reflecting the spirit of the pioneers; through this historical association, they are deserving of respect, honour, and protection.

This populist construction of the past also served to warn of the dangers of implementing government policies that would lead society away from the values and traditions that had been instrumental in the "building" of the Canadian nation. By creating parks and thus restricting forest companies' access to timber, Owen's CORE report was seen as disrupting the regional economy: forest industry employment would decline and have a serious impact on the survival of area families, their value systems, and the very cultural tradition and legacy of the pioneers. Through this metaphorical equation, Owen's CORE report was construed as an assault against the sacred pioneer tradition of Canada.

The coalition's populist rhetoric effectively overshadowed and silenced the voices of dissenting local groups. Claiming to speak for "the people" of the Cariboo-Chilcotin, and claiming to uphold the pioneer legacy of the region, the coalition instead spoke only for those groups in the region that were committed to preserving the status quo of industry access to forest resources. This silencing of competing voices was enabled by the coalition's strategy of drawing on the most sacred symbols of the regional culture to frame its concerns. The coalition was able to bombard the public through radio, television, and newspaper advertisements with a message that was apocalyptic in tone: implementation of the CORE report would destroy the regional culture, lifestyle, and pioneer legacy.

The Cariboo Chilcotin Conservation Council, with a relatively low-key and low-budget media campaign, also engaged in a politics of victimization that emphasized the exploitation of hinterland communities by transnational resource corporations.[47] But their symbolic rhetoric had little strength in a regional culture dominated by a frontier tradition of history as progress, by a popular ideal of the self-made man, and by a pervasive belief in the unlimited abundance of natural resources.[48]

The issue of Aboriginal title was remarkably absent during the course of public discussions of CORE, discussions that ostensibly were to lead to greater certainty over land tenure and to the resolution of regional land-use conflicts. While industry, business, tourism, labour, recreation, and environmental groups debated the future of Cariboo-Chilcotin lands, the very right of the state and various sectors of non-Aboriginal Canadian society to be claiming rights to Crown lands prior to addressing the issue of Aboriginal title was directly challenged by First Nations in the Cariboo-Chilcotin, who refused to participate in the CORE discussions. The use of frontier metaphors and images in the CORE debates – images that enhanced the stereotype of the "invisible Indian" by rendering Aboriginal people absent from the landscape of the past – facilitated the public's ability to ideologically separate these two domains of political activity and to temporarily forget about the overriding issue of Aboriginal title.

A final example will show the creative use of the image of the pioneer in public discussions about contentious events. At the height of conflict over the CORE process, a woman who had recently immigrated from Europe wrote a letter to the Williams Lake *Tribune* criticizing the "outbreak of hatred" between the different sectors. Appealing to the value of tolerance for alternative lifestyles and political opinions, she called on the public to rally behind the spirit of the pioneers to weather the difficult period of change: "We shouldn't forget that hatred consumes energy whereas understanding and goodwill create the strength to go through rough times. This is how this country has been built and it takes the spirit of the pioneers now and again to go into a changing world and to overcome the fear of change. The new frontier is our inventiveness – let's work together."[49] The symbol of the pioneer can serve a variety of competing political interests and can carry a variety of meanings. The spirit of the pioneers – their imagined courage, goodwill, and community spirit – was here evoked not to justify public conflict but to mediate it. That frontier imagery was so quickly adopted by an individual who had only recently immigrated to Canada is testimony to the dominance of the frontier myth of history in the collective Euro-Canadian imagination.

In evoking pioneer values and traditions, Euro-Canadians are making claims to a continuity between the present and the past. They are creating public identities founded on the presumption of a set of unchanging cultural values and traditions that unite old-time settlers and contemporary residents in one cultural community. In reality, the population and the cultural composition of the Cariboo-Chilcotin have undergone dramatic change over the last century. Between 1950 and 1990, the population of area cities quadrupled, largely due to the massive influx of newcomers arriving to take advantage of the booming industrial economy. The majority of Cariboo-Chilcotin residents cannot claim lengthy ancestral roots in the region. A significant proportion cannot claim lengthy histories in Canada. Given the "newness" of the population, it is remarkable that the symbol of the pioneer has attained such a sacred status.

This symbol is ideally suited to addressing a central problem of the regional culture: how to create a sense of collective identity that embraces a diverse group of residents lacking a shared past. The power of the symbol of the pioneer lies in its flexibility: it can embrace a variety of individuals and circumstances. Euro-Canadians use the term not to indicate length of residence in the region but to refer to adherence to a certain set of contemporary values, morals, and ideals that they equate with pioneer traditions. Although Euro-Canadians in the Cariboo-Chilcotin may not share a common past, they do share a common participation in a mythic conception of history. The frontier myth provides a sense of identity, a sense of morality, and a sense of belonging for old-time families and recent immigrants alike, who enthusiastically identify with the heroic processes of colonization and who freely draw on its symbols and metaphors to define their imagined collective histories.

In these formulations, non-Aboriginal people in the Cariboo-Chilcotin do not achieve a sense of connection to the landscape, a place-centred identity, through the process of "indigenization" as suggested by Terry Goldie,[50] in which they identify with Canadian Aboriginal peoples as a medium for identifying with place. Nor do they construct their identity in terms of their direct relationship with the landscape, as Dominy suggests for New Zealand rural settlers. Instead, non-Aboriginal people in the Cariboo-Chilcotin achieve an indigenization through history – specifically through the medium of the pioneer, an icon of the frontier myth.

In celebrating the symbol of the pioneer, Euro-Canadians are putting forth a vision of history that is presumed to be natural, common sense, and shared by all Canadians. Indeed, the moral power of the symbol of the pioneer, when used in the politics of embarrassment, depends on the widespread acceptance of this dominant historical tradition. The frontier myth infuses these symbolic politics, reproducing a selective vision of history less through direct polemics than through understandings that are implicit and conveyed through metaphorical images and associations. Its power as a dominant cultural mode of seeing the past is evident in the subtle ways in which it infiltrates a range of political discourses on a variety of subjects.

At the same time, the frontier myth is capable of serving a variety of political interests. Prologging interests, individuals protesting government regulations, and citizens criticizing local leaders all manipulate the frontier myth for their own purposes. In each evocation of the idea of the pioneer, an imagined past is juxtaposed with the present as a form of cultural critique. In drawing on frontier myth imagery, these groups are staking moral claims to the legitimacy of their struggles. They are using public values and identities as a symbolic currency that validates diverse and often opposing interests. In so doing, they are nevertheless all participating in and reproducing a mythic language that has emerged from the colonial experience and that continues to function in material as well as cultural – and metaphorical – capacities.

# 5
# Indians, Whites, and Common-Sense Racism

Williams Lake, like many other small cities and towns across rural Canada, is often a difficult place for Aboriginal people to live. There is chronic tension between the Aboriginal and non-Aboriginal populations, and racial discrimination against Aboriginal people is evident in subtle gestures and openly demeaning insults and behaviours. These tensions have characterized social relations in the region for many decades and have heightened with the increasing political assertiveness of area First Nations and the onset of treaty negotiations.

At the same time, these tensions are subject to much greater public scrutiny and criticism. Area First Nations leaders are not only speaking out against instances of everyday racism but also challenging their subordinate position within Canadian society on a variety of legal, political, and bureaucratic fronts. The Tsilhqot'in chiefs have declared sovereignty from the Canadian state, the Secwepemc First Nations are participating in Aboriginal treaty talks, and all First Nations organizations are negotiating with government agencies to increase Aboriginal control over the administration of justice, education, and social services in reserve communities. Euro-Canadians are becoming more aware of the Aboriginal presence in the region. The city newspaper now carries regular stories on First Nations political activities and, on rare occasions, even a feature on a social event in a reserve community. These developments have brought questions of past and future roles of Aboriginal people in the regional society and economy to the forefront of public discourse.

In this context of change, Euro-Canadian townspeople engage in a plurality of discourses contemplating their relationships with Aboriginal people. Euro-Canadian attitudes are not homogeneous: there are those who voice strident prejudices; those who oppose Aboriginal treaties and rights and argue for assimilation; those who express ambivalence about their present and future relations with Aboriginal peoples; and those who support land claims and treaty negotiations and who respect and admire the distinctiveness of Aboriginal cultures and traditions. No one set of images captures the complexity of Euro-Canadian attitudes; rather, these discourses often generate conflicting and contradictory images of Aboriginal people.

Despite this diversity, some discourses can be considered dominant by virtue of their ubiquity in the social landscape of Euro-Canadian life in Williams Lake. In this chapter, I trace one of the dominant genres of Euro-Canadian discourse about Aboriginal people, one that is typically encountered in the everyday conversations that occur in casual settings over the dinner table, at the backyard barbecue, and in the pubs and restaurants around town. This genre is dominated by the conventional racist image of the inferior Indian other. In the following pages, I present an account of the casual remarks that I heard in the Euro-Canadian social world, both in interview settings and in informal contexts. I show how Euro-Canadians discuss Indian-white differences, engaging in conversational rituals of solidarity that condemn Aboriginal people as morally and culturally inferior and that create a sense of socialized belonging that celebrates Euro-Canadian frontier values. The two naturalized and opposing categories of Indian and white are not just a feature of popular historical narratives of the Canadian frontier but are also among the most important categories in the symbolic ordering of social relations in Williams Lake today.

A critical question is the extent to which these discourses perpetuate inequalities in Aboriginal/Euro-Canadian relations. Are they simply private ("between-us") discussions that have no impact on the tenor of social relations? What are the "truth effects" of such conversational rituals? Stereotypes themselves may not be problematic. It is critical to consider how these various ideas of Aboriginal identity, and how these constructions of Aboriginal/Euro-Canadian difference, are enacted in specific contexts, how they are applied to certain situations, and what the particular consequences are.

To trace these issues, I turn to a series of discussions with area Aboriginal people who describe their relationships and interactions with Euro-Canadians in the city. These voices contrast sharply with the official public accounts celebrating the friendliness and social harmony of small-town life. Aboriginal perspectives reflect accumulated historical experiences of racial discrimination and show how Euro-Canadians have exercised the power to ascribe negative identities in situations of everyday, informal Aboriginal/Euro-Canadian contact. These processes constitute forms of "status domination,"[1] modes of interpersonal violence that contribute to the personal and political disempowerment of the Aboriginal population.

Aboriginal people's accounts of their experiences in the city also reveal their various forms of resistance to such practices. Withdrawal, verbal and physical challenge, collective political opposition, and humorous parody are all part of the repertoire of oppositional practices that comprise a private and at times public culture of resistance.

## The Dimensions of Difference: Indians in Euro-Canadian Conversational Discourse

Euro-Canadian townspeople frequently discuss and debate the current land claims and treaty process and its potential impact on Williams Lake. Distinct from these serious discussions of the political and historical legitimacy of Aboriginal claims are the everyday conversations through which many Euro-Canadians discuss Aboriginal people. A distinguishing feature of this discourse is its moral focus and lighthearted tone: Aboriginal people are criticized and ridiculed, often through jokes or humorous comments, for a variety of perceived moral deficiencies. Indeed, "joking about Indians" is so common that it could be considered a recreational activity.

Similar patterns of discourse have been discussed among working-class white men in northern Ontario. Thomas Dunk writes: "The image of the Indian which appears most frequently [in young working-class men's discourse] is generally derogatory. In jokes, offhand comments, and general banter and gossip, the Indian stands for negative personality traits ... The idea of the Indian as the living embodiment of pathological behavioural characteristics is never far from the surface of the mind or the tip of the tongue."[2] In the Cariboo-Chilcotin, these conversational patterns are not limited to the working class but engaged in by people from many different sectors: loggers, mill workers, middle-class professionals, businesspeople, politicians, and store clerks. Disparaging remarks about Indians can be heard between friends and acquaintances in the privacy of individual homes, in the workplace, and in the radio conversations of truckers hauling logs out of the Chilcotin. These remarks can occasionally be overheard in public domains: the business offices, coffeeshops, and bars around town. In short, negative beliefs about and attitudes toward Aboriginal people constitute socially constructed truths that pervade the conversational landscape. They are a central part of the dominant culture of Williams Lake, existing as a form of common-sense racism.

The drama, humour, and intense feelings that these discussions of Aboriginal people engender suggest that these discussions are not merely intellectual exchanges of information. In another northwestern Ontario town, David Stymeist similarly noted that discussions of Indians often took on "ritual" qualities. The litany of complaints voiced by Euro-Canadians about Indians created an implicit tone of "us against them," with the complaints being put forth in a very "theatrical" manner.[3] These insights suggest a central feature of Euro-Canadians' casual discourse about Aboriginal people: they are the conversational equivalent of community rituals in which public values, morals, and identities are enacted and affirmed.

These conversational rituals play an important role in the construction of local Euro-Canadian identity and in the socialization of newcomers to the city. In the absence of extensive and permanent lines of communication between the Euro-Canadian city residents and the reserve community members, these informal conversations between Euro-Canadians are among the most important vehicles through which "information" about Aboriginal people is circulated. Through these ritual interchanges, newcomers are informed that to be a resident of Williams Lake is to belong to a small-town community on the fringes of Canadian society and to be a member of a close-knit community held together in moral opposition to Indians.

### Interview Talk and Everyday Conversation

One of the most common images that appears in Euro-Canadian discourse is that of the "drunk Indian." Alcohol problems are not limited to the Aboriginal population; they are widespread in the Cariboo-Chilcotin region generally. Community health surveys have repeatedly identified alcohol abuse as one of the major health concerns in the area. Teenage drinking parties, involving up to 200 youths, occasionally occur in the outlying areas and are a source of much public criticism. In the spring of 1994, a large gathering of youths on the Stampede grounds erupted in violence, requiring RCMP intervention. Although these instances of drinking and lawlessness are occasionally given treatment as public problems, they do not compare to the massive amount of public attention and energy assigned to discussing and moralizing about the problem of "drunk Indians."

A small group of Aboriginal people, known locally as the Troopers, are often seen on the streets of Williams Lake. They are recognizable by their dishevelled appearance, their public inebriation, and their habit of collecting bottles in the city's garbage cans or along the highway. The Troopers have existed as a social category in the city since the early 1970s. To many Williams Lake residents, they are seen as stains on the city's public image and are a source of embarrassment. Although the Troopers represent only a minority of Aboriginal people visible on city streets on any given day, and although not all Troopers are Aboriginal, to many Euro-Canadians they are a frequent reference point for more general criticisms of "drunk Indians": the Troopers are presented as evidence of the moral degradation of the Aboriginal population as a whole. The very name Troopers is spoken in an affectionately patronizing tone that has a sharp derogatory edge.

Despite the frequent discussions and jokes about the Troopers, many Euro-Canadians know little about these individuals. Most Euro-Canadians are unsure of who the Troopers are, how many of them there are, where they go at night, or how long they have been living on the streets. Some theories have the Troopers circulating between reserve communities and the city streets, staying in Williams Lake for only a few days or a few weeks. Others believe that the Troopers are a permanently homeless fixture of the city. These questions, though, do not occupy a great deal of attention or interest. Instead, most Euro-Canadians view the Troopers as a nameless and faceless group of Indian alcoholics.

The Troopers, in fact, are integrated into the extensive kinship networks that connect Aboriginal people across the Cariboo-Chilcotin. Many Aboriginal people know the Troopers by name, by family relation, and by personal history. They know them as individuals who have fallen on hard times, who have come from difficult family situations, or who have suffered extreme abuse in the residential school system. They are not ostracized from the reserve communities of the region; rather than being homeless, many Troopers have relatives in reserve communities with whom they could stay if they choose. In fact, those most frequently seen in Williams Lake actually live on the Sugar Cane reserve in their own homes and merely spend their days in the city.

To most Euro-Canadians, these intricacies of personal history are invisible. Not only are the Troopers an anonymous collective but in many instances the area reserve communities are also rendered invisible. Both are relegated to the peripheral zones of the social world of Euro-Canadians, becoming the subjects of interest only in discussions that reify their difference from Euro-Canadian townspeople.

Jokes about "drunk Indians" are not limited to the Troopers; they extend to Aboriginal people in general. It is an assumed truth that most Aboriginal people have drinking problems. In Euro-Canadians' joking discourse and banter, there is little discussion about why these differences may exist. Instead, it is assumed that drinking is simply an inherent part of Indian culture and/or that Aboriginal people are biologically predisposed to alcoholism. This naturalization of the drunk Indian stereotype was suggested by one older woman. She explained the presumed prevalence of drunkenness among Aboriginal people biologically: Indians have a natural thirst for alcohol. "I think the Troopers evolved out of the high alcohol problem with the Natives when they were allowed into the beer parlours. Because, from what I understand – and you'd have to talk to them, or talk to doctors or whatever – but they have an insatiable thirst for anything sweet. If you've ever watched them drink juice or pop ... we had the highest wine sales in BC at one time! [laughs]" The colonial gaze of the local Euro-Canadians transforms Aboriginal people into natural spectacles to be watched while drinking pop or engaged in other behaviour in public. This is only one example of the way in which Aboriginal people are subjected to a form of hypervisibility through Euro-Canadian scrutiny. Through this public surveillance, the most mundane acts are transformed into highly meaningful events constituting proof of Euro-Canadian assumptions of Aboriginal "difference."

This theme of Aboriginal people as public spectacles was echoed by a woman who, recounting memories of growing up in Williams Lake in the 1950s and 1960s, described Aboriginal people as sexually immoral drunks. She did not see "difference" in a historical context; rather, she blurred past and present as she drew on her memories to portray the contemporary reality of Aboriginal people:

> There was the Famous Café that all of us kids went to when we were teenagers ... I mean, we went there, all the time. And probably five nights out of every week, or at least every weekend, there'd be an Indian man and woman sittin' outside, and half the time they'd be making love, or he'd have his hands up her pants, or her pants would be off or whatever. I mean, it was just ... we just walked around them and went in. That's what they were ... when they were sober they were great people. But that wild juice did things to them! [laughs] But they used to work for my dad, and they were excellent. Some of the nicest people I know are Indian people. But when they're into the bottle, they're not nice. They're different than we are. And they are different.

The belief that sexual immorality and violence are inherent features of Aboriginal life, while being completely unsupported by any documented historical evidence, nevertheless is often heard in Euro-Canadian discussions and at times, as above, is put forth in a very crude manner. The sexual abuse of students at the Oblate-run St. Joseph's Mission residential school has received national media attention, and from recent accounts it is clear that the sexual abuse of children at the mission was occurring at least as early as the 1950s. Many local Euro-Canadians, though, believe that sexual abuse has long been a widespread problem in reserve communities. As one man stated, "They can't blame the Catholic schools for that." A harsher version was expressed by one community leader: "I think that there are real problems in the reserves. I don't think it's any secret by people who are aware of the way things are that the abuse of women is ... much more common than we'd like to see it in the Aboriginal communities. I was talking to a [health care professional] ... [and] he was saying that he believes that a large number of people, maybe 90 percent of Aboriginal females, are sexually abused ... by the time they are ten years old." Most significantly, he was "absolutely convinced" that these social problems are not a recent historical phenomenon, or a manifestation of social crisis and breakdown, but have been an inherent part of Aboriginal culture since before European arrival. These beliefs are among the most chilling and virulent stereotypes with which all Aboriginal people must cope. They are particularly dangerous for Aboriginal women who, objectified as sexually immoral or "loose," then must cope with being targets of unwanted sexual attention and, at times, sexual assault, all rationalized by the same images voiced by the Euro-Canadians quoted here.

A third prevalent image is the Indian as criminal. For many years, Williams Lake and the nearby city of Quesnel have exchanged the dubious honour of having the highest crime rate per capita in the province. This "honour" is in part a product of the way in which these statistics are calculated. Both Williams Lake and Quesnel are service and commercial centres for a much higher regional population, whereas the actual crime rate per capita is calculated only on the basis of the population of city residents.

In Williams Lake, however, it is a widespread belief that Aboriginal people are responsible for the city's high crime rate.[4] The remarks of one community leader were typical: "If you took the court registry and went through it, I mean I can show you ten papers [the "Court Report" published in the city newspaper], and it doesn't take a rocket scientist to figure out that 80 percent of those people going through the court system are the Natives. And that's not the people that are living in Williams Lake. That's out of the fifteen reserves in the surrounding area!"[5] In 1991, the mayor of Williams Lake was incautious enough to share this belief with a reporter from the *Vancouver Sun*. The mayor was quoted as saying that most of the crime was the result of "street people – I shouldn't say native people – breaking into premises to get liquor."[6]

Although his remarks sparked vocal opposition from area First Nations leaders and critical coverage from the provincial media, the mayor later defended his remarks by referring to a city hall task force report. The report, drawing on statistics provided by the attorney general's department regarding individuals charged with offences and processed through the court system, concluded that 53.4 percent of criminal charges between 1990 and 1991 were laid against Aboriginal people. It is debatable to what extent 53 percent can be considered a statistically significant majority, and in this case it arguably demonstrates how statistics are interpreted on the basis of preexisting judgments. For example, gender was not considered a relevant factor, although the same statistics indicated that 95 percent of the individuals being processed through the courts were male.

Aboriginal people, who comprise 10 to 15 percent of the regional population, are clearly overrepresented in the justice system. The causes of this overrepresentation, in the Cariboo-Chilcotin as well as across Canada, are complex and belie simplistic explanations that stereotypes of the Indian criminal offer. As concluded by the commissioners of the recent Aboriginal Justice Inquiry in Manitoba, Aboriginal overrepresentation is linked to both systemic discrimination against Aboriginal people and a higher rate of Aboriginal criminal behaviour. This higher rate itself is "rooted in a long history of discrimination and social inequality that has impoverished Aboriginal people and consigned them to the margins of Manitoban society."[7] This history of discrimination implicates not only the Canadian justice system, which provided "legal sanction for their oppression," but also "a century of paternalism and duplicity in government policies," which "must also be held ultimately responsible for a good portion of the high rates of Aboriginal crime, which are the almost inevitable result of social breakdown and poverty."[8]

Not only is the stereotype of the Indian criminal inadequate as an explanatory device, but it also contributes to this very overrepresentation in creating a situation of RCMP overpolicing of the Aboriginal population. That is, expectations that "Indians are criminals" cause a higher degree of surveillance and scrutiny of Aboriginal people simply because they are Aboriginal. As a result, "many Aboriginal people are arrested and held in custody, where a non-Aboriginal person in the same circumstances either might not be arrested at all, or might not be held."[9] As Cariboo-Chilcotin Justice Inquiry commissioner Anthony Sarich concluded, this attitude "explains these officers' readiness to unquestioningly accept allegations made against natives while keeping a closed mind to anything they raise in answer."[10]

Images of the Indian as drunk, licentious, violent, and criminal recur in the ritual conversations and joking remarks of Euro-Canadians in Williams Lake. But these images are not unique to the Cariboo-Chilcotin; they are prevalent in the conversations and jokes of Euro-Canadians in many other small cities and towns in Canada.[11] These images have filled the pages of Canadian history textbooks, popular literature, pioneer autobiographies, and fur-trade journals for centuries. They are part of the national tradition in Canada of "imagining" Indians.[12] These images, however, are not just inert expressions of a colonial ideology. When they circulate in small-town talk in regions such as the Cariboo-Chilcotin, as I discuss later, they exert a profound influence on Euro-Canadian understandings and attitudes and have devastating consequences in the lives and experiences of Aboriginal men, women, and children.

Another set of images drawn on to describe Aboriginal difference is more closely related to the cultural setting of Williams Lake and to the values and morals that define local Euro-Canadian identities. These images relate to the perceived special status that Aboriginal people enjoy by virtue of their relationship with the federal government. There are several common criticisms, many of them founded on misconceptions: that Indians enjoy a "tax-free" status, that they are given "free" houses and "free" university education, and that they enjoy a wealth of government payments that flow into reserve communities to support highly paid band staff and unrealistic economic development projects that are doomed to fail through mismanagement. This image of the "wealthy, undeserving Indian," for example, is circulated in the frequent jokes about how most Indians are now driving new and expensive trucks "that even I can't afford." There is a strong resentment that Aboriginal people enjoy privileges not available to Euro-Canadians, that they get things for free while Euro-Canadians have to work hard to afford similar luxuries. Thus, Aboriginal peoples' purported laziness, irresponsibility, and alcohol dependence are supported by their special relationship with the federal government. Niels Braroe, David Stymeist, and Thomas Dunk, whose work spans three decades, have described virtually identical attitudes among Euro-Canadians in other rural Canadian towns.

These sentiments were captured in condensed form in an interview with a retired man, who vigorously condemned Aboriginal people:

> I've been in every Indian house in the Cariboo. I have yet to see one Indian house with one vegetable garden. If you look at our vegetable garden up here, it's a quarter of an acre; we produce enough to keep us going right through ... the winter. I have yet to see an Indian get out with a pick and shovel and dig the ground and sweat. They're just not made that way ... I have yet to see an Indian working who's an apprentice for a plumber or an electrician or a carpenter. The Indians want new houses at Sugar Cane, they get a white man to build them, and then they start to wreck them.[13]

In portraying Aboriginal people through these varied images, Euro-Canadians are simultaneously expressing an ideal adherence to a set of values and morals central to the frontier complex: sobriety, respect for the law, self-sufficiency and personal responsibility, punctuality, sexual discretion, materialism, and the capitalist work ethic. These public values emerge from a vision of history captured by the myth of the self-made man. They reflect a deeply held belief in the potential for prosperity and advancement through hard work. These are the values that guide the practical activities of many Euro-Canadian men and women, who, like some Aboriginal people, work for years to pay off high mortgages, afford new vehicles, buy recreational property, enjoy weekend camping, hunting, and fishing, and make occasional shopping trips to Vancouver.

Although these ritualized conversations reinforce a sense of belonging and ideal adherence to public values, they do so at the expense of Aboriginal people, who are perceived to share none of these public values. They are condemned for "living off government money," for being "given" free homes and then "wrecking them," and for being granted tax-free status, all of which are perceived as benefits that unfairly privilege certain special interest groups and that undermine the principle of the equality of all

Canadians. Aboriginal people are seen as the epitome of those who "live off the system" and thus undermine the central values of personal responsibility, thrift, materialism, equality, hard work, and self-sacrifice. These casual remarks and the humorous frame in which they are frequently communicated are vicious expressions that deny the human dignity and individuality of Aboriginal people, that naturalize social problems and violence in a chilling fashion, and that perpetuate assumptions of the special treatment of reserve communities by government that only furthers Euro-Canadian antagonism.

Not all Euro-Canadians are as forthright in their moral condemnation of Aboriginal people, and some may even challenge such remarks if made in their presence. However, it is significant that many of the above remarks were made during formal, taped interviews with middle-class individuals who hold respected positions in the local society. Theirs is not the marginalized voice of the oppressed working class. Their evocation of common-sense racism cannot be explained as an epiphenomenon of their own marginalization in the mode of production, as has elsewhere been suggested.[14] Rather, these individuals potentially wield significant influence in the shaping of public policy and community affairs. As respected citizens, they are among the opinion leaders whose ideas and attitudes are given attention by their peers, by the media, and by the public at large. In this context, their very willingness to speak about Aboriginal people "on the record" to a visiting anthropologist suggests the widespread and supposedly uncontroversial status of these assumed truths of difference.

These conversational practices are not limited to interview settings. Similar images circulate in everyday conversations, in humorous anecdotes, and in offhand comments. Some images are fleeting. One example was a conversation that I had with a professional woman who lived in Williams Lake. At the time, I was living in a house on a nearby Indian reserve. I remarked about the herd of horses, owned by band members, who had the free run of the valley. "Do they feed them?" she asked, somewhat sarcastically. Many Euro-Canadians criticize Aboriginal people, who "get all kinds of government money," for not taking proper care of their livestock.

In some conversations, Indians are praised for living up to Euro-Canadian standards of domestic materialism; implicitly, others are judged for failing to do so. I was visiting with "Don" and "Jennifer." She works as a clerk in a local store, and as part of her work she goes to people's homes to assist with the installation of the goods that she sells. She had recently been to a number of houses on Indian reserves. She knows that the money Aboriginal people get for new houses comes from the Department of Indian Affairs and that the department's budget only allows for mediocre goods for the houses. She discussed how some Aboriginal people are now putting in their own money to upgrade their homes. When I mentioned that the reserve home I was living in had recently been renovated, she responded approvingly: "It's good to see Native people fixing up their houses like that."

Why, we might ask, is it "good" to see this? However well-meaning and sympathetic such individuals are, this type of remark reveals a form of assimilationist thinking that is widespread among ordinary small-town Euro-Canadians who single out Aboriginal people for critical scrutiny and patronizing attention. The speakers take for granted the superiority of their Euro-Canadian value system. The underlying assumption of such subtly patronizing remarks is that Aboriginal people are inadequate as they are, that their comportment is somehow immoral and unacceptable, and that they should strive to live according to the ideal values and standards of Euro-Canadian society. Such remarks exist as small-town forms of what is a long-standing Canadian tradition of manufacturing and discussing the "Indian problem."[15]

Not all constructions of Euro-Canadian-Aboriginal difference are negative. For example, at times I have heard some Euro-Canadians observing that Natives seem to wear layers of clothing even on extremely hot days. They contemplate their observations, suggesting that Natives must have a "different biological tolerance to heat." Alternative explanations – that these are simply individual peculiarities or that there may be different standards of modesty in public – generally do not arise in conversation. Instead, the observations of specific instances are rapidly translated into theories of inherent and collective biological difference.

At other times, some Euro-Canadians speak about Aboriginal people in a manner that alternates between fascination for their cultural differences and disdain for their manner of living. Difference, in the same conversation, is marked by a movement between noble and ignoble imagery. The romantic primitive, the exotic Indian, is eventually transformed into the degraded savage. The following is an edited account from my field notes:

> I was visiting some friends last night. The topic of Natives came up a few times. "Jeff" was remarking on how, when he was recently in Alexis Creek, it was like "being in a different country" because he heard people around him, in the little Japanese store he was in, speaking the Tsilhqot'in language. "It was neat," he said. "And I could sort of understand what they were saying." He went on to explain how an older couple were there in the store. The man went to the self-serve cooler and brought out a bottle of wine. The woman said something to him, and he went back for a second bottle. She again spoke to him, and he returned for a third. "I sort of knew she was telling him to get more wine," he laughed. "Of course, it was stampede time – they needed three bottles to see them through the weekend!" The others laughed.

Similar movements between noble and degraded imagery are evident in the discourses of Euro-Canadian men in which Aboriginal women are discussed as objects alternately of sexual attraction and disgust. This was evident in an anecdote that followed Jeff's story: "'David' [Jeff's friend] then recalled a scene he had witnessed on a curb in town. There were three Native people, two adults and a teenage girl. 'And she didn't look that bad,' David said, referring to her attractiveness. 'They were standing on the curb, and she leaned over and spat out this long stream from a wad of smokeless tobacco. What is it called? Snoose. Right there on the curb!' he laughed. Jeff said, with disdain, 'Oh, she was probably put there by the Chamber of Commerce for tourists to see!'"

These two stories are striking in that both men found themselves initially attracted to Aboriginal people: one appreciated the "neat" language of the Tsilhqot'in people, and one saw a girl who "didn't look that bad." Despite their initial attraction, both men eventually returned to the status quo in which the defiled nature of Aboriginal people is reasserted. Such offhand remarks reveal in chilling ways the casual brutality that Aboriginal women experience through their sexual objectification by non-Aboriginal men. These accounts also illustrate the oscillating tendencies of "fear and temptation" that characterize European attitudes toward indigenous peoples in Canadian, Australian, and New Zealand literature.[16]

At times, the celebration of Indian inferiority takes on an even broader ritual quality that, I suggest, is intricately bound up with the public image of Williams Lake as a rough-and-ready Wild West town, an image celebrated annually in the stampede rodeo and festival. The city is promoted as a modern western town where the frontier lifestyle can still be witnessed in the mingling of cowboys and Indians on the streets, in the aggressive conquest of the wilderness by resource industries, and in the heroic actions of individual workers who – through their drive, independence, and quest for material wealth – affirm the myth of the self-made man.

In this context, Aboriginal people become part of the "colour" of the local setting. Thus, in the above story, Jeff showed an ironic awareness of the role of Aboriginal people as spectacles of tourist interest. He disdained the imaginary staged display but engaged in his own objectification, transforming an observed act of purchasing wine into a humorous account of Aboriginal degradation. The spectacle of this presumed degradation is part of the folklore of Williams Lake. It is part of an unofficial public discourse promoting the city to tourists and socializing newcomers into a comfortable sense of frontier identity and belonging.

### Cautious Discourse

In the Cariboo-Chilcotin, expressions of common-sense racism coexist with an ideology of ethnic tolerance and equality. Television and radio stations carry advertisements condemning racism. Anti-racism editorials, columns, and news stories appear occasionally in the city newspaper. In Williams Lake, public service workers may attend periodic cross-cultural workshops. An annual (although poorly attended) First Nations Awareness Days is sponsored by the school district and facilitated by local First Nations leaders. Ethnic tolerance and equality are key public values in the Cariboo-Chilcotin as in Canada generally.

In the contemporary climate of multiculturalism that bears down on Williams Lake from urban society, there is a widespread awareness among Euro-Canadians about the theoretical issues of ethnic and racial discrimination. As one store clerk mentioned to me, somewhat defensively, "That's all you hear about these days, who's discriminating [against whom]." Many Euro-Canadians are aware that some of their attitudes toward Aboriginal people may be construed as racist, are aware of the pressures of politically correct speech, and resent being branded as racists by outsiders or by First Nations people.

Many Euro-Canadians deflect urban criticisms by claiming special insight into the nature of Aboriginal people by virtue of their long-term personal experience. They claim that urban residents "don't know the Indians up here like we do." They manipulate concepts of Aboriginal/non-Aboriginal difference by refining and localizing their attitudes toward Cariboo-Chilcotin First Nations. These Euro-Canadians argue that there are significant differences between various Aboriginal groups in Canada. As one woman commented, "The [Northwest] Coast Natives are an industrious bunch, and the Prairie Natives are an industrious bunch," but Cariboo-Chilcotin Natives are not. Euro-Canadians thus express a contemporary feature of their "colonial privilege":[17] the privilege of colonizers – those who claim firsthand knowledge of indigenous people – to have special insight into their nature and thus to defend their racism against outside critics "who have never even been to the Cariboo."

Another defensive strategy is that of cautious discourse. One technique involves careful editing of potentially controversial remarks. As one person commented to me, "She's part Native, you have to be careful what you say around her." When a listener may react with charges of racism, representations of Aboriginal people may take more indirect and ambiguous forms. One of the simplest ways to protect the status of the speaker from charges of racism is to qualify the statement: "It's an awful thing to say, but ..." or "I know Indians really well, and have some Indian friends, but ..."

A more complex mechanism for communicating negative views is localized code. This code – a form of colloquial shorthand – can be easily grasped by locals but is more ambiguous to people less familiar with the local culture. For example, a recent newspaper column discussing the problem of "drunk Indians" injuring themselves and wasting taxpayers' money by having to be attended by an ambulance crew communicated these condemnations without making direct reference to Natives or Indians. Another discussed the problem of empty wine bottles left in Boitanio Park. Although Natives or Indians were not explicitly mentioned, the editorial concluded with an admonition that the public should recognize and take action on the problem of the drinking habits of those responsible for the litter.[18]

Critical, joking, and patronizing remarks about Aboriginal people are part of the conversational landscape through which many Euro-Canadians move on a daily basis. These remarks are casually expressed in conversations that easily flow through the topics of recreational sports, work, weekend plans, the weather, and gossip about family and friends. The casualness with which many Euro-Canadians denounce Aboriginal people, and the ease with which they deny Aboriginal people their full dignity, humanity, social worth, and individuality, are two of the most disturbing indicators of how fully racist beliefs and practices have infiltrated the common-sense, lived reality of the non-Aboriginal population.

### Those Who Disagree

Although these conversational patterns are ubiquitous, not all Euro-Canadians participate equally in them. How do those who have more ambivalent attitudes, or who disagree with these attitudes, respond to these conversational rituals?

One man, a professional who had arrived from Vancouver several months earlier and who was employed by an Aboriginal organization, commented about his struggle against the local tradition of "joking about Indians": "I'm totally shocked about how people talk about Indians. I go to the gym all the time – and people know who I am, they know my job. Yet they tell me all these things about Indians, and I'm like, come on! These are people I work with every day, who I have a working relationship with, and who I respect! But it doesn't matter – they just assume that because I'm white it's OK to say these things to me, that I'll agree with them." An older businessman and longtime area resident commented on the frustration that he felt when encountering the drunk Indian stereotype: "We had the liquor store in [the mall], and always I heard 'We've got to get the drunk Indians out of here.' And I said, 'Just back off. We've got to get the drunks out of here, but they're not all Indians.' And I really get mad, because I said, 'We're labelling people that we shouldn't be.' Because there are probably less Natives now that drink than there are whites, percentage wise. And I said, 'We shouldn't be labelling them drunk Indians. It should be drunks, period.'" Rather than directly challenging such comments, as did these two individuals, others may choose to simply ignore them, filtering them from their awareness and perhaps associating with people whom they believe more fully share their own interests, attitudes, and values.

Individuals who do disagree with these prevailing attitudes may cope with having their own values continually negated by dominant conventions by developing what could be called subordinate forms of common sense. A full examination of these processes is beyond the scope of this book, but to pursue such a question would require a shift away from a theoretical definition of common sense as a dominating cultural form and practice and toward a more plural and phenomenologically based definition of the term. Philosopher Alfred Schutz's definition of "common-sense" knowledge, for example, provides one possible starting point.[19] Schutz considers both the biographical locus and the intersubjective character of such knowledge. That is, what one individual construes as taken-for-granted knowledge about the world is shaped both by her unique biographical experience and history and by the processes through which she and those in daily association with her negotiate particular understandings of reality. These social constructions of common sense rest not so much on the reality of a shared worldview – given the uniqueness of each individual's biography, one person's stock of knowledge can never be fully congruent with another's – as on the *presumption* of a "reciprocity of perspectives"[20] among those with whom one associates.

A number of Euro-Canadians who openly support First Nations concerns have described to me not only their frustration about continually struggling against dominant anti-Aboriginal attitudes in Williams Lake but also their distress when, in informal social situations, they have unexpectedly been confronted by friends who have made derogatory remarks about Aboriginal people. Their experiences generate a kind of epistemological crisis in which the presumption of the "reciprocity of perspectives" is shattered by the intrusion of the dominant culture into their private social worlds. It is critical to examine these incidents for what they reveal about how private domains of common sense may coexist with a dominant culture that encodes very different values and attitudes.

One professional woman recounted to me her dilemma when, during a dinner gathering in her home, the subject of the much-publicized Gustafsen Lake standoff was raised. The group of friends, which included older professional and public service workers, agreed that the RCMP should have shot their way into the blockade and arrested all the protesters. There was a general feeling that the Indians had been treated too softly by the government and that armed RCMP aggression is a fitting means of responding to Aboriginal blockades. This woman, who is generally sympathetic to First Nations causes, strongly disagreed with their remarks. She was uncertain how to respond, though, and in the end she remained silent.

The experience was very disturbing to her. The social etiquette of dinner parties usually requires that conversations be polite and relatively non-contentious. That her friends felt comfortable voicing these opinions in this context indicates the degree to which these views – predicated on the stereotype of the Indian criminal – are taken by many area Euro-Canadians to constitute shared assumptions. This woman has lived in Williams Lake for many years and has often heard the kind of anti-Aboriginal attitudes that circulate in everyday conversations. Her distress was caused more by the fact that such comments were unanticipated in the context of an informal gathering in her home. The depth of her distress over this incident suggests the importance of examining both the ways in which individuals may carve out particular spaces of common sense that deviate sharply from dominant constructions and the kinds of epistemological crisis that can be triggered when these protective "bubble zones" of common sense are unexpectedly ruptured by the intrusion of the dominant culture.

## Playing the Categories: Indian, White, and In-Between

It is significant that, unlike on the Canadian prairies in the nineteenth century or in Labrador in the 1990s,[21] no third public category such as Métis has developed to moderate the Indian/white dichotomy and to describe the significant mixed-heritage population in the Cariboo-Chilcotin. Nevertheless, there are many ways in which the Indian/white dichotomy is breached through "discourses of hybridity" that contemplate the partial or mixed qualities of Indian or white identity.

Euro-Canadians may discuss the degrees of "Indian blood" in people who claim a non-Aboriginal identity. The marker of Indian blood is phenotypical: the darkness of skin pigmentation. In some circumstances, a kind of hyperscrutiny, a heightened attention, is paid to outward appearance. A woman from a rural ranching family once commented to me: "My husband can always tell if someone's got Indian blood. Me, I can't tell the difference, but he can always tell – he has an eye for it." This kind of scrutiny is at times matched by a hyperawareness among some Aboriginal people over the stigma that they bear, in the eyes of non-Aboriginal people, by virtue of their skin colour. A woman discussed with me her experience of being in a room full of non-Aboriginal people, some of whom were making obliquely negative remarks about Natives. She felt extremely self-conscious, saying to me that "There was no mistaking I have Indian blood" and suggesting that these insensitive comments were deliberately directed at her. The intensity of skin colour as a locus of stigma is poignantly evoked in the stories that some Aboriginal people tell about their early residential school days. Discovering that it was "bad" to be dark skinned, they desperately attempted to scrub the colour off their hands with soap and water. These are classic examples of what anticolonial writer Frantz Fanon called an "epidermalization" of inferiority.[22]

At other times, Euro-Canadians may evoke notions of the partialness of Indian identity by asserting that particular individuals are not "real" Indians because they have some "white blood." In these cases, it is not phenotype that the speakers point to – the relative lightness of skin colour – but the historical context of long periods of intermarriage between Aboriginal and settler populations.[23] These discourses often appear when speakers wish to denounce the general claims being put forth by area First Nations to Aboriginal title and self-government (see Chapter 6).

Secwepemc, Carrier, and Tsilhqot'in people also engage in discourses of hybridity. Many know that most ranching and pioneer families, as well as some of the prominent old-time families in Williams Lake, have Aboriginal ancestors; in other words, their assumed whiteness is not absolute. Even more frequent are the discourses that Aboriginal people engage in, in certain bureaucratic contexts, to qualify degrees of Indianness.

The federal government's passage in 1985 of Bill C-31 allowed for the reinstatement of official Indian status to a range of individuals previously excluded from eligibility. As a result, a great number of individuals applied for band membership and sought to reestablish ties with and return to reserve communities. Although the federal government retained the authority to define Indian status, it devolved the authority to define band membership to those First Nations willing to assume this responsibility. Many First Nations in the Cariboo-Chilcotin subsequently developed band membership codes based on blood quantum indices; that is, if an individual could prove a minimum degree of genealogical relatedness to existing band members, then his or her application for membership would be put forward for a general band vote of approval. Blood quantum here served as a metaphor for relatedness – children adopted or raised by individuals were considered related by blood – rather than as a philosophy of genetic inheritance. As a result, the concept of degrees of Indianness, tribal identity, and reserve community identity has become heightened. One can now hear individuals on occasion discussing how, for example, their children are "37 percent Native" or "one-sixteenth Tsilhqot'in."

These discourses, however, are limited to bureaucratic contexts. In other settings, most Aboriginal people deny that traces of white ancestry diminish one's Indianness and define Indianness by other criteria: knowing one's language, knowing the land, being proficient at hunting, fishing, and food gathering, and holding a set of cultural values such as sharing, generosity, and respect for elders that they take to define the reserve community ethos.

### Challenging the Categories

Ritual joking naturalizes the category of Indian as a mirror for the construction of a collective self-identity among Euro-Canadians. Yet such discourses do not simply involve an exchange of ideas. Although they may have "truth effects" or cognitive consequences, they also have an affective dimension. Joking remarks are often conveyed with lighthearted laughter, whereas derogatory criticisms are at times expressed with intense anger. The enthusiasm with which people participate in these conversations, and their affective dimension, perhaps in part account for what Braroe has called the "perceptual blindness"[24] of small-town whites to empirical evidence that contradicts their assumptions about Aboriginal people.

Those who challenge these discourses often do so on an empirical level: they discount these generalizations of Indianness as being demonstrably false. Yet, when challenged, Euro-Canadian speakers defend their views not as examples of racism but as valid sociological generalizations. They point to the recent rash of stolen vehicles recovered on Tsilhqot'in reserves to support the stereotype of the Indian as criminal, despite the fact, well known to the local RCMP, that the thefts were carried out by a particular group of youths, most but not all Aboriginal. Euro-Canadians engaging in these conversations typically point to the Troopers to support the stereotype of the drunk Indian, overlooking the fact that the vast majority of Aboriginal individuals whom one sees on the city streets at any time of the day show no signs of drunkenness. In essence, the concepts of Aboriginal difference put forth in these conversational rituals are social constructions generated through the selective perception of reality in which the actions or attributes of one Aboriginal person, or of a small number of Aboriginal people, are taken to characterize the population as a whole.

These conversational practices also render invisible the significant cultural diversity that exists not only between the Secwepemc, Tsilhqot'in, and Carrier, and not only between different reserve communities of the region, but also between Aboriginal individuals. Euro-Canadians who joke about Indians do not mention the numerous First Nations chiefs, community leaders, and ordinary people who have been sober for ten or more years, nor do they mention the many law-abiding Aboriginal people who are themselves concerned about social disorganization and dysfunction in their communities. A number of Aboriginal people in the region have achieved success as measured by Euro-Canadian standards, having obtained university degrees and become lawyers, teachers, social workers, or artists. In the 1980s, a Secwepemc woman from Alkali Lake, Phyllis Chelsea, was awarded an Order of Canada for her work in family and community development. In 1992, Joan Gentles, a Tsilhqot'in, was honoured with an Order of British Columbia for her advocacy of Aboriginal people in the justice system. These accomplishments do not form part of the ritual joking practices. These facts may not be widely known within Euro-Canadian circles, perhaps due to the communicative isolation of the two populations. It may also reflect the selective processes by which information consistent with the dominant Euro-Canadian attitudes is publicly remembered, whereas contradictory information is forgotten.

Finally, in these ritual conversations, the historical context that has generated alcohol abuse, family breakdown, and violence in Aboriginal communities is not discussed. Instead, these traits are presented as essential or natural characteristics of either culture or biology. As various people commented to me, "they're just not made that way," "that's part of their nature," "their culture is different." There is a selective process of dehistoricization occurring here. Although the past is of vital importance in the construction of contemporary public identities and in the defence of the material interests of particular local elites, as described in the previous chapter, it is rendered irrelevant in the everyday conversational rituals through which Euro-Canadians discuss their relationships with Aboriginal communities. Aboriginal difference is presented as ahistorical, as static, as natural. So irrelevant is a historical context that one woman drew on her observations from thirty years earlier to represent current differences between the two populations.

In this way, these discourses conform to Robert Miles's definition of racism as an ideology that distinguishes one group of people as being inherently different from others based on phenotypical characteristics and that assigns certain negatively evaluated characteristics, abilities, or behaviours, whether biological or cultural, as definitive of and natural for this group as a whole.[25] As an ideology of hierarchical difference, racism is not a static set of beliefs; rather, there "have been many significantly different racisms – each historically specific and articulated in a different way with the societies in which they appear."[26]

In Williams Lake in the 1990s, racism is articulated against the backdrop of a dominant set of public values, identities, and material interests. It expresses and reproduces key aspects of the dominant culture. This cultural matrix does not explain the existence of negative stereotypes or racism. It does, however, provide the pool of symbols, themes, and values from which a historically specific and geographically local form of common-sense racism is generated.

Although these kinds of everyday racist discourse prevail in the city, not all joking rituals are racist in the manner in which I have defined the term. The term racism does not capture the complexity of patterns of discussion. Some constructed differences, such as the inherent ability of Aboriginal people to tolerate extreme heat, do not have value judgments associated with them. In yet other conversations, speakers play on the markers of difference, moving between noble and degraded imagery. Discourses of difference are thus fluid and complex processes that defy simple characterization. They are conditioned both by the contemporary material struggles over land and resources and, to some extent, by the contemporary burden of multicultural ideals. In this way, these conversational rituals, although purportedly representing ahistorical differences, are themselves historically contingent: they reflect "strategic reformulations and revaluations of prior discourses"[27] rather than static concepts of us/them.

What remains consistent, and emblematic of a contemporary colonial practice, is the focus on discussing, reproducing, and naturalizing the differences between the colonizing and the colonized populations. The Indian/white opposition is a central device in the construction of a public identity for Euro-Canadians in Williams Lake and in the encouragement of a sense of belonging to a community united in its moral and cultural superiority over Aboriginal people. As I discuss below, these discursive practices are not just innocuous expressions of identity, for they have an ongoing impact on the management of relations of inequality.

## Status Domination and Resistance in Aboriginal/Euro-Canadian Interactions

Racism against Aboriginal people is a common feature of life in rural cities and towns across Canada. Niels Braroe, Yngve Lithman, and David Stymeist have explored different facets of the dynamics of small-town Aboriginal/non-Aboriginal relations in Saskatchewan, Manitoba, and Ontario, respectively.[28] Braroe describes how Aboriginal people in a small ranching town in Saskatchewan in the 1960s suffered the "continual condemnation of their White neighbours in nearly all spheres of human activity."[29] Stymeist, writing of a northern Ontario town in the 1970s, discusses how Aboriginal people were "open targets for abuse by non-Indians. Such abuse ranged from the arched brows and sneering condescension of a [Hudson's] Bay clerk to open mockery and derision or the drunken assaults of a group of white men."[30] Where Aboriginals were routinely denied respect and dignity in their interactions with Euro-Canadians, the dominant coping mechanism employed was withdrawal and social isolation coupled with a private culture of indirect symbolic resistance.[31]

These interactions constitute forms of status domination, practices that involve "humiliation, disprivilege, insults, assaults on dignity."[32] Status domination is one of the most insidious modes of colonial power. Power is expressed not so much in material or ideological modes of domination as in the habitual gestures, casual remarks, and fleeting glances that continually impose on Aboriginal people an inferior and degraded public status. The grinding denial of human worth and dignity, in extreme cases, becomes naturalized as internal racism and self-directed violence among colonized peoples,[33] processes that cripple the potential for forceful public resistance against colonial domination.

The ethnographies of Braroe, Lithman, and Stymeist were carried out in rural communities in the 1960s and 1970s, when racism was as blatant and unquestioned as the "No Indians Allowed" signs posted on small-town café windows and hotel lobbies.[34] In the past twenty years, there have been significant changes in the political, legal, and administrative relationships between Aboriginal peoples and Canadian society. There has been an increased public sympathy and concern for Aboriginal issues, and the ideal of multiculturalism has become a symbol of Canadian national identity. Yet despite the public ideals of equality and multiculturalism, racist discourses of difference continue to appear in the Cariboo-Chilcotin. Despite the absence of public signs, Secwepemc, Carrier, and Tsilhqot'in people continue to be sensitive to the subtle gestures that may communicate that they are unwelcome in certain establishments in Williams Lake. Indeed, subtle mechanisms of exclusion have long been the more effective modes of social segregation in Canadian small towns.[35] The dynamics of racism have been reformulated, but not abolished, in the context of 1990s multiculturalism.

Identity is a transactional construct rather than an inherent aspect of one's selfhood: the fact that many individuals may be of mixed genealogical or cultural heritage is irrelevant unless it is deemed socially relevant in contexts of interaction. How, then, is the assignment of identity, specifically the assignment of Indianness, controlled in Aboriginal/non-Aboriginal interactions?

In previous pages, I have argued that Indian and white are among the most important categories operating in the symbolic ordering of social life in Williams Lake. Yet there are many possible settings in which Indianness may be deemed irrelevant and in which Aboriginal people may successfully assert other identities during their interactions with non-Aboriginals. Aboriginal and non-Aboriginal people may cooperate as sports teammates or schoolmates. In band offices on reserves and in tribal council offices in the city, they may interact as employer and employee. In stores and government offices, they may interact as customer and clerk, as client and service provider. In some informal social settings, gender rather than ethnicity may be an overriding factor shaping the interactions.

Yet in these varied contexts, the key issue remains: does one party have greater power to determine which identities become relevant during the course of interaction? Today, the most common sites of face-to-face interaction occur in the city businesses, stores, schools, and government agencies in which Aboriginal people are consumers of goods and services offered largely by non-Aboriginal providers. These providers may "know" about Aboriginal people through the anecdotes and jokes exchanged during conversational rituals but perhaps not through personal relationships with them. As a result, when an Aboriginal person enters a store, an office, or a school classroom, his or her Indianness – and the assumptions that accompany that designation – may predetermine the manner in which the provider relates to him or her. Because area Aboriginal people are largely dependent on the stores and services of Williams Lake in order to secure goods, services, education, health care, and so on, there is an implicit power imbalance in their interactions with these providers. Although Aboriginal people may choose to deal with demeaning treatment by withdrawing from or challenging it, they may also simply put up with disrespectful treatment for the sake of completing the transaction.

These negotiations of identity occur in many contexts of interaction around Williams Lake: between Aboriginal students and non-Aboriginal teachers in the public schools, between young Aboriginal athletes and their coaches, between prospective Aboriginal renters and landlords. In each setting, multiple identities could theoretically be asserted in the course of interaction; yet in each setting, the non-Aboriginal provider, by virtue of his or her control over resources, may exert greater control over determining if an individual's Indianness will be relevant: if a student will be labelled "slow" because Indians are assumed to be poor learners; if a hockey player will be benched because the coach prefers to play the white players; if a tenant will be rejected because it is assumed that "Indians don't take care of their houses." That these experiences happen is common knowledge among Aboriginal people in the region.

Not all contexts of interaction, of course, have such obvious power imbalances, where non-Aboriginal people control access to desired resources – education, employment, and so on. The point is that identity is continually being assessed and negotiated during all transactions and that it is important to examine the dynamic of power in these processes, not only to explore how one party may assert greater control over which identities become relevant but also to explore which forms of resistance Aboriginal people may reasonably enact.

To what extent, then, are negative attitudes and assumptions about Aboriginal people made relevant during everyday interactions in Williams Lake? The degree to which racism persists in Williams Lake is hotly debated. Many of the Euro-Canadian community leaders whom I spoke with asserted that there was very little or no racism against Aboriginal people in the city. If some racist attitudes and practices persisted, they claimed, they were limited to marginalized pockets of the community. "We all get along pretty well" and "It's the white lawyers and band managers who cause the problems" were typical responses. Although these were the official responses of prominent individuals speaking on the record, they echo the views of many other Euro-Canadian residents with whom I spoke.

In contrast, many Secwepemc, Carrier, and Tsilhqot'in people state that racism is a pervasive element in their relationships with Euro-Canadians. These different perspectives on racism were clearly evident in a 1992 assessment of the needs of Aboriginal students in the Cariboo-Chilcotin School District.[36] An educational consultant surveyed Aboriginal students, their families, district educational staff, principals, teachers, and counsellors. Students and their families reported that racial discrimination – ranging in expression from direct racial taunts to more subtle forms of being excluded or being expected to be low achievers – was among the most important problems that Aboriginal students faced. In contrast, few of the teachers, and none of the administrators, identified racial discrimination as an issue facing Aboriginal students.[37] To what extent this gulf in perception continues to exist is an open question. The Cariboo-Chilcotin School District, however, has long recognized that First Nations students face particular difficulties in the public school system, and it was one of the first school districts in the province to hire an educator specifically to coordinate First Nations education. There is therefore a structural commitment to seriously addressing the situation of Aboriginal students in the local schools, even if a consensus on what the difficulties are remains elusive.

Accounts by Aboriginal people of being treated rudely by cashiers, of being followed by store clerks who suspect them of shoplifting, and of being subjected to subtly demeaning treatment are part of the taken-for-granted reality of Aboriginal life in Williams Lake. Aboriginal women throughout the region are familiar with the social consequences of the Indian squaw stereotype: dealing with non-Aboriginal men who assume that sexual passes will be accepted and who may resort to violence if their advances are turned down. These attitudes and practices toward Aboriginal women continue to be found in rural regions of Canada.[38] As Janice Acoose points out, the highly publicized death of Helen Betty Osborne in La Pas, Manitoba, is only one instance of the chronic abuse that Aboriginal women have experienced and that has been encouraged by the Indian squaw stereotype.[39]

On occasion, a particular incident draws media coverage and public attention to these issues. The 1992-3 Cariboo-Chilcotin Justice Inquiry, one of a series of recent task forces and public inquiries into Aboriginal justice in Canada,[40] documented a widespread "attitude" problem among area police officers in their dealings with Aboriginal people. The Secwepemc, Carrier, and Tsilhqot'in people who testified at the inquiry told of being assaulted in jail cells by RCMP officers, of RCMP abuses of authority and invasions of privacy, and of being taken by the RCMP to the city "drunk tank" while sober.[41] Various stereotypes legitimate these practices. That of the Indian criminal underlies the reported overpolicing and harassment of law-abiding Aboriginal people throughout the Cariboo-Chilcotin. That of the drunk Indian supports some RCMP officers' apparent abuse of authority in using the city drunk tank as an unofficial means of social control for sober individuals.

Many Aboriginal people, intimidated by the adversarial nature of the inquiry forum that allowed RCMP lawyers to cross-examine complainants, did not give testimony to the justice inquiry. Incidents now part of the written record of the inquiry reflect only a small portion of the accounts of discrimination, demeaning treatment, and brutality that are freely discussed in private circumstances. For the most part, the accounts of everyday discrimination that circulate in the Aboriginal communities are excluded from the official public record of Williams Lake.[42]

In the remaining pages of this chapter, I turn to these private contexts in which Aboriginal people described to me some of their interactions with Euro-Canadians. This is only a cursory discussion of the diverse forms of status domination that impinge on Aboriginal lives. These accounts also suggest the various ways in which people struggle to resist instances of demeaning treatment. Most of those telling these accounts are Secwepemc, thirty to seventy years old, and longtime residents of reserves. Many of these individuals have attended the residential school at the mission, in which they received a powerful indoctrination into notions of cultural and moral inferiority. It is from this particular constellation of life experiences that they speak.

**Examples**

One of the most common issues raised by Aboriginal people is their experience of being rudely treated or followed around as suspected shoplifters in the stores in Williams Lake. One man in his fifties recounted his experiences:

> You see that often when a Native person walks into a store. You watch them, the clerk will be just watching you, following you around. Or right away, as soon as you get in there, they'll come up to you and say, "Can I help you?" One time, this lady was watching me, following me wherever I went. Then she came up to me and said, "Can I help you?" I told her, "If I'm going to steal something, I don't need your help!" After that she never did bother me. She'd just say "Hi" when she saw me come in, that was all.

A middle-aged woman commented: "Look at when you go to the mall to go shopping at Saan's or Woolco. They follow you around in there. It's like, it pisses me off. I tell one of those women, 'What's your problem?' and she'll look at me and say, 'Oh, I don't have a problem,' and she'll walk away. But ... you go in there to buy clothes, and all you do is get followed around. It kind of pisses me off."

A woman in her forties described being in line at a local department store and waiting to purchase some items. She waited for five minutes while the clerk carried on a pleasant conversation with the white woman ahead of her, who had just bought some goods. The clerk finally turned to her, her smile vanishing and a coldness appearing. Offering no apology for having made the Native woman wait so long, the clerk took her money and threw it down on the counter. Her customer angrily slammed down the goods on the counter, snatched her money back, and stormed out saying, "If that's the way you're going to treat me, I'll keep my money!" Being suspected of shoplifting, being ignored or receiving poor service in stores and restaurants, and being subjected to the icy stares of store clerks are typical experiences of Aboriginal people in many rural communities in Canada and have been documented in other small-town ethnographies.[43]

A second context of interaction occurs in the public spaces in Williams Lake: on the streets, in the park, in the shopping mall, in the bars and cafés. Going to town – whether to play bingo, drink, shop, or simply socialize – is an enjoyable activity for many people. Most Aboriginal people, however, do not see the city as neutral territory; rather, it is a place controlled by Euro-Canadians where they must remain on guard against acts of disrespect and abuse. One woman, for example, commented about her apprehension when entering stores. Her careful scrutiny of the comportment of clerks stands as a parallel to the kind of scrutiny to which Aboriginal people are often subjected in public places: "I'm always a little apprehensive when I go in [to a store] until I know the attitude of them, and then I either relax or get defensive. But I'm always, when I go into a new place, if I don't know the place, I'm kind of like watching for little telltale signs of their attitudes."

The city's indoor shopping mall is one of the most popular gathering places, where people mingle in the corridors, on the benches, or at the tables in the food court. It is also one of the best barometers of local Aboriginal/Euro-Canadian tensions. During the two-month armed confrontation between Aboriginal people and the RCMP at Gustafsen Lake in 1995, relations across the Cariboo-Chilcotin were tense: Aboriginal people in 100 Mile House reported being refused service in local restaurants, and T-shirts with anti-Aboriginal slogans were reportedly selling "like hotcakes" at one rural café.[44] These tensions spilled over into interactions at the Williams Lake mall. One mother told me of the trouble experienced by her teenage daughter, who, tired of the stares and hostile glances of a group of Euro-Canadian adults seated nearby, finally turned and said angrily, "Yes, I *am* from Gustafsen Lake!" The mother was proud that her daughter had defended her dignity.

More blatant acts of harassment occurred when the Cariboo-Chilcotin Justice Inquiry hearings were in session. Aboriginal customers in the mall reported being harassed by security guards, who were walking through the mall videotaping Aboriginal customers and evicting some (including one prominent Tsilhqot'in chief) purportedly for loitering. These tensions intensified due to allegations raised at the inquiry, allegations that received provincial news headlines, that a mall security guard had on several occasions used excessive force and had physically assaulted Aboriginal patrons.[45] In response to growing complaints, area First Nations leaders met privately with the mall manager. They pointed out the economic importance of Aboriginal shoppers to the mall and threatened a boycott unless the harassment ended. Subsequently, new security guards were hired.

In this way, area First Nations are transforming their economic power as consumers into public forms of political resistance. Despite the growing recognition by local businesses of the importance of Aboriginal consumer dollars to the city's economy, patrons at the mall continue to describe instances of harassment. Recently, one woman has taken the strategy of writing to the city newspaper to complain of such discriminatory treatment.[46] These challenges are thus increasingly entering public forums of debate.

Status domination occurs through the forcible ascription of negative identities. One of the most common of these imposed identities is that of the "drunk Indian." So pervasive is this stereotype that on occasion sober Aboriginal people are perceived by Euro-Canadians as drunks. On one occasion, I was in the mall on a Friday afternoon and was seated on the benches watching people pass by. A woman of about my age was seated across from me, also by herself. After sitting there for a few minutes, I spotted "Eddie" coming along. Eddie, an older Secwepemc man whom I had recently met on one of the reserves, is a wiry, bowlegged cowboy with long grey hair pulled back in a ponytail. As he passed by me, smiling broadly, he greeted me with his characteristic friendliness in his thick Secwepemc accent: "Hi! How you doing!" I returned the hello and smiled back. After he had passed, the woman across from me turned to me, caught my eye, and remarked in a conspiratorial but laughing tone, "Looks like he's had a bit too much to drink!" Because I had detected no evidence that Eddie was drunk, and because he had just celebrated his ninth Alcoholics Anonymous birthday on the reserve, I turned to her and said, "That man has been sober for nine years." She looked quite surprised, and with a nervous laugh she soon got up and walked away. Particularly remarkable about this incident was not only that an individual showing no signs to me of drunkenness was immediately labelled as a drunk Indian but also that this woman assumed that the social distance between me and her was closer than that between Eddie and me and that it was safe for her to make such disparaging remarks. Rather than taking the friendly interchange as a sign of a personal relationship, she interpreted it as a drunken breach of the normal rules that guide social relations and that encourage an avoidance of contact between Aboriginal and non-Aboriginal people. Her misinterpretation of this event indicates just how deeply the idea of the social isolation of the two populations is embedded in the ordinary understandings of city residents.

The prevalence of the drunk Indian stereotype in Williams Lake is particularly remarkable given that one nearby Secwepemc community, Alkali Lake, has become internationally known for successfully dealing with the problem of alcoholism. An older man who has been sober for many years spoke of his frustration with this stereotype:

> A lot of places I went – I haven't had a drink for fifteen years, and ... that's what they keep saying, "You're this," no matter who you are. If you seen me walk through the door, there, a lot of places I go, the first thing you think of is "Well, here comes another one of them drunk Indians off the street." And this is the kind of thing that goes before us, a lot of the times, "Another stupid Indian coming along, drunk." This is what we have to pack. That's why, a lot of times, a person walks in the room, he either wants to walk out he's so scared, or he's going to fight.

The weight of stereotypes is felt as a physical burden, as something that Aboriginal people have to "pack" around, as an image that precedes them in their interactions with non-Aboriginal people. So powerful are these images in the Euro-Canadian imagination that individuals such as this man feel that effective forms of resistance are limited to two strategies: withdrawal and physical violence.

Status domination also plays out as struggles over the control of public spaces. The tensions in the mall, in cafés, and in bars raise the issue of Aboriginal people's right to be treated with the same respect and dignity as other citizens occupying public spaces. Some of these tensions may be very subtly played out. For example, one quiet weekday evening, "Stewart" and I were playing pool in one of the local bars. A group of four non-Aboriginal men came in and sat at the next table. As I was at the table, Stewart, sitting on a chair, began drumming the end of his pool cue on the floor. A man at the next table said to his friends in a voice loud enough to be overheard: "What is this, a fucking powwow?" After a minute, Stewart said, "Come on, let's leave," and we left immediately. As a result of this kind of interaction, Aboriginal people may choose to frequent only those stores and restaurants in which they are treated respectfully. Some public spaces – the bar at the foot of Oliver Street, the Chinese café downtown – are known as "Indian places." Although also patronized by non-Aboriginals, these establishments are considered comfortable places for Aboriginal customers. This form of informal spatial segregation of establishments, perhaps in a more extreme form, has been described for other rural Canadian towns as well.[47]

These struggles over the control of public spaces also occur in more mundane contexts such as city sidewalks. Forty years ago, it was conventional for Euro-Canadian townspeople to expect Aboriginal people to step off the sidewalks when they approached. Such an extreme form of domination and public deferral to Euro-Canadian authority is no longer conventional. However, city streets continue to be sites of struggle. "Stanley," a man in his thirties, and "Andrea," a woman in her forties, described what for them were the common-sense realities of being Native in Williams Lake:

> *Stanley:* It's not always an out-and-out thing ... It's just the looks you get, or being cut off in traffic, or being made to step aside. It's there.
> *Andrea:* Walking down the street – [they] expect you to get off the road. I used to do that before, but I won't anymore.
> *Stanley:* Now I'm getting so I'll walk into their chest if I have to. Because they wouldn't do that for anyone else – they see someone else coming along, their own colour, it's "Oh, excuse me!" But if they see you coming, they won't look you in the eyes or anything, they keep on talking or whatever. But they know they're going to walk into you unless you move.

Here domination translates not into forms of hypervisibility in public places, as described earlier, but into its opposite: the hyperinvisibility of Aboriginal people in the public landscape. This invisibility brings with it a form of enforced physical subservience. Through the avoidance of eye contact, Euro-Canadians negate the very existence of Aboriginal people as human beings occupying physical space. In response, both these individuals now enact physical forms of resistance, refusing to yield even if it means a physical collision.

This enforced invisibility is a pervasive form of domination in Aboriginal/non-Aboriginal relations. Many Aboriginal people whom I spoke with described their relationship with the Euro-Canadian community as nonexistent: Euro-Canadians in Williams Lake simply ignore their presence in numerous ways. The rendering of Aboriginal people as irrelevant and nonexistent has long been one of the most peculiar features of small-town relations.[48] For example, one ethnographer, writing of the northern BC settlement of Fort St. James in the 1950s, noted: "Discrimination takes a curious form in Fort St. James. There appears to be a complete disregard of the fact of [the] Indian presence. The White shuts his eyes to the Indian until his presence needs to be noted. Indians are not ill-treated individually but they are not recognized as part of the social life of the town."[49] Indeed, the "invisible Indian" is such a common theme in local interactions (or noninteractions) that it should be considered an important stereotype in itself. More generally, rendering invisible colonized populations, whether in history books, in public consciousness, or in everyday social interaction, can be seen as a characteristic feature of all colonial relationships. The Tunisian anticolonial writer Albert Memmi argues that this tendency denies the injustice of relations of inequality by negating the very existence of the dominated. In the process, power is both exercised and rendered invisible.[50]

Status domination operates through the shaming, the humiliation, and the denial of worth communicated in a variety of subtle and habitual practices: sharp glances, passing remarks, turned backs, verbal insults. These interpersonal modes of power and violence, when practised over a long term against a population already made vulnerable through other modes of domination, have a profoundly demoralizing impact. Certainly, not all Euro-Canadians engage in these practices. On any day, one can observe numerous instances of friendliness and politeness in the interchanges between Aboriginal people and Euro-Canadians and can talk to a number of Euro-Canadians who will defend Aboriginal people's right to be treated with dignity and respect. Yet because these instances of interpersonal violence have been so prevalent in the past, and because they continue in the present, Aboriginal people still guard and limit their interactions with Euro-Canadians. These practices account in part for the fact that many Aboriginal people prefer to remain in reserve communities rather than move to Williams Lake or to other Euro-Canadian cities.[51] Euro-Canadian practices of status domination and everyday racism have contributed significantly to the internalized racism with which many Aboriginal people struggle and have contributed significantly to the forms in which this racism is expressed: in the violence, the suicides, and the slow deaths from alcoholism that have prevailed in many Secwepemc, Tsilhqot'in, and Carrier communities since the 1950s. It is against this legacy of continual denial of moral worth and dignity that many Aboriginal people in the Cariboo-Chilcotin now struggle.

**Plural Forms of Aboriginal Resistance**

These accounts also indicate the various forms of emerging resistance, of Aboriginal people's refusal to give way, either physically or morally, to Euro-Canadian domination. Although most of the Aboriginal people whom I spoke with thought that non-Aboriginal attitudes have not changed significantly over recent years, they believed that their own unwillingness to tolerate such treatment has changed. There are more instances in which Aboriginal people are refusing to be rendered invisible: by speaking up, by claiming space. Area First Nations leaders – through their work with band offices, their interactions with government ministries, and their public advocacy of Aboriginal rights and treaties (and through media coverage of these activities) – are becoming known to a broader cross-section of the Williams Lake public. Being known as public figures, these individuals said, has lessened their experiences with the kind of blind discrimination that other Aboriginal people continue to experience. Many leaders are now simply ignoring racist remarks and attitudes, instead concentrating their energies on higher levels of political activity in which they are challenging the structural basis – government laws and policies – that underlie Aboriginal people's subordination.

Yet Aboriginal people imbue these personal stories of discrimination with a great deal of significance and emotion when told to non-Aboriginal audiences, whether in private or public contexts. Perhaps what makes these stories of discrimination and resistance so significant to the tellers is that they represent what James Scott refers to as the "political electricity," the sense of release, elation, and personal satisfaction, that comes from the first public challenge to long-standing systems of domination.[52] Although some forms of resistance described through these stories are limited to interpersonal exchanges – the customer who challenged the store clerk for assuming that he might shoplift, or the woman who exploded at the cashier who treated her rudely – others are more organized, such as area First Nations leaders' threatened boycott of the mall to protest the harassment of customers or the efforts of Tsilhqot'in leaders to have a public inquiry into the treatment of Aboriginal people by area RCMP and the provincial justice system in the Cariboo-Chilcotin. These forms of resistance to interpersonal modes of status domination parallel the political efforts of First Nations leaders to redress other historical injustices: the government's long-standing denial of Aboriginal rights and title and the long-term impact of coercive assimilation experienced by students at St. Joseph's Mission residential school.

These multiple modes of resistance contrast significantly with the circumscribed forms of opposition enacted by Aboriginal people in the small Saskatchewan ranching community studied by Braroe in the late 1960s. The primary modes of opposition then were "covering" or attempting to hide one's Aboriginal identity, withdrawal from Euro-Canadian contact, and a form of what Erik Schwimmer has called "symbolic competition."[53] Having few avenues in which to challenge their stigmatized identities, Aboriginal people openly demonstrated "profane" behaviours or characteristics but imbued them with positive symbolic meaning as compared with non-Aboriginal interpretations. Aggressive public drunkenness, for example, can be interpreted as a form of symbolic opposition, a defiant assertion of the drunk Indian stereotype and an intentional violation of Euro-Canadian rules of public conduct. Along these lines, Nancy Lurie has described Aboriginal public drunkenness as "the world's oldest on-going protest demonstration," arguing that these assertions of Indian identity take place in the absence of other means of securing a positive recognition of Indianness and that they are an effective means of protest precisely because they disturb non-Aboriginal people and force their attention to the distinctiveness of Indian identity – even if construed in negative terms.[54] These forms of symbolic opposition, which only confirm dominant negative stereotypes of Indians, are a reflection of the limited resources available for direct resistance. In contrast, the various modes of resistance now evident in the Cariboo-Chilcotin are testimony to the increasing empowerment of Aboriginal peoples in many small-town settings across Canada.

At the same time, forms of organized political resistance are matched by these symbolic modes of resistance. This rich, dramatic, and playful culture of resistance is largely invisible to, and unappreciated by, non-Aboriginal people. This is essentially a culture of humour in which Aboriginal people play with dominant stereotypes, defusing their power through inversion, parody, and ambiguity.

One mode is through joking. Indian jokes are widespread among Secwepemc, Carrier, and Tsilhqot'in people. Some jokes play on the failure of modern Aboriginal people to live up to Euro-Canadian expectations of noble savagery. In one example, a young boy was searching his home for some matches. His older sister joked with him: "Rub two sticks together! What kind of Indian are you, anyway!" Another example occurred when I was a passenger in a carload of Aboriginal people. It was an early fall afternoon. As we drove through a residential district of Williams Lake, passing many homes in which newly cut wood was stacked for winter use, the driver, a Secwepemc man in his forties, turned to us and said: "How do Indians know it will be a hard winter?" When none of us replied, he said: "White man make a lot of wood!" His shift to the broken Indian-speak of Hollywood movies added a particularly humorous edge to his parody of Euro-Canadian expectations of the noble savage.[55]

Many other jokes play on the negative stereotypes that surround Aboriginal people's public identity in Williams Lake, particularly those of the drunk Indian and the Indian criminal. These jokes twist the stereotypes into a form of self-parody that is also a form of symbolic opposition. One example is a joke once told to a gathering of people in a reserve home: "What did the little Indian boy get for his birthday? The neighbour's bike!" At a local powwow on a hot summer day, two young boys who had just completed a dance passed a bottle of water between them; the announcer joked to the audience: "Look at that! Old Indian tradition, sharing a bottle!"

Occasionally, these jokes are dramatized. I vividly recall one occasion some years ago. It was late in the evening, and some Secwepemc friends – "Joe," his wife, and three other adults – and I were just leaving the Friendship Centre in Williams Lake after a powwow.[56] Drumming and singing could still be heard in the background. As we began to cross the street to Joe's pickup, he called out "Hey!" to the others to get their attention and started staggering across the street, acting like a drunk. He, his wife, and his friends began laughing at his antics. We got into the truck and drove off. Joe is a prominent member of the reserve community, and at that time he was the leader of the reserve's Alcoholics Anonymous group and had been sober for nine years.

In their attempts to renegotiate their public identities as Indians, Joe and other sober members of his community struggle against the prevalent assumption among Euro-Canadians that "all Indians are drunks." "Playing drunk," particularly in the context of city streets, is a dangerous activity, for Joe was likely to be perceived as one by Euro-Canadian onlookers. In facing the continual possibility of being labelled a drunk Indian, he carved out a private space of resistance: his playful self-parody was humorous precisely because he and his audience knew he is now sober. In this way, "playing drunk" continues the long tradition of staging public drunkenness as a defiant mode of symbolic opposition to Euro-Canadian domination as noted by Schwimmer and Lurie some twenty years ago.

But the language of opposition, the performance of the drunk Indian stereotype, gains additional meaning within the context of a community of sober Aboriginal people. It becomes not only a form of symbolic opposition to ongoing Euro-Canadian evaluations but also an assertion of a new code of values that distinguishes a sober Aboriginal present from a debauched Aboriginal past. Anthropologists Frederick Errington and Deborah Gewertz have discussed similar processes among Duke of York Islanders in Papua New Guinea's East New Britain province, where, in their annual performance of the arrival of the first Methodist missionaries, villagers depict their ancestors in a highly humorous light as "bumbling savages" who were eventually transformed into civilized Christians.[57] Errington and Gewertz argue that these performances are humorous to local audiences not because they express anticolonial resistance by demonstrating the outrageous falsity of colonial stereotypes of the savage; instead, Duke of York Islanders, since gaining independence in 1975, have developed a "postcolonial" consciousness in which they see themselves not as subordinated but "as the most sophisticated – as the most advanced, the most cultivated – of Papua New Guineans."[58] Their annual performances are humorous to local audiences now because they have accepted their transformation from savagery to civilized Christianity as official, positive, and authentic history: these performances "rerealized Papua New Guineans as citizens of their own country by separating them from their common precultural pasts."[59]

Similar processes, I suggest, underlie the act of drunkenness that Joe performed for his friends. Although Aboriginal people in the Cariboo-Chilcotin clearly have not moved beyond the structures of colonial domination that continue to impinge on their lives, this subtle performance of the "drunk Indian" articulated the official local history of one reserve community that had made great strides in dealing with the problem of alcohol abuse. The juxtaposition of this new local history with the dominant assumptions of the regional Euro-Canadian society imbues these performances with meaning: they are at once acts of resistance and statements about a new Indian identity. Aboriginal performers are at once embracing their past and distancing themselves from it, mimicking the drunk Indian stereotype, and stating, in effect, "We were like that once, and you may think we're still like that, but in reality we're different today."

In voicing Indian jokes in private, and in performing jokes in Euro-Canadian contexts, Aboriginal people are enacting forms of indirect resistance to the pervasive colonial discourse that they encounter in Williams Lake. Through ambiguity, humour, and parody, these joke tellers and performers are subverting the concepts of difference that prevail in Euro-Canadian constructions. It is the frame of humour that enables this process. Because joking conveys meanings presumed to differ from those conveyed when acts are performed seriously,[60] Aboriginal forms of "joking about Indians," when performed against the backdrop of dominant stereotypes, render the literal truth of stereotypes questionable. If they are not to be taken literally, then what are their meanings? It is precisely the ambiguity of these joking practices – the fact that meaning is left hanging in the air, undefined – that momentarily suspends the power of a colonial discourse. Epistemological power is defused, and meaning dissolves into fragments of possibility, opening the way for multiple interpretations and subordinate histories and identities to emerge.

The everyday Euro-Canadian discourses of difference and the various modes of Aboriginal resistance to forms of interpersonal domination occur alongside more general political and economic challenges in relations between First Nations organizations, local and provincial governments, and regional forestry and mining companies. I have presented a snapshot of how Aboriginal people and Euro-Canadians are attempting to comprehend, to maintain, or to reconfigure their relations with one another. These mundane dynamics of interpersonal relations are an important but frequently overlooked dimension of colonial domination and resistance.

Two recent works provide ethnographic portraits of Euro-Canadian racism against Aboriginal people. Thomas Dunk, in an ethnography of male working-class culture in northern Ontario, presents anti-Aboriginal racism as a form of false consciousness, a scapegoat ideology that blinds workers to the reality of their own domination and exploitation within the capitalist system.[61] Charles Menzies examines racist discourses among Euro-Canadian fishermen in Prince Rupert, portraying them as understandable reactions rooted in fishermen's fear of losing their livelihood should settlements of land claims involve a transfer of fisheries to First Nations.[62]

While documenting the existence of common-sense racism, the cost of portraying Euro-Canadian workers as victims of the capitalist system is a significant lack of attention not only to Aboriginal people's accounts of their experiences as the victims of chronic racism but also to ordinary Euro-Canadians' ongoing complicity as powerful local agents in a system of colonial domination. Racism becomes more intense and overt in times of economic crisis, but it is not simply *caused* by economic competition. Rather, racism has been a defining characteristic of Canadian culture, and of small-town social relations, for over a century. These analyses restrict "real" power to corporate boardrooms and metropolitan governments.[63] In so doing, they detract attention from the complexity of colonial practices and deny what philosopher Michel Foucault would call the diffuse, "capillary" forms in which colonial power is exercised in Canada.[64] At worst, these analyses could be read as offering a structural rationale and apology for racism, inadvertently contributing to the very hegemonic colonial system that such authors might wish to challenge.

Racism, and constructions of Aboriginal difference more generally, are central ingredients of rural Euro-Canadian cultural traditions. These conventional forms of racist beliefs and practices have served as effective modes of power that over the long term have maintained the subordinate position of Aboriginal peoples. It is this more general set of taken-for-granted cultural assumptions from which other dominant discourses, which indeed become more public in times of economic conflict, emerge. In the next chapter, I examine current public conflicts over Aboriginal land claims, how certain discourses are mobilized to defend Euro-Canadian interests, and how First Nations leaders are adopting various strategies to challenge these dominant discourses.

# 6
# Encountering Histories: The Land Claims Public Forum

In 1990, the provincial Social Credit government announced its intention to cooperate with the federal government in the negotiation of outstanding Aboriginal land claims. Months later, the newly elected NDP government affirmed this commitment. In 1992, the tripartite BC Treaty Commission was established to oversee treaty negotiations. These developments signified a historic shift in a provincial policy that had denied Aboriginal title for over 120 years. They also marked the beginning of a new stage in regional struggles between Aboriginal and non-Aboriginal people in the Cariboo-Chilcotin that have been ongoing since the arrival of the first non-Aboriginal settlers over a century ago. First Nations' claims to land, resources, and self-government call into question not only the presumed right of governments, industries, and individual non-Aboriginal users to control the lands and resources of the region but also the cultural apparatus that has been used to legitimate the control and regulation of Aboriginal peoples: the official histories celebrating "discovery" and "conquest," the public identities of Canadian benevolent paternalism and Aboriginal cultural-racial inferiority, and the liberal democratic myth of the self-made man. These competing visions of history, society, and Aboriginal/Euro-Canadian relations are at the centre of public debates on Aboriginal land claims in the Cariboo-Chilcotin.

In this chapter, I explore how Aboriginal and non-Aboriginal (particularly Euro-Canadian) people, in public forums and debates, are discussing the issues of land claims and Aboriginal treaties. These issues are presented through an account of one public forum on land claims held in Williams Lake in March 1995. The forum was organized by the federal Reform Party and was one of eight "town hall" meetings held across the province in the spring of 1995 to rally public opposition to the Aboriginal treaty process. The discussions at this meeting echoed the prevalent views that I encountered during interviews with civic leaders, at other public land claims forums, and in letters to the city newspaper, views that I weave into this narrative account.

My main goal in tracing public discourses on Aboriginal land claims and treaties is to provide an interpretation of the conceptual structure of Euro-Canadian oppositional discourse. First, I show how land claims opponents draw on key assumptions of the local dominant culture: public values, regional identities, beliefs about Aboriginal people, and theories of society and history. Second, I show that, in engaging in the politics of embarrassment, these individuals and groups draw attention to perceived contradictions in the dominant culture in order to reveal inconsistencies in government ideology and practice and to pressure governments to abandon (or modify) their treaty negotiation policies.

One of the arguments of this chapter is that the concept of racism is inadequate to account for the mechanisms that maintain the disempowerment of Aboriginal populations in British Columbia. Again, I am defining racism as an ideology that distinguishes one group of people as being inherently different from other groups based on phenotypical characteristics and that assigns certain negatively evaluated characteristics, abilities, or behaviours, whether biological or cultural, as definitive and natural of this group. Euro-Canadian discourses opposing land claims, although they obviously attempt to deny Aboriginal rights and title and to perpetuate existing relations of power, cannot be simply characterized as expressions of racism. These discourses are not all centred on the continual assertion of Aboriginal/non-Aboriginal difference; they do not all involve a reification of the inferior Indian other. However, Euro-Canadian oppositional discourses do not simply reflect the opposite: the promotion of assimilation as the solution to the "Indian problem" by denying Aboriginal difference. The hegemonic workings of the dominant culture involve much more complex processes of the situational manipulation of concepts of similarity and difference in order to defend existing material privileges. The exercise of power involves, as its central feature, the ability of dominant groups to control public definitions of identities, historical relationships, and contemporary conflicts.

Just as Euro-Canadian oppositional discourses on land claims are varied, so are the discourses engaged in by First Nations leaders who seek public support for Aboriginal treaties. When speaking to audiences in public forums, First Nations leaders attempt to challenge both the official histories that have erased Aboriginal people from the landscape and the negative and demeaning public identities that they have been ascribed. Much of Aboriginal politics in Canada is concerned with the continued assertion of cultural difference. This has been especially true in the context of court challenges, in which Aboriginal leaders have had to demonstrate the perpetuation of Aboriginal rights and title via the survival of distinct

Aboriginal cultural practices. However, in other contexts of confrontation, Aboriginal speakers engage in much more complex strategies to communicate with non-Aboriginal audiences.

I trace some of these strategies in the final pages of this chapter. Although Aboriginal leaders solicit public recognition of their right to practise distinct cultures and to live in self-governing communities, their strategies for securing public support involve more than just a juxtaposition of Aboriginal and Euro-Canadian worldviews, cultural values, and histories. They involve more than a reification of "difference." Instead, Aboriginal leaders stategically use dominant genres of discourse, and make appeals to dominant Euro-Canadian cultural values and symbols of power, as they attempt to make the terms of the dominant culture work for their specific purposes. Aboriginal discourses on land claims reflect the plurality of Aboriginal voices and identities and the varied degrees to which First Nations cultures, at times, are strategically articulated with the culture of dominant Euro-Canadian society.

## Background

In 1993, the BC Treaty Commission, comprised of representatives from the federal and provincial governments and the BC First Nations Summit, began overseeing negotiations with those First Nations in the province that had agreed to participate in the process. In 1995, the Nisga'a – negotiating since 1976 under the federal government's comprehensive claims process – signed an agreement in principle with the federal and provincial governments, marking one more step toward the signing of the first modern treaty in the province. The speed at which current treaty negotiations are proceeding[1] is parallelled by intensifying public opposition to treaties among non-Aboriginal people in rural resource communities.

Unlike most other regions in Canada that have been the sites of recent treaties, in British Columbia, and the Cariboo-Chilcotin region especially, virtually all of the traditional Aboriginal territories – those portions called unoccupied Crown lands – are tied up in parks, forest licences, grazing leases, and mining tenures. The transfer of blocks of Crown land to Aboriginal organizations through the treaty process will necessarily involve a reallocation of lands, resources, and rights. To what extent this reallocation will involve economic disruptions to industry, employment, and related businesses in small towns and cities across the interior is debatable. But there exists a growing common-sense belief in resource communities that Aboriginal treaties pose a serious threat to the survival of resource-dependent jobs, industries, and communities.

Not all non-Aboriginal people in Williams Lake are opposed to the treaty process, and a number of individuals and sectors fully support Aboriginal peoples and their struggles. Various perspectives on the land claims process are voiced in the city newspaper, in public forums and meetings, and in homes and workplaces across the city. Even forest companies, strongly encouraged by provincial government policies, are anticipating a future in which area First Nations are significant resource holders and are establishing formal relationships and joint forestry ventures with area First Nations.

On the political front, though, there is a groundswell of opposition to the treaty process among forestry, business, and some local government leaders. Williams Lake community leaders have described Aboriginal treaties as the "single most important issue" facing the region, as the greatest "threat" to the Cariboo-Chilcotin forest companies, and as having the "greatest socioeconomic impact on the next generation." As treaty negotiations proceed, and as First Nations leaders become increasingly assertive politically, private racist attitudes intensify against First Nations people.

Since 1990, there has been a marked shift in the way that Euro-Canadians publicly discuss Aboriginal land claims and issues. More and more city residents and civic leaders are unwilling to go on the record to voice their opposition to the treaty process. In the context of what is perceived as a growing trend toward political correctness emanating from urban society, Euro-Canadians are increasingly leery of publicly opposing the treaty process for fear of being branded as racist. In this climate, the Reform Party has emerged to champion the cause of the "average citizen" who opposes land claims. Reform representatives have developed a rhetoric designed to weather the politically correct climate of the 1990s while espousing an assimilationist policy toward Aboriginal people.[2] This political rhetoric, particularly the Reform Party's call for "cash only" settlements, is one of the dominant discourses drawn on by Euro-Canadians speaking out publicly against treaty settlements.

Reform's critique of Aboriginal treaties is based on two basic principles, which are variously elaborated and interpreted in local discourses. The first and most powerful ideological critique is that Aboriginal treaties and their self-government provisions contravene the Canadian ideals of equality, democracy, and individualism by perpetuating a division of Canadians along racial lines by setting up racially based territorial enclaves and by granting special rights and status to Indian people. The second critique draws on the public value of participatory democracy and the party's own emphasis on grassroots populism. Reformers claim that the federal and provincial governments do not have the mandate to settle land claims without consulting the public. The Reform Party criticizes negotiations for going on "behind closed doors" and demands that any land claims agreements be put to a public referendum for approval.

Debates about the legitimacy of the current BC Treaty Commission forum are also occurring within First Nations communities across the province. Not all First Nations in the Cariboo-Chilcotin support the BC Treaty Commission. The five northern Secwepemc First Nations and one southern Carrier First Nation are currently participating in treaty negotiations. In contrast, the six Tsilhqot'in and three southern Carrier First Nations are not. Like the James Bay Cree,[3] the Kanawake Mohawk,[4] and the Labrador Innu,[5] they are asserting a sovereign political stance with respect to Canada. The Tsilhqot'in and southern Carrier First Nations argue that treaties are to be negotiated only on a nation-to-nation basis with the federal government, and they openly criticize the BC Treaty Commission for including the province at the negotiating table.[6] These First Nations, and others across the province, object to the governments' demands that they extinguish Aboriginal title through the treaty process, fearing that doing so will diminish any currently unspecified Aboriginal rights they may wish to exercise in the future. Whether the current treaty process is the most appropriate, whether First Nations should participate in it, and what the outcomes of this process will be are topics of much discussion, and at times heated debate, within all Secwepemc, Carrier, and Tsilhqot'in communities.

These competing political views and interests came to a head in the Reform Party's town hall meeting. The intensity of feeling about Aboriginal land claims and treaties was readily apparent. By the end of the meeting, there were over 100 people, Aboriginal and non-Aboriginal, packed into the hall. The debates that evening were not merely intellectual clashes of competing worldviews but also at times highly charged emotional confrontations that are typical of public challenges to long-standing systems of power and domination.

## The Reform Town Hall Meeting

The meeting was held on a blustery March evening at the Elks Hall, a downtown building owned by one of the most prominent service organizations in the city. By the start of the meeting, eighty people have filed into the hall. Their spatial arrangement in the room reproduces the conventional social hierarchy: non-Aboriginal people, many from fifty to seventy years old, have taken seats toward the front of the room, whereas clusters of Aboriginal people have gathered at the sides and the back, some seated, others standing. Several First Nations chiefs and community leaders are present. A number of Euro-Canadian civic leaders are there: the mayor, a city councillor, regional district representatives (known as Reform Party supporters), and the local figure representing the Council of Forest Industries at the Nisga'a negotiating table. A city newspaper reporter and the NDP MLA's executive assistant are there to record the event. In short, First Nations leaders and at least some Euro-Canadian political leaders, particularly those openly opposed to the current Aboriginal treaty process, have deemed the town hall meeting significant.

The meeting is called to order. The moderator is a Euro-Canadian man and a former RCMP assistant commissioner. He announces: "We're here to address the issues that rank number one on the minds of at least 50 percent of the people in this province. Of course, I'm speaking of Indian land claims and self-government." The panel of speakers is introduced: Cariboo-Chilcotin MP Phillip Mayfield, North Island-Powell River MP John Duncan, and Skeena MP Mike Scott, all Reform Party members. The fourth panel member is Mel Smith, an elderly lawyer, career bureaucrat, and former BC deputy minister in the Social Credit government who "is recognized throughout Canada, I believe, as an authority on constitutional matters pertaining to the Aboriginal scene."

The ominous weight of the topic emerges almost immediately. The moderator reassures us that the town hall meeting is a public forum, designed for "two-way communication." Paradoxically, to enable this communication, the chair informs us that he will exercise "benevolent dictatorship" in regulating comments. The meeting is to proceed with speeches from the local MP, the lawyer, and the two other MPs. The meeting is then to be opened up for "questions to the panel," facilitated by two roving men with microphones. Questioners are asked to line up in an orderly fashion. "I encourage every one of you please to be respectful to one another. We Canadians have a reputation for tolerance in the face of disagreement – perhaps there will be some disagreement here." His evocation of Canadian benevolence and the ideal values of fairness, equality, tolerance, and freedom of speech is in sharp contrast to the angry, tense air emanating from the panelists, who, stiff and frowning, are staring out at the crowd.

Over the next hour, the panelists present their reasons for opposing Aboriginal treaties and land claims. Lawyer Mel Smith outlines his critique of the legal and historical basis for Aboriginal land claims, a critique that he has recently published.[7] Much of his argument is based on a creative, unconventional, and misleading interpretation of legal and historical facts. For example, he states that there is no legal basis for supporting Aboriginal claims to title and argues that Aboriginal rights to the land were extinguished over a century ago when British colonial authority was established. His argument, however, relies on a selective reading of the legal record, drawing on the 1991 BC Supreme Court decision in the *Delgamuukw* case but ignoring the 1993 BC Court of Appeal's later conclusion that unextinguished Aboriginal rights and interests in the land continue today.[8]

Smith tells the audience that it is a "myth" that the province has never properly acquired Indian lands. Instead, BC governments have "proceeded in a different way" by establishing Indian reserves. The province, he suggests, has been extremely generous in this regard: "Do you know ... [that]

70 percent of the reserves in Canada are in British Columbia! It is a myth to say the government has not met its obligations to the Indians!" Many of the reserves in British Columbia, in contrast with the large prairie treaty lands, are only a few acres in size, established to cover small fishing stations, burial grounds, hay meadows, or village sites. This fact, however, is obscured in Smith's rhetoric of generosity. He continues, suggesting that there is no legal reason for treaties to involve the transfer of land. Instead, they can be settled through cash payments. He criticizes the treaty settlements in the Canadian north, which, in his words, "have virtually sacrificed our northern inheritance to a very very few Native people!" Finally, Smith argues that the idea of the inherent right to Aboriginal self-government has no foundation in the law. The idea of Aboriginal self-government, now recognized and supported by the federal government, "causes all sorts of problems, because it raises expectations, it causes the Native people, the leadership, to feel that they have their own rights."

The images of history, of identity, and of Aboriginal/non-Aboriginal relations that flow through Smith's argument resonate with prevalent assumptions within the local Euro-Canadian culture. Frontier history is evoked by negating Aboriginal title and by affirming the legitimacy of European "conquest." The lands of Canada are seen as being acquired through an "inheritance," a term that suggests the rightful transfer of wealth and equates the Canadian nation with a "family" in which all members share equally the national patrimony. This rhetoric erases the fundamental historical fact that the lands of Canada were appropriated from Aboriginal peoples through coercion and force. By asserting the image of the homogeneous Canadian nation, this rhetoric erases the principle of Aboriginal rights: that Aboriginal peoples, by virtue of their original occupancy, have rights that distinguish them from immigrant Canadians. These lands, Smith suggests, are being "sacrificed" and "given away" to Aboriginal groups – terms that presuppose the rightful ownership by the Crown – rather than being transferred back to Aboriginal groups in recognition of the need to redress historical wrongs.

Weaving through Smith's rhetoric is the image of benevolent paternalism: the persistent assumption, central to Canadian national identity and myths of history, that in Canada "We have treated our Aboriginal people well." The Euro-Canadian image of paternalism is matched by the stereotypes of the "wealthy, ungrateful Indian" who is unfairly benefiting from outlandish government generosity and the passive, childlike Indian who is being misled by sympathetic governments into false expectations of Aboriginal rights. Aboriginal political activity is dismissed as the influence of outside agitators. Over and above these images is the paternal assumption of superiority that enables the critique: Smith dismisses Aboriginal politicians as incapable of responsible decision making, and he reaffirms the burden of Euro-Canadians, by virtue of their privileged vision, to direct Aboriginal lives.

**The Moral Discourse of Equality**

The following speakers develop the ideological critique of Aboriginal land claims as violations of the Canadian public ideals of participatory democracy and equality. John Duncan criticizes governments for negotiating with the Nisga'a without consulting the public. He extends this critique of the lack of representation to political processes within the Aboriginal communities. Ethnocentrically presuming that the Canadian ideals of democratic decision making (or majority rule) hold true for traditional forms of government in all First Nations societies of British Columbia, he claims that the Aboriginal leadership is out of touch with the grassroots Aboriginal population. He cites a survey by Statistics Canada in which Aboriginal people were asked which steps could be taken to resolve "problems in Indian reserves." The most common response was "more policing" and "family counselling," whereas "self-government" was "way down near the bottom of the list." He announces, "I have believed quite firmly for some time that the Indian-led leadership which views self-government as an answer for everything is thinking very differently from the membership."

The most forceful critique of the evening is launched by the Skeena Reform MP. Mike Scott begins by warning the crowd that he will not be adhering to ideas of "politically correct speech." "As you've probably noticed, some non-Indians think it's respectful never to tell Indians anything that they think they aren't prepared to hear. I don't agree!" Framing his own critique in the comfortable language of paternal benevolence, he begins by suggesting that land claims are not in the best interests of Aboriginal people. The province's resource economy will be destroyed by land claims settlements, he tells the audience. Thus, "As the least well-off British Columbians, Indians more than anyone will be harmed if the government makes deals that help destroy the economy."

The central theme of his argument is that Aboriginal land claims and treaties violate the fundamental Canadian principle of the equality of all citizens. He states: "We should all be equal before the law ... We should all be subject to the same laws in the same way. This is a fundamental principle of democracy. Anyone who draws distinctions on the basis of race, regardless of whether they have good intentions or not, is a racist by definition." The problems that Aboriginal people now face, he claims, are due to the fact that they were not granted equality before the law in the past:

> A lot of people, strangely enough, believe that the solution to these problems is to do more of what caused them in the first place. They think that what we need is laws that give Indians special privileges, status, and rights.

> Why would anyone think that this would work when it has failed so miserably to this point in time? ... This would be bad for Indians as well ... This is ... not a pitched battle between those who want to help Indians and those who want to hurt them ... but a battle between those who believe in individual rights and those who believe in group rights.

Scott's rhetoric of equality, however, involves more than an upholding of Canadian principles. His argument is explicitly framed by an evolutionary theory of history presuming that Aboriginal cultures will, and must, assimilate into the modern capitalist society and economy that encompass them. Equality, in this second sense, is not the right to maintain distinct social and cultural traditions, but the natural historical imperative of cultural assimilation of "primitive" cultures into more complex, "civilized" societies. This implicit theory of history is one of the defining characteristics of colonial ideologies.[9] In Canada, this assumption has long been a central feature of Indian policy, and in the 1940s and 1950s it was central to the acculturationist approach to Aboriginal cultures,[10] an approach that has since been refuted by anthropological studies documenting the viability and persistence of hunting societies and cultures within industrial capitalist society.[11]

Nevertheless, these ideas of cultural evolution and the incompatibility of Aboriginal and Western cultures are widespread among the Canadian public. Scott's rhetoric draws upon these common-sense assumptions. Aboriginal treaties, he argues, are invalid because Aboriginal political leaders are trying to "re-create a way of life that never existed!" He continues: "It is something of a scam to say that they could re-create traditional life" today with the added luxuries of Western technology. "That way of life is gone. And it isn't coming back." Culture is defined as material technology rather than the more intangible and encompassing modes of social organization, values, and worldviews. From within this narrow perspective, Scott denies the very feasibility of distinct Aboriginal societies, with their own political structures and cultural orders, within contemporary Canadian society.

Public opposition to land claims through the assertion of the value of equality is occasionally expressed by other groups and individuals. Recently, a group calling itself the BC Foundation for Individual Rights and Equality formed to oppose the NDP policy of negotiating settlements of Aboriginal title.[12] A Williams Lake-area community leader is one of the group's directors. He recently wrote to the city newspaper, voicing opposition to Aboriginal treaties through a similar rhetoric. The target of his criticism, once again, was not the First Nations leaders but the federal and provincial governments. There was a similar denial of difference and of historical rights and a similar image of the naïve, childlike Aboriginal person being misled by government:

> This summer we are witnessing a flood of disputes over native assertions of their so-called "Aboriginal rights" ... The real villains in all this are the federal and provincial governments and their bureaucrats. Since 1982, these culprits have been leading the native people to expect that their wish lists would be fulfilled, that indeed Canada's native people have a right to expect preferential treatment. The fact is, these "rights" exist only in government policies ... Our governments – and the Indians – had better get the message: there is one law for all Canadians. The people in this country will never tolerate any policies or actions that disregard our equality and individual rights ... [Natives] have no rights beyond what every other citizen has ... The time has come to put an end to governments, bureaucracies and policies that have headed too far down a road that will lead this country to ruin.[13]

Such discourses engage in a selective organization of history, and of knowledge, in which the ideal of equality is situationally mobilized to protect the power and the privilege of members of the dominant society. These speakers protect themselves from accusations of racism by not criticizing land claims through a rhetoric of Aboriginal difference, particularly notions of difference constructed as cultural backwardness or moral inferiority. Instead, they turn the tables and argue that the very mention of difference constitutes an expression of racism. In championing equality and denouncing Aboriginal treaties as furthering racism, these discourses are among the most powerful oppositional forms now circulating in Aboriginal rights discussions.

Similar debates are occurring in other settler societies where indigenous assertions to special rights and self-determination are increasingly recognized by governments and the courts and, at the same time, opposed by public groups. In Australia, the federal government's passage of the Aboriginal Land Rights (Northern Territory) Act in 1976 enabled Aboriginal groups in the Northern Territory to obtain grants to tracts of vacant Crown land over which they held traditional affiliations. A groundswell of public opposition coalesced into the Land Rights Action Group in 1977, and in 1978 the group became known as "One Nation, One Law."[14] Concerned that Aboriginal groups would be able to exert control over national park lands and popular tourism destinations, the group argued that the Land Rights Act granted Aboriginal people special rights and thus violated the fundamental principle of the equality of all Australian citizens.[15]

In 1996, a more extreme, right-wing group formed as Pauline Hanson's One Nation Party. One Nation emerged in the wake of the High Court's 1992 *Mabo* decision, which for the first time recognized the existence of Native title under Australian common law, and the 1993 federal government's passage of the Native Title Act, which set up a procedure by which

Aboriginal groups could lodge and negotiate the settlement of outstanding Native title claims. The One Nation Party is explicitly opposed to Native title, multiculturalism policy, and what it sees as the government's liberal allowance of Asian immigration into the country. While being roundly condemned for espousing openly racist views and an assimilationist mentality, the party claims to be the voice of the "ordinary Australian" defending the principles of equality and freedom. It has won much support in rural Australia.

Similarly, in New Zealand, Maori claims to distinct rights to land and self-determination have been countered by what Andrew Sharp calls a pervasive "Pakeha ideology of equality."[16] As in the "self-made man" vision of history, this ideology holds that all individuals enjoy equal opportunity, that those who succeed and prosper do so on their own initiative, and that those who do not are left behind by their own failings. Consequently, Pakeha opponents argue that any special legislation recognizing the distinctiveness of Maori rights is "racist" by definition.[17]

Given the similarities in the public ideals of liberal democratic societies – the equality and freedom of all individual citizens, and democratic (majority rule) government – it is not unexpected that the public values mobilized in Canada, Australia, and New Zealand to oppose indigenous rights should be identical. The fundamental challenge is also basically the same: How can liberal democratic societies accommodate the distinct collective rights of indigenous minorities while maintaining the principles of fairness and the equality and freedom of individual citizens?[18] While the Reform Party of Canada may seek to answer this question by denying the collective rights of Aboriginal peoples, arguing that Aboriginal people must assimilate as individuals indistinct from other citizens of the country, this solution, in reality, is no longer feasible. Distinct Aboriginal societies have persisted in Canada despite centuries of colonization and their encapsulation within Canadian society and its institutions. Today Aboriginal people reject the assimilation solution and are insisting on the right to maintain their social collectives through the exercise of rights to land and self-government. The Canadian government and the Canadian courts have increasingly recognized the persistence of the distinct rights of Aboriginal peoples, rights that include not only traditional forms of sustenance – hunting and fishing – but also Aboriginal title, the "exclusive use and occupation" of the land itself. Finally, the Canadian Constitution has affirmed the distinct rights of Aboriginal peoples. Since the 1970s the federal government has enacted policies – treaty settlements being one example – which have been based on the recognition that indigenous peoples hold collective rights not shared by immigrant Canadians.

The problem, however, remains: How can these collective rights be reconciled with individual rights? Does the recognition of Aboriginal rights contravene the basic Canadian principles of the equality of all citizens? To answer this question, and to respond to critiques such as those launched by the Reform Party, we need to distinguish the ideology of equality from the actual way in which the Canadian legal system and public policy operate. While a full discussion of this is not possible here, some basic observations can be made.[19]

All individuals in Canada, contrary to the assertions of the Reform Party, are not equal before the law, nor are they treated equally in government policy. In practice, the collective rights of minority groups are recognized in a number of ways, as has already been indicated for Aboriginal peoples. The Canadian Charter of Rights and Freedoms acknowledges and preserves the "multicultural" heritage of Canadians and can be interpreted as affirming the collective rights of distinct ethnic groups.[20] In particular, the collective political, linguistic, and cultural rights of French-Canadians have been accommodated (to varying degrees of success) in several ways within the structure of the Canadian state. As Michael Asch points out, these rights are indirectly accommodated through the system of provincial jurisdiction. The majority of French-Canadians reside in Quebec, and as the ethnic majority of that province, they may exercise the right to control a variety of provincial matters, from the administration of justice and education to the designation of the province's official language. As a province, Quebec may "opt out" of any constitutional change to which it is opposed.[21] The linguistic rights of French-speaking Canadians are recognized in the federal government's designation of French as one of Canada's two official languages. Residents outside of Quebec have the right to obtain federal government services through the French language. French-speaking parents living outside of Quebec, with some restrictions, have the right to have their children educated in French through the Constitution's "minority language education" clause.[22]

The Canadian Charter of Rights and Freedoms protects the right of all citizens to be treated equally before the law. But the Charter's equality clause is not interpreted by legal scholars to mean that all individuals must be treated the *same* before the law.[23] Differential treatment based on factors such as level of income, physical capability, and religion are all acknowledged as necessary to ensure just treatment. Some forms of selective differentiation exist to protect the individual's right to freedom of cultural and religious practice (in other words, their collective cultural and religious rights). Other forms of differentiation exist to further the *outcome* of equality, by ensuring a fair access to and a just distribution of resources and opportunities. For example, affirmative action hiring strategies seek to increase the representation of ethnic minorities previously excluded by discriminatory hiring practices. This does not mean, however, that tensions between equality and "special rights," or "discrimination," are not debated. One scholar, for example, has argued that any law can be defended or attacked on the basis of the Charter's equality provision.[24]

Furthermore, it is important to note that Aboriginal treaties are not being created as a form of "distributive justice"[25] to ameliorate existing inequalities in society or to bring Aboriginal peoples up to the same standards of living, health, education, and prosperity as other Canadians. Instead, they are being implemented as a form of "reparative justice," to restore or compensate for rights that have been wrongly breached or taken away from Aboriginal peoples in the past.[26]

In short, there are inherent contradictions between Canadian ideals and legal and government practice. The Reform Party, while seeking to draw attention to these contradictions in order to oppose Aboriginal treaties, is not alone in manipulating the ideals of equality and freedom for partisan interests. Yet their rallying cry of "one law for all Canadians" does not reflect the reality of Canadian society and its institutions. For Aboriginal people, justice cannot be achieved by taking away collective rights already recognized in law, policy, and practice. It requires a political process of negotiating new arrangements by which Aboriginal communities can exercise forms of self-government that enable them to maintain their social organization, forms of governance, and cultural traditions while also contributing to and existing within the framework of Canadian society. The Reform Party's assimilationist solution is only one extreme along a continuum of possibilities for addressing the problem of reconciling Aboriginal rights within a liberal democratic framework. As Michael Asch has argued, given the fact that Canada, as well as other liberal democracies such as Switzerland and Belgium, already recognize collective minority rights within the structures of the state, the barrier to incorporating a fuller recognition of Aboriginal rights in Canada is more ideological that structural.[27] Yet in rural settings in Canada, these ideological barriers are significant. Public opposition is being voiced through a variety of discourses that rest not just on an assertion of the ideals of equality and individualism, and not just on the denial of Aboriginal "difference," but also on varied, shifting definitions of Aboriginality and Aboriginal/Euro-Canadian relationships.

### Other Discourses: Naturalizing Conquest and Denying Aboriginality

Some Euro-Canadians oppose land claims by relativizing the brutalities of history. They argue that the "conquest" of one group by another, although perhaps tragic and regrettable, has long been a natural feature of Western history. If Aboriginal groups are to be compensated for their loss of land, other groups, with equally valid claims for compensation, will also have to be recompensed. In one recent letter, a resident of the Williams Lake area asked, "How far back do we have to go?" – suggesting that, if Aboriginal claims are to be accepted, then the British should also be compensated for the invasion by the Romans. These individuals detach the issue of Aboriginal rights from the context of colonialism and render it a natural feature of world history. These arguments deny both the specificity of Aboriginal rights and the responsibility of contemporary society to address past practices. Instead, opponents suggest that "The past should be forgotten." They defend the silences of official history and reject the efforts of First Nations leaders to recover these silences.

The denial of Aboriginality is another rhetorical strategy frequently heard in opposition to land claims. One occasionally hears non-Aboriginal people remark that "There are no real Indians around anymore." They suggest, consequently, that Aboriginal people have no valid claims to Aboriginal rights. Indianness, in these contexts, is constructed according to blood quantum. Some Euro-Canadians argue that there has been such a degree of intermarriage over the past two centuries that "full-blooded Indians" no longer exist.[28] So absolute are the categories of Indian and white in local discourse that any hint of non-Aboriginal ancestry is taken, under these circumstances, to invalidate true Aboriginality. This appropriation of the power to confer authentic Indian identity, and to render invisible Aboriginal people who do not conform to imposed standards, has long been a feature of the practices of various segments of colonial society, including Euro-Canadian politicians, Indian Affairs administrators, artists, journalists, writers, and anthropologists. In discourses surrounding land claims, these struggles over the authenticity of Aboriginal identity continue to be central to the processes of power.

### Moral Discourses of Aboriginal Inferiority

Some Euro-Canadians, despite concerns with being branded as racists, also engage in moral discourses of Aboriginal inferiority to oppose Aboriginal land claims and treaties. These discourses are evident not only in public meetings and forums but also in letters to the Williams Lake *Tribune* and in the interviews that I conducted with community leaders. Many local Euro-Canadians, in unabashed paternal fashion, argue that Aboriginal people "are not ready" for treaties or self-government and that treaties, in fostering the segregation of Aboriginal people from mainstream society, would be a "disaster for Natives." The prevalence of these attitudes reflects how deeply ingrained are the assumptions of Euro-Canadian superiority and paternal benevolence.

Many Euro-Canadians define the problems that Aboriginal people face not in terms of government oppression or racial discrimination – actions in which Euro-Canadian society is implicated – but in terms of social ills: unemployment, poverty, alcoholism, and poor living conditions. To many, the solution to these perceived problems is relatively simple: Aboriginal people must develop the will to go out and find work. Thus, the social, economic, and historical inequalities that divide the Aboriginal and Euro-Canadian populations are comprehended within the framework of the self-made man vision of history, in which Aboriginal people are blamed for the difficulties that they now face. These problems can only be solved, these Euro-Canadians argue, if Aboriginal people adopt the appropriate set of values of the dominant culture.

There is little room for cultural pluralism in this scenario. Many community leaders believe that Canadian society, despite its multicultural fabric, offers little potential for Aboriginal people to exist as distinct political, social, and cultural collectives. Instead, Euro-Canadians propose that Aboriginal people become economically assimilated while retaining only surface cultural traits such as powwow dancing and crafts. Negative difference is lost; in its place remains the exoticized and innocuous difference celebrated in events such as the Williams Lake Stampede and easily accommodated within constructions of official multiculturalism.

This common-sense view of assimilation is accompanied by an overwhelmingly negative image of reserve life. It is only the rare non-Aboriginal person, it seems, who has been to an Indian reserve or visited with people in their reserve homes. Few Euro-Canadians seem to know the names, or the locations, of the area's fifteen reserves. Instead, they know of reserve life through the anecdotes exchanged between friends and acquaintances, through reading about incidents of crime reported in the city newspaper, and through passing the more visible reserves, such as Sugar Cane, Soda Creek, and Anaham, along the highways. The image of reserve life that prevails is bleak: run-down housing, strewn garbage, broken-down cars, violence, alcoholism, and social pathology.

Although the negative features of reserve life are also debated by Aboriginal people, the positive and redeeming values remain invisible to Euro-Canadians: the strong bonds within families, the sense of belonging to a community, of commitment to the land, to cultural traditions, and to a collective future. Passing these reserves, Euro-Canadians do not see the well-kept houses, the thriving businesses, the homes where family life is happy and harmonious. Lacking any sense of these positive aspects, many judge reserve life through the ethnocentric screens of Euro-Canadian values, morals, and stereotypes.

These assumptions easily find their way into public discussions of land claims. Many critics oppose land claims as yet another massive government "giveaway" to Aboriginal people. Treaties, if they perpetuate the "segregation" of Aboriginal people in reserves, will only exacerbate the problems of unemployment, poverty, poor social conditions, apathy, dependency, and alcoholism. A typical expression of these beliefs, founded on the image of the "wealthy, undeserving Indian," was provided in one woman's recent letter to the editor: "Everyone agrees that land claims should be settled, but how? How many years have we been pouring funds into this abyss [reserve communities]? It apparently has done the natives on the reserves no good at all ... Where has this money gone? The native people of Canada should be the best dressed, the best housed, the best educated people in the world! The people on the reserves seem to be desperate and hopeless."[29] Another woman similarly drew on the images of Canadian benevolence and Aboriginal ingratitude, couching her argument further by evoking frontier histories of Aboriginal savagery and the benefits brought to Aboriginal people through colonization:

> There's a lot of concern over the land claims issues. It appears this is a preparation for a more serious next step. Who and what is really behind this, as we get along well with the native Indians? They now have warm houses to live in, warm clothing to wear, education privileges, and much more [than] before the white people came. No more one tribe killing off another Indian tribe either. We are nice to everyone ... When the white people fled from persecution and death in Europe, they settled in this undeveloped land, hundreds of miles from the Indian settlements because the Indians burned their cabins, wheat fields and made sport as to who could get the most white man's scalps. I read this in many early history books, which seem to have disappeared from the libraries ... Canadians are nice people and try to give everyone a fair chance. Some are taking advantage of this goodness.[30]

Yet others argue that treaty settlements will not solve the problems that Aboriginal people now face because of their incapacity to manage their own lives: "A note to negotiators for their lack of foresight on First Nations credibility. Does no one understand that giving [to] people who have proved themselves incapable of management will create a catastrophe? ... We give them millions of dollars for programs and enterprises; most of which have been mismanaged and failed."[31] And others argue that land claims are invalid because Aboriginal people already have land that they do not use. They criticize them for not cultivating their hay fields, for littering their reserves with old cars, and for allowing their houses to become run down. Euro-Canadian standards are again imposed on Aboriginal communities; their failure to live up to these ideals is used as evidence for the inappropriateness of land claims settlements to resolve the "real" problem.

## Moral Inferiority Historicized

The land claims issue has brought First Nations and Euro-Canadian leaders of the Cariboo-Chilcotin into unprecedented formal contact. In public forums and private meetings, First Nations leaders have drawn attention to some of the hidden aspects of their historical experience: the negative impact of the residential school system, the coercive relationship with the Indian Affairs bureaucracy, the limitations imposed on them by the Indian Act. In drawing attention to these aspects of history, First Nations leaders attempt to accomplish two things. First, they challenge prevalent assumptions that the social ills, violence, alcohol abuse, and chronic unemployment in reserve communities are innate aspects of being Indian. Instead, these problems are presented as a consequence of historical forces – the Indian Act, the residential school system – that have created Aboriginal marginalization and dependency. Second, First Nations leaders point to the settlement of Aboriginal land claims as a means of resolving social problems and creating thriving, self-sufficient communities.

Just as First Nations leaders are attempting to historicize notions of Aboriginal difference in order to combat the essentialist negative stereotypes that prevail in Euro-Canadian understandings, so many non-Aboriginal people who oppose land claims and treaties are now articulating notions of Aboriginal difference not based on inherent features but due to learned cultural behaviours and habits. Although their interpretation of the cause of social ills is now historical, their solution remains the same: assimilation.

> The problem that Caucasians have had over the years, we've always felt we were superior ... "We're far superior, we have better weapons, we suppress those people and live happily ever after" kind of attitude ... The problems that we have nowadays is because of that suppression. I don't think the culture of the Natives is as proud as they once were. You can't keep people dumb and uneducated on a specific little parcel and expect them to grow as the rest of the community has grown. So when they do try to integrate – I mean, when I worked at the mill, they hired Natives. They'd show up three days and would be gone. That was the way they were brought up. They had no responsibilities. There was food on the table; they could get it from somewhere without having to work ... I know for myself, my father worked his tail off. That's what I saw, so I knew in order for me to make it I had to work my tail off. And I hope my son's getting the same education ... Where I think that same thing's happening in the Native community. They see their dad drinking, staying home and sleeping in, abusing the mother. It becomes acceptable, I guess.

Similar views were voiced by another community leader:

> Well, I think a big part of the problem is our history. When I talked to the Natives, anyway, a big part was the restrictions that was put on them through the federal, what do you call it? The Indian Act, yeah ... When

> other people came from Europe, they gave them, if they went and homesteaded, they got certain pieces of land. And that was theirs as long as they did certain things ... I guess that's one of the things that went wrong. They were stuck on that piece of [reserve] land; they weren't told "You have to do this to be able to keep it." And they put them there, they basically made them a welfare state because they didn't force the issue and make them, "OK, you've got to do this, you've got to do this." But they started building houses for them; they did this and that. And they became dependent on the government. And everything they did had to be approved by the government. Instead of setting themselves up like any other community. I mean, that's how Williams Lake started. There's no reason why these reserves couldn't have grown if they were allowed the same jurisdiction that everybody else had.

Both speakers now understand the current difficulties Aboriginal people face as a product of historical factors. The first speaker perceives Aboriginal dependence and irresponsibility as a result of government suppression; the second, as a result of government benevolence and over-protection. In both cases, the historical problem is construed as the denial of equal rights; the solution is the restoration of equal rights and assimilation. Thus, the confrontations occurring over Aboriginal treaty processes involve more than efforts of First Nations leaders to draw public attention to hidden historical matters. They also involve challenges to the very terms of the frontier myth. In response, Euro-Canadians who oppose treaties argue not so much from a position of historical amnesia, but from within a particular historical worldview that, while according the existence of past injustice, suggests that if Aboriginal people had been allowed the same "freedom" as the pioneers they would not be in their current predicament.

### The Audience's Response

By the end of the panel's presentation, the atmosphere in the room is tense. Now is the time for questions from the audience, and the tight control that the moderator attempts to wield over the public forum begins to slip. His attempts to limit public responses to questions posed to the panel – which would implicitly affirm the credibility of those seated on the stage – ultimately fail. Instead, speaker after speaker challenges the panelists, accusing them of distorting legal and historical facts and condemning them for their lack of support for Aboriginal treaties. The moderator successfully cuts off the first speaker after two minutes, but subsequent audience members refuse to submit, and the moderator eventually gives up his attempts to cut off their responses. Under the force of this vociferous opposition, other audience members, if they agree with the presentation, are silent in their support. The two audience members who do quietly question the panelists are outnumbered by eight others who condemn the presentation. The majority of those who speak out are Aboriginal; others are non-Aboriginal people employed by and known to be sympathetic to Aboriginal peoples and causes.

Among those who speak are three First Nations chiefs and leaders. Their responses indicate the manner in which Aboriginal people are employing public values and various discursive modes to press their interests.

The first audience member to speak to the panel is Chief Ervin Charleyboy, the elected chief of the Alexis Creek First Nation.[32] Although not participating in the BC Treaty Commission process, many Tsilhqot'in leaders continue to be active in lobbying for wider recognition of Aboriginal rights. Chief Charleyboy is becoming well known in the regional non-Aboriginal community. He gained some notoriety a few years ago when, on behalf of his band, he asserted Aboriginal title by expanding the official boundaries of the reserve to incorporate a parcel of Crown land where the band planned to build a trailer park. He has since been featured, without apparent irony, in the "Friends and Neighbours" section of the city newspaper. The chief is an imposing figure, tall and with a strong voice, and he is shaking with rage as he stands up to speak. In forceful and uncompromising terms, he loudly condemns the panel for voicing racist views: "I want to comment on some of the things [the lawyer] has said ... I think some of the things that he said is based on racism ... We were shoved onto these goddamned reserves without our consent! The Indian Act was pushed on us without our consent! That's unconstitutional! And you guys talk about equality – that's bullshit! There is no equality in this country!" After a minute, the moderator interrupts him, deflecting his speech. Frustrated, Chief Charleyboy concludes: "The Reform Party is a racist party, and that's all I have to say!"

In making recourse to the sanctity of equality and the legitimacy of the Constitution – and in pointing out how past actions of governments have violated these principles – the chief speaks from within the terms of the dominant culture, attempting to draw attention to apparent contradictions in that culture and to the historical injustices glossed over by the Reform speakers. His moral weapons are identical to those of the Reform Party: equality, the Constitution, the evils of racism. But these terms have vastly different meanings when used by individuals positioned on opposite sides of the divide of power and rooted in different cultural and historical experiences.

To the Secwepemc, Tsilhqot'in, and Carrier people of the Cariboo-Chilcotin, to whom racial prejudice, marginalization, and unequal treatment have been part of everyday life for over four generations, the Reform Party's appeals to equality are highly offensive if not infuriating. In public forums such as this one, Aboriginal speakers attempt to convey to the public precisely this reality: that Aboriginal people have been subjected to a variety of legal, bureaucratic, and ideological modes of domination based on the concept of their difference from other Canadians and that these inequalities must be rectified through Aboriginal treaties.

Yet First Nations leaders, in asserting their political rights, also make recourse to a rhetoric that alternately highlights Aboriginal people's similarity to and difference from other Canadians. First Nations in Canada are demanding not only equality – the right to be treated with dignity, respect, and fairness – but also recognition of their differences based on the legal and political rights flowing from their distinct historical status as indigenous peoples. In response, Euro-Canadian opponents selectively apply key features of the dominant culture – the ideal of equality – to affirm existing relations of power. The impasse created by these confrontational rhetorics is evident as waves of tension pass through the audience in the wake of the chief's speech.

Following several more responses, another man, standing at the back of the room, takes the microphone. He is "Frank Peters," a leader in his thirties from the Ulkatcho Carrier community in the west Chilcotin. Like the Tsilhqot'in, the Ulkatcho First Nation is not participating in treaty talks, but its leaders are also attempting to negotiate new relationships with non-Aboriginal society. In contrast to the Tsilhqot'in chief, who relies on standard public values and who uses a confrontational rhetoric, Peters takes a more moderate and personal approach. He appeals to the audience's common humanity, its love of family, and its commitment to living in harmony with its Aboriginal neighbours – in short, the key public values by which Euro-Canadians, in quite different contexts, have defended their own notions of Cariboo-Chilcotin identity.

Peters's appeal for public understanding draws on another mainstream discourse, that of the popular psychology "healing" movement first introduced to Cariboo-Chilcotin Aboriginal communities in the guise of Alcoholics Anonymous groups some twenty years ago. Since that time, a variety of training programs for personal growth, including offshoots of the California-based EST human-potential training, have been held in many reserve communities. Individuals from one Secwepemc community, Alkali Lake, now run their own personal-training company, New Directions, and are frequently contracted to run sessions in western Canada. The local, Aboriginal-run Nenqayni Treatment Centre and many other centres for treating Aboriginal alcohol and drug abuse, such as Round Lake in Vernon, Kakawis on Vancouver Island, and the Nechi Institute in Edmonton, have developed a healing philosophy that blends popular psychology with Aboriginal cultural revitalization. Many adults, as the first step in "sobering up," attend one of these residential treatment centres for four to six weeks. "Going for treatment" is a common phrase and event in reserve communities, one with no shame attached. It is not unusual for a person struggling with alcohol to attend a treatment centre several times.

Over the last twenty years, Aboriginal people in the Cariboo-Chilcotin have incorporated this discourse of Western popular psychology, interpreting and reshaping it to become meaningful within their particular circumstances. The creativity with which Aboriginal people are using this discourse is evident in Peters's address to the audience. He likens Indian-white relations to those of a dysfunctional family, and he uses this metaphor to appeal for reason and understanding:

> We all know about this dysfunctional [family] ... I was going through treatment and personally realized everything that's happened, I'm seeing it, everything that I find out about myself, this is how society is. A lot of injustices have happened to our people – people refusing to admit to it. It's like society is stuck in denial. And the government is like an alcoholic father, and we're kind of Indians stuck on the reserve. And we want to protect our parent, by being quiet or staying in our place so he doesn't get angry at us, cut off our funding, or whatever. So ... by being quiet, we agree to this suppression. And become codependents ... And imagine you guys going home and feeling that you have to stay on the reserve and fight amongst each other for who's going to get a house next year! It's like that every year!

His speech is interrupted by a Euro-Canadian man in his fifties, who has been sitting by himself in the middle of the room. With his back to the speaker, he yells out loudly, to no one in particular, a condensed assertion of the self-made man myth of history: "Go to work for once! Like we do! Asshole! Enough of this shit!" He stands up and storms out of the hall as his words reverberate among the shocked audience – shocked not just by his rudeness but also because he has dared to publicly state what many consider to be common-sense "truths." Frank Peters, however, continues to speak: "These are all things that Canadian society has to be reminded of. I think the more people understand how our situation is, I think there would be more compassion. Our kids are going to grow up together ... Our children, your children. To find a better place to live. We love the non-Native society, but we love ourselves too. We love ourselves enough to keep fighting these injustices that keep happening to our people."

Such healing discourse is a regular part of public discussions in many reserve communities, where the psychodynamics of alcoholic families, and the problems of alcohol-related violence, have been recognized and discussed for years. In the context of a potentially hostile audience in a public political forum, Peters's speech, in its personal emotion, its appeal for compassion, and its use of the concepts of "codependency" and "dysfunction," challenges some deeper norms of Euro-Canadian culture. His speech violates a widespread Euro-Canadian cultural norm that marks public expressions of personal issues and emotions – and, indeed, the public acknowledgment of one's identity as an alcoholic – as inappropriate, shameful, and a sign of personal weakness. Furthermore, the language of popular psychology, and the concepts of dysfunctional relationships and alcoholic family dynamics, are not commonplace among most Euro-Canadians in the Cariboo-Chilcotin. His stretching of the metaphor of the dysfunctional family to comprehend Aboriginal/Euro-Canadian relations is creative and compelling; yet, to an audience of older and conservative Euro-Canadians, these metaphors are not rooted in a context of shared cultural experience and meaning. Peters offers the audience a bridge to understanding that requires listeners to actively set aside their own cultural assumptions in order to comprehend Aboriginal people's experiences and their common humanity.

The last audience member to speak is Rick Gilbert. He is fairly well known in Euro-Canadian business circles. For many years, he was the chief of the Williams Lake First Nation, the Secwepemc reserve community closest to the city. As chief, Gilbert developed a variety of contacts with small businesses and municipal officials, due in part to the need to negotiate terms of the many leases and rights of way through the band's reserves. He stands up from his seat at the side of the room, and as he takes the microphone the moderator recognizes him and acknowledges him by name. Gilbert, in contrast, speaks to the non-Aboriginal audience in its own idiom. As he proceeds, something of a calm settles over the audience. Many of those seated turn to face him as he speaks:

> Some of the comments I heard tonight regarding the way government is handling land claims ... like some of the fear that has been felt by people, I think – anybody that has been involved in business, logging business, or department store business, knows that at certain times there needs to be negotiations. And as a worker, you're going to ask for 100 percent of what you think you should make, and your employers or government are going to offer you the minimum amount that they want to give. My feeling, at this time, is that the Reform Party is offering 2 percent ... but that doesn't mean anything, because in the end we're going to end up somewhere in the middle. The province of BC is not going to be given away, and hopefully the standard of living for Indian people is going to be a lot better than it is, has been in the past. And that's all we're looking for, a better way of life for ourselves.

Rick Gilbert, like Frank Peters, also makes use of a powerful metaphor to appeal for public understanding of the land claims process. But his metaphor, in contrast, is rooted in the culture of small-town, right-wing entrepreneurialism. By extending the concept of labour-management negotiations to the land claims process, he not only offers Euro-Canadians a conceptual framework in which to understand these processes but also implicitly acknowledges and affirms the central values of the dominant Euro-Canadian culture: the importance of the resource industries and small businesses and the value of the capitalist work ethic. In asking the audience to accept this analogy, he is indirectly appealing to the public values that are central to the dominant Euro-Canadian regional culture.

Gilbert continues to address some of the main stereotypes used to oppose the land claims process. He struggles to bridge the gulf created by negative stereotypes of the "wealthy, undeserving Indian" and the "lazy Indian living off government money." Instead, he affirms the many similarities in values between Aboriginal people and Euro-Canadians. Aboriginal people, he insists, do not want to be on social assistance. They want to be self-supporting, a goal currently blocked by the difficulties of initiating economic development projects on reserve land controlled by Indian Act legislation and Indian Affairs regulations. "All we want is land that's not improved a lot. And people ... we're tired of it. And I think the people of Canada are tired of the arguing that they're giving us welfare money for Native people. And we're tired of getting welfare money. Our people want to work, they want to pay taxes, they want to pay for everything they can get. But we have to create the opportunities. And that's why we need to get the resources, and that's how we're going to get them, is through negotiations."

Rick Gilbert's comments mark the end of audience responses. The meeting is concluded, and there is little lingering as the audience files out of the hall and into the darkness.

In various ways, First Nations leaders in the Cariboo-Chilcotin are drawing on the symbols, values, and emblems of the dominant culture to appeal for public support for Aboriginal land claims. In so doing, they are attempting to negotiate the terms of a new coexistence between Aboriginal and non-Aboriginal populations that will include respect for the right of Aboriginal people to live in their own communities, to be self-sufficient and self-governing, and to practise distinct cultural lifestyles. In these public forums, individuals such as Frank Peters are pointing out "things that Canadians need to be reminded of," the ways in which the historical experiences of Aboriginal Canadians have differed from those of non-Aboriginal Canadians, and the injustices and inequalities imposed on reserve communities through Indian Affairs policies, federal legislation, residential schools, and racial prejudice.

Yet First Nations leaders are not only attempting to recover the silenced components of history. Their efforts to show the differences in Aboriginal and non-Aboriginal historical experiences are accompanied by efforts to draw similarities between the two populations, to bridge the symbolic divide between Indian and white, and to demonstrate a commitment to a common future. Through the use of creative analogies, First Nations leaders are appealing to common shared values: family harmony, neighbourliness, independence, self-sufficiency, and pride through hard work. In so doing, First Nations leaders are attempting to show how treaties will bring about a realization of these mutual values and goals. Thus, Aboriginal discourses on land claims are fuelled not only by assertions of cultural difference but also by claims to similarity with members of the dominant society. These strategies for communicating with non-Aboriginal audiences explicitly affirm the dominant values and symbols of Euro-Canadian culture: they employ a rhetorical strategy defined by the metaphorical presentation of "strategic equivalences" between the Aboriginal and Euro-Canadian worlds.

Aboriginal discourses about land claims and treaties are highly influenced by context; in this case, by virtue of the format of this public forum, First Nations speakers reacted defensively against a dominant discourse opposing treaties presented to an audience comprised mainly of older, conservative Euro-Canadians. A more forceful political rhetoric, emphasizing historical rights, Aboriginal title, and sovereignty, can be heard in other forums. In yet other contexts in which Aboriginal leaders are invited to speak to Euro-Canadian audiences, a more gentle and indirect style of discourse may be used.[33]

Furthermore, the discourses presented here are only one component of a complex and multilayered process through which First Nations are resisting and challenging Euro-Canadian authority over lands and resources – challenges enacted in the courts, at road blockades, in formal meetings with government officials and industry executives, and in the open defiance of Canadian laws through the public assertion of Aboriginal rights.

Even within this public forum, the varied responses of the Aboriginal speakers reflect the diversity of discourses among Aboriginal people themselves, discourses shaped by the varying influences of one's age, gender, cultural heritage, political philosophy, and position and experience within local and regional politics. For example, since the mid-1970s, Secwepemc bands have been propelled into new and intense bureaucratic relationships with various provincial and federal government agencies. Through this experience, Rick Gilbert has learned, in his words, "how to talk to politicians at high levels." As he described it, this strategy is not a confrontational style of discourse but a reasoned and calm approach that attempts to identify common interests between both parties engaged in negotiations while advancing one's own particular interests. As he mentioned to me in a later discussion, he consciously adopted this discursive strategy at the Reform Party meeting: he was speaking directly to the Reform panelists and to white audience members whom he recognized.[34]

A central characteristic of these discourses is their creativity. Despite the historical and ongoing forms of domination of Aboriginal lives – as captured by the violent verbal outburst by the Euro-Canadian audience member – Aboriginal responses reflect an inventive energy through which new identities and new metaphors of Aboriginal/non-Aboriginal relations are continually being forged, attempted, and tested in public contexts as speakers attempt to manoeuvre around plural forms of domination. These discourses suggest that the competing views on the land claims issue are best characterized not as a simple dialectic of domination and resistance but as being situated in more complex, intersecting "zones of transcourse,"[35] where multiple discourses and multiple identities are voiced by individuals variously positioned within the fields of power that comprise colonial relations.

Non-Aboriginal discourses on land claims are equally complex; here I have limited my discussion to those Euro-Canadian oppositional discourses that, in the Cariboo-Chilcotin, are shared by a group of powerful civic and industry leaders and are frequently voiced in public forums and in everyday conversations. These forms of opposition draw on multiple strands of a colonial culture – common-sense assumptions of history, of identity, of society – that facilitate the continued subordination of the Aboriginal populations. The idea of the inherent moral inferiority of Aboriginal people – whether due to race, culture, or historical circumstance – underlies the widespread conviction that Aboriginal people simply do not "deserve" treaty settlements. It underlies the conventional, common-sense assimilationist view that the proper answer to the question of land claims is the abolition of reserves, the abandonment of most aspects of Aboriginal culture, and the blending of Aboriginal people into the Euro-Canadian society and economy.

Opposition to land claims and treaties, however, is more generally grounded in a historical consciousness defined by the myth of the frontier. This myth encodes a set of assumptions about the nature of Canadian history, which is seen as the outcome of the courageous actions of heroic individuals. By extension, any individual with sufficient courage and ambition can prosper in life today. The myth of the frontier, as articulated in the Cariboo-Chilcotin, encompasses both a celebration of the ideal of equality and a rationale for the collective inequalities experienced by Aboriginal peoples. Thus, the apparent contradictions perceived by some scholars between egalitarianism and racist ideology in Canada[36] are not experienced in the everyday lives of most Euro-Canadians in the Cariboo-Chilcotin. Euro-Canadians do not seem to perceive or experience any inherent "fundamental dissonance"[37] in espousing racist views and upholding egalitarian ideals, although they are frequently criticized by *others* for these perceived disjunctions between ideal and actual conduct. Rather, racism and egalitarianism are compatible with their most fundamental cultural assumptions about history, the individual, and society.

The frontier myth, in its celebration of the self-made man, provides not only an explanation of the past but also a map for future relationships between Aboriginal and non-Aboriginal Canadians. When Aboriginal speakers point out the injustice of colonial domination and the unresolved issue of Aboriginal title, Euro-Canadians opposing land claims respond by rendering "conquest" as a natural, universal, and inevitable process of Western history. History is reduced to the axiom of "survival of the fittest." When First Nations leaders point to the historical forms of state domination that have resulted in poverty, marginalization, and social ills in reserve communities, these Euro-Canadians blame Aboriginal people for their dependency, laziness, and lack of a work ethic: structural inequalities are reduced to individual failings. Although the surface facts of history may be debated, it is the underlying historical epistemology that serves to orient discourses opposing land claims and that continues to exert a conservative and hegemonic force in these debates.

# 7

# Re-creating the Wild West: Negotiating Indianness in the Williams Lake Stampede

No aspect of public culture captures the frontier ethos of the Cariboo-Chilcotin more fully than the annual Williams Lake Stampede. During the four-day festival, the city transforms itself into an imaginary Wild West frontier settlement. Billed as a tribute to the region's ranching and rodeo heritage, the festival consists of a professional rodeo, "barn dances," pancake breakfasts, a parade, and a stampede queen contest. Local businesses and stores remodel their interiors into make-believe Western frontier saloons, hotels, and gold mines, and images of cowboys, cattle, horses, and hay bales fill the downtown store windows. Local residents are encouraged to "dress Western" to get into the spirit of the festival. It is within this symbolic field that Aboriginal people, as Indians, emerge as an important component of the ritual process.

In no other context do area Aboriginal people, as Indians, become as visible and as positively valued by town residents than in the ritual festivities of the stampede. Aboriginal people occasionally participate in the parade wearing buckskin, powwow regalia, and headdresses and performing drum songs and dances before the crowd. Booths for Indian arts and crafts might be set up outside the rodeo grandstand, and in the past tipis have been erected on the stampede grounds. These images of Indianness stand as a counterpoint to the Western identity represented through the stampede festivities. The dichotomy of Indian and white found elsewhere in frontier histories and in everyday Euro-Canadian conversations is reproduced here in a ritual context. Indian and white are opposite yet interdependent identities; both are required to complete the scripts of identity and history performed during the stampede.

In this chapter, I assess how public identities are represented and contested within the context of the Williams Lake Stampede. I ask two questions. First, given the many other domains in which Aboriginal people are rendered invisible or insignificant in the public landscape, why do stampede organizers deem Indian participation in the event so important for its success? To explore this question, I review the origin and development of the stampede. This historical analysis is critical for revealing the core symbols and events of this ritual complex. Although the stampede has undergone some significant changes over time – new events have been added, and old ones have been dropped or modified – there is a consistent core of symbolic associations and events that have their roots in the Wild West performances of the late nineteenth century. These performances were later incorporated into small-town stampedes and rodeos that were popular throughout Canada and the United States and that, in turn, evolved into professional rodeo. Throughout this evolution, there has remained a consistent emphasis on the dramatic performance of frontier identities and of the binary contrasts between Indian and white. It is this ritual tradition that underlies the desire of the stampede's Euro-Canadian organizers to encourage Aboriginal participation as Indians and the disappointment at their reluctance to fully join in the festivities.

Second, how do stampede organizers and area First Nations leaders understand the meanings and implications of Indian participation in the festival?[1] After a brief overview of the organization and events of the contemporary stampede, I describe how stampede organizers and First Nations leaders understand Indian participation through radically different cultural frameworks. First Nations people are highly ambivalent about staging cultural displays and performances during the stampede. Yet the willingness of some to consider setting up mock Indian villages, powwow performances, and displays of arts and crafts does not reflect an unwitting capitulation to hegemonic symbols and identities. Rather, these individuals are critically aware of the hegemonic implications of presenting their cultural identity in terms that could be assimilated into stereotypical images of noble savages and of the potential for the public to misinterpret the full meaning of Aboriginal cultural practices. They are struggling not over the symbols, images, or roles that they have been assigned within the ritual script but over the power to control the overarching contexts in which cultural identities are being performed. Their willingness to consider participating in the stampede should be considered a case of "strategic essentialism"[2]: a form of political action through which symbols of Indianness are deliberately and carefully mobilized to bring about specific political effects.

### The Origin and Development of the Stampede

The village of Williams Lake was "born" in 1919 with the arrival of the Pacific Great Eastern Railway from the Lower Mainland. That year also marks the beginning of the Williams Lake Stampede. The event was initiated by two local cowboys and several village merchants, who decided to host a small rodeo to gather townspeople, regional residents, and tourists alike to celebrate the birth of the new settlement.

By the 1920s, the stampede had become a regular annual celebration. From the outset, it was organized and run by the elite of the regional society: town businessmen and area ranchers organized the event, and the Roman Catholic priest from St. Joseph's Mission, the local Indian agent, and the area MP and MLA were the judges and honorary presidents. Aboriginal people, particularly Secwepemc and Tsilhqot'in, were enthusiastic participants and spectators, and the stampede soon became the most important annual gathering of Aboriginal people from across the Cariboo-Chilcotin.

The 1920s stampedes consisted of several events now commonly associated with rodeo: roping competitions and bull- and bronc-riding events. Horse races were also featured. There were several novelty races. The most popular were the Roman Race, in which a rider stood astride two horses and galloped down the track, and the Mountain Race, in which challengers raced down a sheer mountainside opposite the stampede grounds. The early stampedes were widely known as occasions for celebrating and drinking, when participants "were a thirsty bunch and later even a little tipsy."[3] The drunkenness and wild abandon of the stampedes were symbolically associated with the imagined Western frontier culture. The stereotypical association between alcohol and the Western cowboy[4] was captured in one novelty event, the Drunken Ride, in which a well-known cowboy feigned drunkenness and ended his performance with one leg over the saddle and his head hanging inches from the ground.[5]

By the 1920s, Aboriginal people of the Cariboo-Chilcotin had become integrated into the ranching economy. They were working as cowboys and labourers on non-Aboriginal ranches and farms or were raising their own small herds of cattle and horses, and many men and women were skilled riders. Aboriginal men actively competed in the stampede events, and certain renowned Aboriginal cowboys dominated the Roman and Mountain Races. At the same time, Aboriginal people's participation as "Indians" was even more symbolically important to the ritual festivities. To understand why this was so requires tracing the ritual genre of the stampede back to its roots in the American Wild West exhibitions of the late 1800s.

Buffalo Bill Cody is credited with developing the first Wild West exhibitions. Outgrowths of travelling circuses, menageries, and vaudeville shows, the Wild West exhibitions, first performed in 1882, continued this tradition of entertaining spectacle. What they presented to the public, however, were dramatizations of purportedly authentic events of American history, specifically the "conquest" and settlement of the Western frontier. This commitment to educating the American (and later the European) public about the real events of American history was evident in Cody's refusal to have the Wild West spectacles billed as "shows." In fact, the Wild West exhibitions and performances enjoyed tremendous popularity, at times playing to audiences of 40,000. Between 1883 and 1916, Buffalo Bill's Wild West toured every major American city and performed throughout Canada and Europe.[6] These events became the most important vehicle for shaping American and Canadian public understandings of the history of the American frontier.[7]

The Wild West exhibitions featured demonstrations of cowboy skills of roping and trick riding. But it was their dramatic reenactments of scenarios from the history of the Western frontier that captured the audience's attention and enthusiasm. These reenactments included displays of precontact Indian life, such as the setting up of mock Indian camps and the performance of Indian dancing. The most exciting reenactments were scenes of the Pony Express rides, buffalo hunts, and Indian attacks on stagecoaches and settlers' cabins. The authenticity of these events was dramatically enhanced by the participation of actual historical figures such as Sitting Bull, Geronimo, and Buffalo Bill Cody himself.[8]

The commodification of Aboriginal people as public spectacles was occurring elsewhere at this time: in the Chicago world exposition of 1893[9] and in the Indian Congresses of the 1890s and the first decade of 1900.[10] These processes parallelled the depiction of the noble savage in museum displays and in artists' renditions of the American west. In the Wild West exhibitions, however, Native Americans were not presented as static curiosities but were incorporated into dramatic scripts of history constructed through the epistemological framework of the frontier myth. As Indians, they were critical to this colonial script: their exotic cultures represented the "primitiveness" of the early inhabitants that would naturally give way to European "civilization"; their resistance to the settlers was essential for the affirmation of a narrative of history as heroic conquest.

These ritual genres soon spread to festivals and fairs across both Canada and the United States. The most prominent public festival in Canada became the Calgary Exhibition and Stampede. Originating in 1923, the annual event featured a rodeo and displays of Indians and Indian culture. As in the later Williams Lake Stampedes, the downtown stores in Calgary erected false fronts to give the appearance of a Western frontier town, and residents were encouraged to dress in Western clothing to add to the festive air.[11]

This ritual complex also provided the symbolic forms for small settler communities to represent and celebrate regional identities and histories.[12] Although horse racing and roping and riding competitions had been popular spectator activities throughout the 1800s, they now became overlaid with Wild West-influenced dramatic reenactments and displays of Indian culture. In the prairie region, Aboriginal people were encouraged to attend small-town fairs, agricultural exhibitions, and rodeos, where they set up camps and performed songs and dances to appreciative audiences.[13]

Aboriginal involvement in both the large city stampedes in Calgary,[14] Banff,[15] and Winnipeg as well as in the small-town fairs was not universally welcomed.[16] Christian missionaries, Indian agents, and government officials in Ottawa believed that these cultural performances encouraged resistance to assimilation, distracted people from farming, and fanned the "excitement of celebrations."[17] In 1914, the Indian Act was amended to prohibit Aboriginal people in Western Canada from participating in "any show, exhibition, performance, stampede or pageant in Aboriginal costume" without government permission. Yet the public support for Indian participation was so great that by 1920 the law had become ineffectual.[18]

In Williams Lake, this ritual genre laid the foundation for the early stampedes. Rodeo contests were the central events. In addition, throughout the 1920s, there was a series of dramatic performances and contests that highlighted frontier themes and Indian-white contrasts. Some novelty races were for Indians only. The Indian Race of 1924 required participants to wear "war bonnets." When Aboriginal people refused to participate, non-Aboriginal people dressed as Indians to play their part. The Squaw Race of 1923 featured two non-Aboriginal women, one wearing a wig made from a horse's tail that "streamed around her shoulders like a squaw's hair would."[19] Spectators were treated to displays of "Indians dancing in their old-time costumes accompanied by the tom-toms and other implements of torture" during the 1926 stampede.[20] The most obvious import from the Wild West exhibitions was the 1924 dramatic performance of "a spectacular stage coach holdup and attack on a Hudson's Bay fort" enacted by "real Indians, Cowboys and Pioneers."[21]

Here the symbols of the American Wild West exhibitions were adapted to the local setting of the Cariboo-Chilcotin. The famous Wild West scene of the Indian attack on the Deadwood stagecoach was Canadianized: it became an attack on an HBC fort. But whereas the symbols were adapted to the Cariboo-Chilcotin context, the frontier history dramatized during the early stampedes had a distinctively American flavour. The master narrative portrayed history as a narrative of regeneration through violence rather than as the narrative of conquest through benevolence that would later emerge as dominant in Canadian versions.

The early stampedes reflected the performative components of the hegemonic culture-as-history. They communicated public myths of identity and history that celebrated the arrival of European settlers and the subordination of the Secwepemc, Tsilhqot'in, and Carrier populations and that relegated conflict over the land and resistance to colonial authority to the comfortable domain of the distant past. Yet the history portrayed was stylized. In the Cariboo-Chilcotin, there is no record of an Aboriginal attack on an HBC fort, nor is their any validity to tom-tom drums being used as implements of torture. In contrast to these dramatizations of Indian-white conflict, throughout the 1800s and early 1900s relations between Aboriginal peoples and settlers in the Cariboo-Chilcotin had been relatively free of violence. What these scenes communicated was a historical fantasy constructed through the framework of the American version of the frontier myth, now popularized through ritual performance.

In the decades that followed, the stampede continued to be the most popular annual gathering for both townspeople and regional residents. Over time, some events were modified and new ones added. Changing images of women were evident in the creation in 1933 of the stampede queen contest. Women had been active competitors in the 1920s stampedes; now, in the queen contests, they were represented in demure, passive roles that stood in sharp contrast to the masculine images of the rodeo cowboys. This changing role for women in rodeo parallelled developments elsewhere in North America as rodeo began to be professionalized in the late 1920s and early 1930s. The gradual exclusion of female competitors from professional rodeo occurred simultaneously to the appearance of "sponsor girls" contests – the precursor of rodeo queen competitions – in which women were selected on the criteria of appearance, dress, and basic horsemanship to represent their communities at regional rodeos.[22]

By the 1950s, the dramatic performance of frontier conflicts was no longer a part of the stampede program. The displays of Indian culture, Indian people, and the Indian/white dichotomy, though, were still central symbolic themes. In the postwar context of a booming economy and a rapid influx of newcomers to the region, organizers of the stampede sought to rejuvenate it. The atrocities of the Nazi Holocaust had raised issues of racial prejudice and violence to the forefront of international public concern. At the same time, Aboriginal people were becoming increasingly visible in romantic, noble savage stereotypes in popular culture, from the tremendous resurgence of Hollywood westerns[23] to the recreational clubs in which non-Aboriginal people learned the dress, arts and crafts, and dances of Native Americans.[24]

In this context, the stampedes of the 1950s enacted new rituals of community identity through which Aboriginal and non-Aboriginal people were represented as existing in a balanced, harmonious relationship. The colonial categories of Indian and white were elevated to new heights of reification with the modification of the stampede queen contest to include both an Indian and a white queen. At the coronation ceremony, the Indian and white queens sat on matched thrones, the Indian queen in decorated buckskin and feathered headband, the white queen in a long white satin gown, tiara, and gloves. Aboriginal people, as Indians, were viewed as an essential component of the stampede festivities. As a newspaper editor of the time said, Indians added "colour and variety" to the event; they were spectacles of curiosity, of exotic interest, that enhanced and completed the town's festive portrait of Western identity and culture.[25]

The 1960s and early 1970s are widely known as the heyday of the Williams Lake Stampede. The economy was prospering, the population was growing, and tourists from across Canada and the United States were flocking to the annual July celebration to watch the rodeo, drink alcohol and party, and attend the all-night dances at Squaw Hall, the open-air dance hall on the stampede grounds. In the 1960s climate of civil rights protests and increased movements toward racial integration, organizers of the stampede decided to amalgamate the Indian and white queen contests into one. But the duality of Indian-white identities was preserved in other aspects. Aboriginal people dressed in buckskin and regalia continued to enter the parade. Secwepemc, Carrier, and Tsilhqot'in families from all across the Cariboo-Chilcotin travelled to the stampede in horse-drawn wagons and vehicles, setting up their canvas tents on the stampede grounds, where they remained for the week visiting with friends and family. The "Indian Camp," as it was known to Euro-Canadian townspeople, became a spectacle of tourist interest and was preserved in tourists' snapshots and artists' paintings.

The decision of stampede organizers to charge fees for camping, and the availability of automobiles for transportation to and from reserve communities, eventually brought an end to the Indian Camp at the stampede grounds. In the 1970s and 1980s, the increased politicization of the Aboriginal communities, and their struggles to address the many dimensions of political, economic, and bureaucratic domination that they experienced, inevitably led to public debates about the role of Aboriginal people in the Williams Lake Stampede. Secwepemc, Tsilhqot'in, and Carrier people had long had their own motives for gathering during stampede time; indeed, by the 1950s, the stampede had become the most important annual occasion for area Aboriginal people to gather and to celebrate an intertribal community that largely excluded townspeople. With camping no longer allowed on the grounds, other dimensions of Aboriginal participation were undergoing scrutiny. Aboriginal people expressed resentment over being assigned the role of noble savages and being economically exploited as tourist attractions. For the first time, both Aboriginal people and Euro-Canadians began to publicly criticize the derogatory image of Aboriginal women contained in the name of Squaw Hall. These criticisms intensified following the publicity and extremely lenient court sentences given to two non-Aboriginal men involved in the 1967 brutal assault and death of Rose Roper, an area Secwepemc woman.

At the same time, area Secwepemc, Tsilhqot'in, and Carrier people were undergoing a cultural revitalization that involved not only a revival of cultural traditions but also an incorporation of significant components of "pan-Indian" cultural traditions of powwows, drumming, dancing, and sweatlodge ceremonies. These cultural traditions increasingly served as a currency for Aboriginal people to communicate to themselves, and to non-Aboriginal audiences, the distinctiveness of their cultural and political identities.[26] In short, symbols of culture that had long been part of the ritual complex of the stampede, as well as part of the symbolic language of identity within the regional Aboriginal communities, now became invigorated as symbols of political power. The political contest ultimately was not over the symbols themselves – feathered headbands, decorated buckskin, and Indian dances – but over their significance and meaning and over how these symbols of cultural identity were to be read and comprehended by the public.

For eight decades, the stampede has served as the major occasion for the ritual performance of the collective identity of Williams Lake as a frontier town, an identity performed not only for local residents but also for tourists and visiting dignitaries, including Princess Margaret and Prime Minister Pierre Trudeau. Throughout its history, there has been a consistent ritual core. What began as historical reenactments of the imagined confrontations between Indians and settlers on the frontier evolved into symbolic displays of the Indian/white dichotomy. Aboriginal people were represented as Indians in highly stylized and restricted roles: as exotic, noble, natural, "colourful" figures. These images fulfilled non-Aboriginal expectations of authenticity that were created and reinforced through other popular cultural representations in movies, literature, and Hobbyist movements. In the context of a town's annual celebration, the Indian-white juxtaposition became a core element, an archetype, in the construction of the town's public identity and history. This archetype, and the frontier myth of history in which it is embedded, continue to provide the major symbols of public identification in the city today.

### Theoretical Frame: Negotiating Identity through Performance

Why have Aboriginal people willingly participated in the stampede? Why have they demonstrated an apparent willingness to adopt the role of "noble savages" and, in Rayna Green's words, to "play Indian"[27] in Euro-Canadian ritual performances?

The stampede, like all small-town festivals, can be read as a narrative performance of the city's myths of history and public ideology. There is a wealth of anthropological literature on cultural performances in which the symbolism and ritual structure of varied events such as rodeo,[28] parades,[29] and small-town festivals[30] can be approached as texts encoding implicit cultural meanings and dramatizing contradictions in the cultural and social order. Because an overriding theme of small-town festivals is community solidarity and harmony, these events can serve to perpetuate public myths that mask social conflict, domination, and inequality. They can be read as rituals of the dominant in which the participation of subordinate groups only symbolizes their compliance with, and acceptance of, the inequalities that have rendered them powerless and marginalized. From this analytical approach, though, agency is underemphasized, and the participation of subordinate groups can be read as evidence of how fully the hegemonic culture has infiltrated their consciousness and practices.

Some anthropologists are now shifting attention away from a textual reading of cultural performances and toward exploring how subordinate groups are using rituals and festivals as occasions to challenge the dominant ideologies and structures of power in which they are enmeshed.[31] Meaning is approached not as a disembodied text but as construed through social action, becoming the subject of struggle by different groups within the context of the ritual itself. For example, Dorothy Holland and Debra Skinner show how the participation of Nepalese women in Tij festivals provides a rare opportunity for women to generate and express new and politicized identities concerning their subordinate position within the patriarchal family and structures of the state. Fred Myers, analyzing the performance of Australian Aboriginal sand-painting ritual in a New York art gallery, discusses how the Aboriginal artists sought to capitalize on Western fascination with Aboriginal exoticism while at the same time subverting static colonial stereotypes through the *performance* of multiple constructions of Aboriginality. Julie Cruikshank identifies similar processes at a Yukon Aboriginal storytelling festival. In the context of recent land claims settlements and shifting political relationships between Aboriginal and non-Aboriginal populations of the territory, storytellers challenged the Euro-Canadian audience's notions of static traditional culture by using stories to assert a variety of contemporary Aboriginal identities and to comment on and critique the past and present state of Aboriginal/non-Aboriginal relations.

In short, what may appear to be a submission to colonial stereotypes, and what may appear to be instances of Aboriginal people "playing Indian," emerge from a lack of appreciation for the multiple meanings at play in ritual contexts and for the way in which Aboriginal people are using modes of cultural performance not only to express distinct cultural meanings and identities but also to subvert and challenge dominant colonial stereotypes. Ritual performance itself may constitute a mode of resistance to the dominant culture.

In the following pages, I present a brief overview of the Williams Lake Stampede today: its organization, its major events, and the domains in which Aboriginal people participate. I then turn to a series of interviews that I conducted with stampede organizers and area First Nations leaders regarding Aboriginal participation. I show how Euro-Canadian organizers of the stampede and First Nations leaders understand the implications of Aboriginal participation, especially under the rubric of cultural displays, through radically different frameworks of meaning and signification. I show how Aboriginal people are attempting to negotiate their way through the minefield of hegemonic symbols to carve out a space for the expression of their identities and concerns and to promote positive images of Indianness to both Aboriginal and non-Aboriginal audiences.

## The Stampede Today: Organization, Events, and Aboriginal Involvement

The stampede remains the most important annual celebration in Williams Lake. Stampede pictures and murals are displayed in the local library, in the museum, and in city hall. The city promotes itself as the stampede capital; its official mascot is a humorous cowboy figure, Williams Lake Willie, that represents the city in other regional summer festivals and parades. The stampede is not only a major source of symbols of community identity but also a major economic event. Virtually every motel and hotel room is booked for the four-day period in early July. One retailer referred to the stampede period as a "cowboy Christmas," the second most important time of the year for retail sales. The Chamber of Commerce unofficially estimates that the stampede brings in almost $1 million to the city's economy.

The festival is run by a nonprofit society, the Stampede Association, led by a board of directors who are elected to two-year terms. In 1994, almost half the board had some background in ranching or rodeo and about a third were small-business owners, and the majority were relative newcomers to the association. The Stampede Association, in fact, has for decades had strong ties to the city's business community, which has financially supported the festival through loans, annual donations, and sponsorships. The Stampede Association's political relationship with the municipal government, in contrast, is delicate. In the past, the association has criticized city council for not providing more financial and political support, given that the stampede is a major economic boon to the city and that the event is organized entirely by volunteer labour. Apart from one city councillor who represents the city on the stampede board of directors, there is no overlap in personnel. Finally, despite the active involvement of many Aboriginal people in the regional rodeo circuit, the Stampede Association is overwhelmingly a non-Aboriginal organization. No Aboriginal people are on the board of directors. Of the ninety-two volunteers recognized in the city newspaper in 1994, none was publicly recognized as Aboriginal, although eight volunteers were privately known to have mixed ancestry.

In short, a small sector of the regional society is responsible for controlling the public culture presented through the stampede festivities. An equally important factor in shaping the stampede is the weight of its ritual legacy. Although the directors may introduce a certain amount of change and innovation, there is a consistent core. The same events are found in many other small festivals across Canada and the United States.[32] Local service groups hold pancake breakfasts and steak dinners in the grocery store parking lots. Midway rides and games of chance are set up outside the rodeo grounds. Street sales, children's amusements, and musical entertainment fill the downtown streets. In the evenings, various dances are held, from the relatively quiet Kiwanis Club's Klondike dance to the rowdy barn dances in the civic arena. Finally, there is the stampede queen contest and the parade, the latter typically drawing huge crowds.

The centrepiece of the stampede, though, is the three-day professional rodeo. The rodeo is on the Canadian Professional Rodeo Association circuit and draws competitors from across Canada and the United States to enter events such as saddle bronc riding, bareback riding, bull riding, calf roping, steer wrestling, and women's barrel racing. Although hometown riders may enter the stampede on a "local" card, the high quality of the competition has dissuaded many from competing, and for the most part the rodeo has lost its earlier local flavour.

Contemporary rodeo has evolved from the turn-of-the-century Wild West exhibitions and the small-town rodeo competitions,[33] and what it retains is the symbolic legacy of earlier dramatizations of frontier history. Elizabeth Atwood Lawrence, in her symbolic analysis of rodeo, finds that the contests between men and wild animals – bulls and bucking broncs – are performative representations of America's imagined past. These events symbolize the human conquest of nature and the bringing of the wild into the domain of the civilized: "Rodeo embodies the frontier spirit as manifested through the aggressive and exploitative conquest of the West, and deals with nature and the reordering of nature according to the dictates of this ethos. It supports the value of subjugating nature, and reenacts the 'taming' process whereby the wild is brought under control."[34] The persistence of frontier imagery in contemporary professional rodeos is apparent in the mock Indian villages that continue to be set up at the Calgary Stampede as well as at the major rodeos at Omak, Washington, and Pendleton, Oregon. Williams Lake Stampede organizers, aware of the Indian presence in these other rodeos, continue to encourage Aboriginal participation as part of what the organizers define as the rodeo tradition.

Aboriginal people do participate in the stampede's events. Secwepemc and Tsilhqot'in riders enter the rodeo events and are highly competitive. On occasion, an Aboriginal woman enters the stampede queen contest, and in 1997 a Tsilhqot'in woman, Daana Gilpin, won the title. Aboriginal and non-Aboriginal people alike fill the rodeo grandstands and line the streets to watch the stampede parade.

The parade typically includes several Aboriginal entries. In 1994, there were two Aboriginal country-rock bands. One float carried the Alkali Lake First Nation girls' soccer team, which had done very well in a city soccer league. There was an entry representing the First Nations-run Nenqayni Alcohol and Drug Treatment Centre, carrying old-time fiddlers and assorted men, women, children, and elders. Some wore regular dress, whereas others wore buckskin or powwow regalia. One teenager carried a hand drum.

In 1994, two Aboriginal entries drew on explicitly cultural themes to present themselves to the audience. The Anaham First Nation's float presented a potpourri of cultural images. Children, adults, and elders, some in regular dress and others in powwow regalia or buckskin clothing, sat or stood on the back of a flatbed truck. A banner announced "the Anaham Band proudly presents the Chilcotin Dancers." Two *lahal* teams were seated facing each other, one side singing and playing hand drums.[35] One man wore a headdress of bright red, orange, and yellow feathers. There was a small tipi draped in an orange-and-blue plastic covering. In the midst of this was a baby swinging in a cradle suspended between two uprights. The second Aboriginal entry presented two young women: the Miss Chief Anaham Princess, and the runner-up to the Miss First Nations Awareness Days contest of 1994. The women wore ribboned powwow dresses and moccasins and sat on the hood of a pickup truck, waving to the crowd as they passed.[36]

In short, Aboriginal participation in the stampede occurs in a variety of contexts: as spectators, as competitors, and as performers. Parades can be considered symbolic representations of community;[37] Aboriginal people, by presenting themselves in this forum, are publicly demanding the right to be acknowledged as visible and respectable members of the regional society. Their participation in the parade under the banner of various symbols – musical bands, sports teams, and distinct cultural groups – reflects the diverse ways in which they construct their identity in various social contexts of everyday life and the diverse ways in which they attempt to negotiate their visibility to non-Aboriginal society.

The cultural entries, however, entail the greatest risk. In a regional society in which racial discrimination is prevalent, the cultural groups are claiming the right to be publicly recognized and respected as Indians.[38] Given this context, it is somewhat ironic that the First Nations princess entry consistently drew the loudest and most enthusiastic applause of all the parade's floats.[39] The image of the Indian princess, of course, is a key stereotype of North American culture. This stereotype has long been evoked to symbolize the receptivity of Native North America to European colonizers.[40] In the Pocahontas myth, the Indian princess intervenes to save the life of her European male captor, becoming the ultimate goodwill ambassador and an ideal model of Aboriginal/non-Aboriginal relations.[41] In the contemporary setting of the Cariboo-Chilcotin, ideological space continues to be allotted to this stereotype.

The symbolic currency that Aboriginal people use to represent their identities to non-Aboriginal audiences includes images that resonate with the stereotypes found in mainstream popular culture – tipis, artificial feathered headdresses, Indian princesses – and images of hand drumming, *lahal,* and baby swaddling, common practices in reserve communities. It makes little sense, though, to attempt to analytically distinguish the "authentic" from the "invented" cultural symbols. For over seven decades, images from North American popular culture have been incorporated into the ritual symbolism of the stampede. For over seven decades, and probably longer, Aboriginal peoples in the region have presented themselves to the non-Aboriginal public in formal regalia of headdresses and buckskin. To chase the origins of these ritual symbols – whether they are "traditional" to the Secwepemc, Tsilhqot'in, and Carrier, or whether they are "invented" traditions adopted from the dominant Euro-Canadian culture – is largely irrelevant. What is critical to appreciate is how symbols of identity evolve in the context of historical relationships between Aboriginal and non-Aboriginal populations, how the meaning of these symbols is subject to varying interpretations and becomes transformed over time, and how today these symbols continue to provide a currency for the ongoing negotiation of identities.

## Performing Indianness in the Stampede: Euro-Canadian and Aboriginal Perspectives

### Stampede Organizers' Perspectives

The organizers of the Williams Lake Stampede whom I spoke with unanimously want area Aboriginal people to set up tipi villages, craft displays, and drumming/dancing performances on the stampede grounds. In recent years, the stampede has been declining in popularity. As part of their project to encourage public participation, stampede organizers are attempting to rejuvenate the festival to bring back the local emphasis that characterized the stampedes of the 1960s and early 1970s. Aboriginal people, organizers claim, have always been a part of the stampede tradition. In particular, many organizers referred to the way that Aboriginal people would arrive at the stampede in horse-drawn wagons to camp out on the grounds for the week. The Indian Camp was the focal point of Aboriginal participation, and current organizers would like to see parallel displays of culture in the present. Organizers realize that displays of Aboriginal culture would be of major economic benefit to the Williams Lake Stampede and would draw tourists and their dollars, as do the Indian displays at the Omak and Pendleton rodeos.

Stampede organizers also believe strongly that Aboriginal people would benefit from displaying their culture during the stampede. As one organizer commented, "We approached the Native community to participate, like they do at Omak and Pendleton, where they set up tipi villages. It gives them an opportunity to display their heritage, to sell and market arts and crafts, displays of Native dancing. Unfortunately, nothing happened on that. They were part of it before and should be a part ... The whole Native thing is a touchy situation. We have put invitations out, we will help them financially. We've put the ball in their court. They have all the opportunity to display their culture." Organizers see the advantages of Aboriginal involvement through the lens of small-town entrepreneurial values: it would give them an opportunity to market their culture to the public and to engage in the capitalist economy. Stampede organizers think that Aboriginal people are missing a chance to display their heritage. They know that audiences would be highly appreciative, and they see nothing problematic about representing identity through these cultural displays.

When Aboriginal people conform to Euro-Canadian expectations of comportment, they are praised; when they resist, they are criticized. Stampede organizers recognize that local Aboriginal/Euro-Canadian relations are "touchy," and most respect Aboriginal peoples' decision not to participate. But in frustration, some slipped into moral judgments. One mentioned that in 1993 an Aboriginal man from the Chilcotin offered to organize a powwow during the stampede, but "two months before the stampede he came back and said it couldn't be done." He continued: "We'd love to have something Native on the grounds, but they can't seem to get it organized."[42] Another commented: "We tried [to get Aboriginal people involved]. They just weren't interested. They ... it's an awful thing to say, and I don't know how to word it any other way ... are lazy. I hate to say that, but basically that's what it boiled down to, when we were trying. None of them wanted to come in and do it."

These remarks do not characterize the stampede organization as a whole, but nevertheless they are worthy of analysis. They reflect a classical Canadian tradition in which Euro-Canadians – often with the best of intentions – have persistently sought to mould Aboriginal people into various ideals of dress and comportment and have responded with collective condemnations of Aboriginal people when they have resisted non-Aboriginal forms of control.[43] Aboriginal resistance is comprehended only as confirmation of their inferiority – their laziness, their lack of organizational skills – and their inability to know what is in their best interests.

It is not only these traditions that contribute to the gulf of understanding between the stampede organizers and area First Nations leaders but also the very nature of local Aboriginal/non-Aboriginal relations, where social contact between the groups is circumscribed. Stampede organizers have made tentative overtures to First Nations people through informal networks: they contact those Aboriginal individuals whom they know through the rodeo circuit or with whom they have had dealings. Organizers, as far as I know, have not approached reserve communities through formal channels by contacting the official political leaders of area reserves or tribal councils, although one individual hoped that in the following year a person on the board would be explicitly designated to solicit Aboriginal input and involvement. Furthermore, the "touchiness" of Aboriginal/non-Aboriginal relations is mutual; First Nations leaders are equally reluctant to enter into these discussions. Their reluctance, however, is due not to laziness or a lack of incentive but to their concern with the more complex issues of power, relations of inequality, and symbolic modes of domination.

**First Nations Perspectives**

Since the 1970s Aboriginal people in the region have been using a variety of symbols and ritual practices to express and convey their Aboriginal identities. But there is also a debate within Secwepemc, Tsilhqot'in, and Carrier communities regarding the legitimacy of these symbols of identity, and to what extent they can, or should, be used to represent cultural identity to non-Aboriginal audiences. I will limit my discussion to the various Secwepemc opinions on this matter, with whom most of my ethnographic work has been carried out.

Some Secwepemc people debate the legitimacy of these cultural symbols and rituals in terms of their "authenticity." Not all Secwepemc people attend powwows or sweatlodge ceremonies. Some individuals dismiss sweatlodge ceremonies, as well as other recently popular spiritual practices such as the Plains Indian pipe ceremonies and Sun Dances, as "imported culture." They argue that these practices are not traditional to the Secwepemc. They see these ceremonies as carrying no meaning, and they worry that those who engage in them are being misled by spiritual leaders of dubious integrity.

Other Secwepemc people find meaning in powwow dances and sweatlodge ceremonies, but they do not personally support the idea of performing such rituals for non-Aboriginal audiences. Their concern is not with the legitimacy of cultural symbols of identity, but with the meanings that may be conveyed, and the stereotypes that may be affirmed. Some argue that dressing in Indian regalia and "parading for whites" is a degrading spectacle. Others argue that conveying identity through these essentialist images ultimately limits the audience's ability to appreciate the full individuality, diversity, and humanity of Aboriginal people. They voice resentment at the power of the Euro-Canadian festival organizers to control the terms – and the symbols – for their participation in the event. Commenting on the manner in which Euro-Canadians have assigned Aboriginal people a status of virtual invisibility in the regional social landscape, one leader remarked in frustration, "There's no room for us as tourist attractions, but when we want to be human, the door is shut." Ultimately, these individuals are drawing attention to the fact that the meaning of cultural performance is derived from the broader context of power relations, in which non-Aboriginal residents still hold privileged control over when Aboriginal people will be acknowledged and on whose terms. At the everyday level of informal social interaction, these terms of recognition often are limited to a restricted range of identities: the drunk Indian, the Indian criminal, the noble savage.

Mediating these positions are a few First Nations individuals who are willing to act as "cultural bridges" and who on occasion do coordinate Aboriginal cultural performances and displays for non-Aboriginal audiences. Among these are elected First Nations chiefs and past chiefs as well as individuals employed in the public service. All, by virtue of their position, have taken on roles of advocacy for Aboriginal people in their dealings with non-Aboriginal society. In the last few years, for example, these leaders have organized cross-cultural training workshops to introduce the regional police, court workers, judges, social services workers, and school teachers to Aboriginal cultural beliefs, values, and spiritual practices such as pipe ceremonies and sweatlodge ceremonies. They believe in the potential for such cultural performances to bridge the gap in understanding between the Aboriginal and non-Aboriginal populations and to improve the tenor of social relations in the city.

Yet these First Nations leaders also have ambivalent attitudes toward participating in the stampede festivities as adjunct sideshows to the larger ritual and where they lack the full control over the terms of their participation. They share a strong conviction that stampede organization, and the Williams Lake community generally, take the Aboriginal presence for granted, misinterpret cultural performances, and benefit economically from displays of Aboriginal heritage while returning little to the reserve communities. One individual commented: "What I want to know is, what is Williams Lake willing to put in? Let's talk money! The stampede has been commercialized now. It's a money-making thing. We want to benefit too ... The town of Williams Lake doesn't do nothing for [our] Band. We spend between $100,000 and $120,000 every month in town, in the local businesses ... and the town doesn't do nothing for us!"

Some leaders are concerned about being spatially marginalized during the stampede festivities, about being sequestered in small spaces and forced into secondary roles that diminish the importance of Aboriginal culture. One individual commented, with some frustration: "There isn't a place in the stampede grounds big enough for us to do anything during stampede. If we're going to put up ten or twelve tipis, as well as a place to sell arts and crafts, and what we need for Native awareness – bannock, jarred fruit – also big enough to hold a powwow and *lahal* games, we're going to need lots of space. They [the stampede organizers] said 'Great!' But we said, 'No: there's no place big enough during stampede week!'"

One individual saw these issues in a deeper historical context, arguing that the history of Aboriginal involvement in the stampede is one in which Euro-Canadians have controlled the terms of Aboriginal participation, including and excluding them when convenient: "In the beginning stages, Native people were the rodeo. And then the white people came in and they took control over it. And then they had their dances, and First Nations people weren't allowed to go there, so they built this other hall [Squaw Hall] that the people were having so much fun at, then that place was taken over!"

The most controversial event, still resented by those area Aboriginal people who remember the earlier stampedes, was the Stampede Association's decision in the 1970s to charge Aboriginal people for camping on the grounds. In earlier times, the fact that Aboriginal people camped on the grounds and were allowed into the rodeo for free was taken as a sign of Euro-Canadian recognition that the stampede grounds were located on traditional Aboriginal territory. With the policy shifts of the 1970s, Aboriginal people were "pushed out" of the stampede and their traditional rights were denied.

Given this historical context, First Nations leaders see the current tensions with the stampede organizers as rooted in the issues of control: "I don't think they want to see First Nations people empowering themselves. They want to keep control ... Our people have always responded to them when they tell our people what to do. But now our people are becoming empowered, so [Aboriginal people] don't [respond] ... We do speak up. I think people are very uncomfortable about that."

Conflicts over representation in the stampede are rooted in two drastically different conceptions of history. To First Nations people, their increasing struggle to control the terms in which Aboriginal cultural identity is publicly defined is part of a broader process in which they are challenging the multiple dimensions of more concrete forms of political and economic domination by the Indian Affairs bureaucracy, the Canadian justice system, the provincial agencies managing Crown lands, or the forestry and mining companies exploiting natural resources. The control of public definitions of Aboriginal identity has long been an important part of these processes of domination.

In contrast, many non-Aboriginal people approach these issues from a historical perspective in which relations of power have become so naturalized as to become invisible. Many do not acknowledge racism to exist in the Cariboo-Chilcotin; they do not question the legitimacy of the histories they read in school textbooks or popular pioneer autobiographies; and they do not consider their own common-sense beliefs about Aboriginal people – whether seen in negative or romantic images – to have any bearing on relations of power. In fact, the very existence of relations of power, and their own implication in these relations, are not recognized. Community festivals, further, are widely promoted as lighthearted forms of family entertainment devoid of ideological and political content.[44] The politicization of festivals, through Aboriginal boycott or protest, is typically seen as an inappropriate introduction of contentious issues into an apolitical event.[45] As a result, there remains a gulf in understanding between stampede organizers and First Nations leaders over the problematic nature of Aboriginal involvement in the festival.

### The Strategies of Performance: Aboriginal Rationales

Despite their concerns, a few First Nations leaders did express an interest in participating in the stampede under certain conditions. These leaders are willing to represent cultural identity through a variety of symbols of Indianness: putting up tipis; setting up booths selling bannock, jarred fruit, and crafts; and staging *lahal* games, powwows, and drumming performances. These leaders are not unconcerned with the potential for general audiences to misconstrue the meaning of cultural performances. Their willingness to use these symbols of cultural identity to communicate with non-Aboriginal audiences must be understood in terms of the broader constraints on their ability to negotiate identity in the Cariboo-Chilcotin and, given these limitations, their pragmatic political intentions and their strategic considerations of the dual audiences to whom they are directing their displays and performances.

The hegemony of colonial stereotypes lies not in the symbols themselves but in the epistemological power exercised by dominant groups to control the meanings of these symbols. As Patrick Wolfe has argued with regard to Australian Aborigines' entanglement within the symbols of colonialism, "to acquire a hegemonic language is to submit to a framework in which local meanings can take on unpredictable significance in relation to oppositions or associations whose determination is independent of local factors."[46] When Aboriginal people in the Cariboo-Chilcotin engage in powwow drumming, dancing, and sweatlodge ceremonies in reserve settings, how individuals experience and interpret these events is contained within local fields of understanding (although as I have indicated, these local fields also are heterogeneous). For a number of people, these practices have become the means for expressing deeply rooted feelings of identity, spirituality, and belonging. But to non-Aboriginal audiences reared on Hollywood movies and pulp Western novels, these practices may take on quite different signification, resonating instead with the stereotypical images of the noble savage that are embedded in popular Canadian culture. At the very least, the manner in which audiences understand and interpret these performances becomes unpredictable when these practices are transported beyond contexts controlled by Aboriginal people. The use of such symbols and practices, so easily absorbed into hegemonic constructs of exotic otherness, does not necessarily contribute to the subjugation and powerlessness of the Aboriginal population. What it does mean is that public performances of Aboriginality are sites defined by the confrontation of multiple epistemologies variously privileged by social fields of power.

Aboriginal people of the Cariboo-Chilcotin are acutely sensitive to the epistemological power of the dominant society: the ability of non-Aboriginal people to misconstrue Aboriginal behaviours and utterances as evidence of the drunk Indian or the Indian criminal stereotype, the ability of non-Aboriginal politicians and lawyers to misconstrue the history of British Columbia so as to deflect and deny claims of Aboriginal rights. They are also sensitive to the hegemonic potential of images of the noble savage. Non-Aboriginal people, one Tsilhqot'in leader pointed out, frequently overlook the way in which powwows, dancing, and drumming embody the most central values of Aboriginal societies, treating these performances as if they were shows or spectacles, "like the Shrine circus." He continued: "They don't see the importance of our spiritual and cultural values that are exercised through powwows and drumming. The drummers are into their own spirituality for the drum, eh, and the dancers are also into their own spirituality for honouring the great spirit and mother earth. It's not just a cultural show, but there is spirituality involved."

The risk is not only that non-Aboriginal audiences will misinterpret these performances but also that these performances will be dismissed as inauthentic by some Aboriginal people themselves. Nevertheless, most leaders were not overly concerned with tracing the authenticity of these practices. Instead, they responded by adopting a model of culture remarkably similar to those now advocated by contemporary anthropologists, through which notions of a static, bounded, traditional culture have been deconstructed and replaced by a model that highlights the dynamic and creative nature of cultural systems. This very fluidity, one Secwepemc individual claimed, constitutes Aboriginal tradition:

> All people from the past have learned to borrow. There has been a lot of borrowing. It's a continuation of that trend from the past. What it does is build on the model, the model style ... If you look at some of our elders, when they dance – that's a borrowed thing. That's been going on for years. See, the other thing too is that we lost a lot of our cultural traditions. It's not what it is today. Yet that's part of ... our people are searching for

> identity. And that's what we're taking back from the earth. That's who we're becoming. We're slowly becoming this style. We use whatever it is. We're still following our traditions.

A similar understanding of tradition was voiced by another Secwepemc leader:

> What else can we do? We've lost everything. We don't have any memory of what we did before ... I think sometimes you get fooled into thinking the only way we can be a true Indian is to live how people did 100 years ago ... Tradition evolves. It's ongoing every day. It's not something that happened 100 years ago. People start traditions today, and people do, every day ... And if it doesn't work, it disappears. If it does, it gets lodged as tradition ... and that's what we're doing now, saying that some of the things we did then aren't good for us now ... We don't have to keep going as they did.

When engaging in cultural performances, then, First Nations leaders are aware that they are entering into fields of competing definitions of the very nature of Aboriginal culture and tradition.

Despite these endemic risks, some First Nations leaders were willing to consider organizing cultural displays and performances in the overarching context of stampede festivities. Their motivations had to do with their own pragmatic political concerns and with their assessments of their potential audiences. Furthermore, they were willing to become involved only if they could exercise total control over the terms, conditions, and processes through which these performances would be held.

These leaders thought that cultural performances, when directed to general audiences, could only raise the public profile of Aboriginal people of the region. These individuals are explicitly attempting to counter not only the negative stereotypes of Indianness but also the widespread invisibility of Aboriginal people to the regional society. Thus, one individual believed that not participating would only further Aboriginal invisibility to Euro-Canadians. Aboriginal culture "gets most misunderstood when you don't see anything," he commented. Another thought that participating in the stampede would counteract Euro-Canadian tendencies to "see" only Aboriginal people who conform to their preconceived stereotypes of the drunk Indian, as epitomized by the category of the Troopers. Aboriginal cultural displays "would be an eye opener for the people of Williams Lake," because people would realize that the Aboriginal people "they see on the streets aren't the only ones around." While these strategies may reflect the degree to which the dominant culture has restricted Aboriginal modes of resistance – that Aboriginal people have to submit to images of cultural exoticism to capture "positive" non-Aboriginal attention – Aboriginal agency has nevertheless survived. These decisions are being taken with an eye to their practical implications: positive images of Indianness may afford some temporary relief to the continual denial of worth to which Aboriginal people are subjected through many forms of everyday racism.

Furthermore, such performances may create a context for people to express and renew positive cultural identities among themselves. First Nations leaders felt strongly that these positive, public assertions of Indianness within the context of stampede festivities would also be of great benefit to area Aboriginal people in boosting their cultural pride and self-esteem. As one individual remarked, "I think all of these types of activities [tipis, *lahal,* fish barbecues, booths for arts and crafts] will ... make our young people, and even our older people, be proud of who we are. We need to be very visible. In a positive way." The fact that these performances would be enacted in the risky setting of a Euro-Canadian festival only enhances their political significance: rather than undermining Aboriginal meanings, the public Euro-Canadian festival context transforms these performances into defiant assertions of moral worth and integrity. When directed at Aboriginal audiences, the question of non-Aboriginal audience response becomes irrelevant to these leaders. It is the very juxtaposition of dominant and subordinate constructions of the meaning of Aboriginal culture that would empower these performances as modes of resistance to the dominant Euro-Canadian culture.

In order to negotiate issues of identity and history with non-Aboriginal audiences, First Nations leaders of the Cariboo-Chilcotin must first develop a means to command public attention. They must develop a means to counteract their widespread invisibility in many other dimensions of their relations with non-Aboriginal people. Previous chapters have described how Aboriginal people are mobilizing their economic power as consumers, their political strength in current provincial treaty policies, and their moral power as victims of racial discrimination in order to challenge various aspects of their position within the regional society. In the ritual context of the Williams Lake Stampede, First Nations leaders are contemplating manipulating the power inherent in the public's fascination with "Indian culture," and the centrality of Indians in the stampede's ritual script, in order to draw attention to issues of cultural pride, power, and racism in local social relations. First Nations leaders are making use of the unwitting power that they can draw from the "colonial gaze" to begin this process of renegotiating the meaning of Aboriginality.

As James Carrier points out, there are dangers inherent in "ethno-Orientalisms," essentialist representations of Aboriginality by Aboriginal people themselves. These constructions can "mislead and have unfortunate consequences if they are applied unreflectively in novel situations."[47] The danger of these homogeneous representations of otherness, however, lies not in the representations themselves but in how they are used and in their social, political, and economic consequences. Furthermore, the leaders whom I interviewed are not unreflective or naïve but are experienced players in the contemporary politics of identity. As various scholars of colonialism have argued, strategic essentialisms may be extremely powerful representational strategies both for mobilizing indigenous peoples into collective political action and for advancing their collective political interests in particular historical and political contexts.[48] But First Nations leaders in the Cariboo-Chilcotin are not rhetorically committed to these essentialisms. In many other contexts, as I have discussed, Aboriginal people are deconstructing essentialist stereotypes and/or are making claims to equality and similarity with other non-Aboriginal Canadians through a rhetoric based on drawing "strategic *equivalences*" with their non-Aboriginal audiences. In the ritual context, however, by virtue of the power engendered in the colonial category of the Indian, engaging in cultural displays and performances of Indianness is a powerful political strategy.

First Nations leaders, like anthropologists, at times *are* concerned with tradition, authenticity, and the hegemony of colonial symbols. In private settings, powwow songs, dancing, sweatlodge ceremonies, and other spiritual events are providing the means for experiencing and expressing unique identities. Increasingly, these practices and performances are being used as a language to express identity to non-Aboriginal audiences. These individuals are concerned with the difficulties of cross-cultural translation and the potential for general audiences to misinterpret cultural performances. The risks of miscommunication, though, are outweighed by the pragmatic political potential that these performances bring to the enhancement of Aboriginal self pride and the improvement in local social relations. Although neither First Nations leaders nor anthropologists can predict with certainty the outcomes of their representations, the intentionality of those agents, and the considerations and forces that guide and constrain their choices of action, are critical to trace for understanding the continuing and determined efforts of Aboriginal people to use "old" symbols to negotiate new identities and relationships with non-Aboriginal audiences.

# 8
# The Frontier Complex: Conclusions and Comments

The dominant culture of the Williams Lake region is strongly marked by its economic dependence on resource industries. As a northern resource city, it has a distinctly working-class ethos, in which manual labour, small-business entrepreneurialism, competitiveness, materialism, and right-wing populist egalitarianism are primary public values, and in which there exists a strong sense of marginalization, powerlessness, and resentment of urban government forms of regulation and control. Yet the dominant culture is not just an outgrowth of the economic structures and relationships common to hinterland resource communities. The regional culture is rooted in a much deeper complex of understandings about history, society, and identity, a complex that can be thematically ordered by the idea of the frontier. To unravel the threads of this cultural complex is to reveal how deeply imprinted it is by Canada's colonial legacy.

I have followed some of the more important threads of this complex through vignettes of different domains of cultural representation and practice. Similar cultural processes could have been traced in other settings: in debates over developments in heritage tourism, such as the Alexander Mackenzie Grease Trail; in the public discourse surrounding the Cariboo-Chilcotin Justice Inquiry of 1992-3; in the more confrontational debates about history that are arising in public meetings discussing Aboriginal treaties; or in the daily struggles that occur between the chiefs, councillors, and staff of First Nations band offices and the officers of the Department of Indian and Northern Affairs, where the culture of paternal control takes an extreme form. My goal has been to draw out the connections between these different aspects of ordinary life; in particular, I have tried to draw together the cultural themes and processes that link explicit histories, historical consciousness, and everyday practice among Euro-Canadians. More concretely, my goal has been to identify how a modern colonial culture works at the level of everyday life not only through the manipulation of concepts of Aboriginal/Euro-Canadian difference but also through the control of definitions of public identities, histories, and present realities; through aligning experience within a contemporary historical epistemology profoundly shaped by the colonial context; and through attempts to counter competing definitions of history, identity, and experience put forth by Aboriginal people.

In this final chapter, I summarize some of the main features of the frontier complex, suggest some of the ways in which this local cultural complex corresponds to cultural traditions found in Canada more generally, and highlight some implications for understanding the current political debates regarding Aboriginal title, rights, and treaties in British Columbia.

At its most immediate level, the frontier complex is framed by a particular historical epistemology that celebrates the "discovery" of a rich, "empty" land by non-Aboriginal explorers and settlers. These heroic figures tame the wilderness and subdue Aboriginal populations through a process of benevolent conquest, in so doing rendering colonization a natural and desired process of the domination by a superior civilization over primitive, inferior peoples. Vignettes of the encounter, conflict, and conquest of nature and Aboriginal peoples become the epitomizing events in Canadian national histories and are a continual source of symbols for the creation and re-creation of Canadian national identity.

In contrast to the narrative theme of regeneration through violence that dominates American versions of the frontier myth, in the public histories that prevail in the Cariboo-Chilcotin region "conquest" was achieved not only through violence but also through benevolence: through Aboriginal peoples' purported acknowledgment of and childlike submission to the benevolent paternalism and superiority of the settlers, missionaries, and government agents. The rhetoric of benevolence as a justification of colonization, of course, is not unique to Canadian popular histories or to Canadian Indian Affairs policies. What is significant is the degree to which the idea of benevolence has come to frame contemporary assertions of Canadian national identity. Despite the centrality of the rhetoric of benevolence in the development of Indian policy in the United States,[1] in Canada benevolence has been transformed into an icon of national identity, serving as a founding concept by which non-Aboriginal people understand and legitimate their ongoing relationships with Aboriginal peoples.

The frontier myth is ubiquitous in public settings: bookstores, tourism pamphlets, museum displays, restaurant placemats, advertising slogans, and public festivals. The frontier myth, through its set of symbols, metaphors, and narrative structures, provides a structured way of looking at history in which "truths" are communicated intuitively and indirectly, appealing to imagination, fantasy, and emotion rather than through the direct, intellectual argument of scholarly historical narratives. Nevertheless, the frontier myth is capable of great flexibility and is regularly drawn upon to express a variety of interests and identities. The nationalistic agenda of high school history textbooks contrasts with the localized expression of historical identities through settler reminiscences and pioneer autobiographies; both, though, draw on the frontier myth's narratives and images to celebrate the process of colonization. The degree to which this historical epistemology is drawn upon by local residents to structure their life histories indicates how deeply the frontier myth has become lodged in everyday cultural practice.

The hegemonic potential of frontier histories lies not only in the way that they celebrate European settlement of Canada and the subjugation of Aboriginal peoples. It also lies in their sheer bulk. Non-Aboriginal Canadians, for the most part, have privileged access to the material forces that control the production of public history, and frontier histories dominate the public landscape in Williams Lake. Aboriginal perspectives are almost completely absent. History, we are told, began with European arrival in the Cariboo-Chilcotin; the pre-European history of the Secwepemc, Tsilhqot'in, and Carrier people is dismissed. The impact of European settlement, the Aboriginal land question and the failure of governments to acquire Aboriginal lands by due process, and the repressive modes of legal and bureaucratic control exercised over Aboriginal communities in the Cariboo-Chilcotin go virtually unmentioned. In contrast to the highly stylized, scripted appearance of Indians as hostile warriors, noble childlike savages, squaws, or drunks, the existence of Aboriginal peoples with complex cultures and histories that extend back far beyond the recent arrival of Europeans is rendered invisible.

First Nations leaders throughout the Cariboo-Chilcotin are forced to confront the terms of the frontier myth as they work to gain public recognition for Aboriginal title and rights and to secure a respected place as autonomous and self-governing communities within the context of non-Aboriginal society. Yet their struggle is not just against texts, not just against a literary tradition of imagining the past. The frontier myth as a selective historical tradition exists at a much deeper level, as a historical epistemology that provides a conceptual framework and a symbolic language for understanding past and present. The frontier myth also weaves through prevalent representations of Euro-Canadian identity and public values, and it is occasionally the source of powerful symbols embedded in the rhetoric of Euro-Canadian political discourse.

The clearest example of this process is in the way that Euro-Canadians use the symbol of the pioneer to criticize government actions and to defend their varied political interests. Speakers create populist versions of a frontier history that they juxtapose with the reality of the present as a form of social and political critique. The language of the frontier myth may be drawn upon to create local identities and histories that alternately resonate with Canadian nationalist histories or distinguish Cariboo-Chilcotin residents from urban Canadian society. Yet the very use of the term "pioneer" in political discourse implicitly affirms the unquestioned legitimacy and morality of the process of colonization. These "clichés of historical memory" are powerful condensed symbols that intuitively convey an entire historical scenario valorizing colonial conquest. Again, that these key symbols and metaphors flow through everyday language and political discourse demonstrates how fully the frontier myth, as a selective historical tradition that has emerged within the colonial context, has come to define the common-sense cultural assumptions and views of rural Euro-Canadians.

The frontier complex also finds expression in the way that Euro-Canadian community leaders represent public values and regional identities. At times, members of the public create a collective sense of belonging by evoking historical traditions captured by the image of the pioneer. In associating the pioneer with a set of ideal values, moral qualities, and personal characteristics rather than a lengthy period of occupation, this image thus provides a means by which a recent group of diverse immigrants is able to claim a common identity, a shared sense of belonging, and a legitimate place in the Cariboo-Chilcotin. At other times, Euro-Canadian community leaders express a collective identity centrally concerned with relationships to place. Community leaders speak of Williams Lake as a small city on the periphery of mainstream society and of having to continually fend off the domineering powers of urban governments. Leaders have a strong sense of being closely associated with a natural wilderness that is unoccupied and rich in resources free for the taking. These spatialized identities, the binary contrasts between urban and rural, between centralized governments and individual freedom on the periphery, and the image of an untouched, empty wilderness rich in resources, all reflect the continuing legacy of a frontier mythos.

The frontier complex also consists of a set of public values – independence, autonomy, self-sufficiency, competitiveness, materialism, and equality – that are frequently cited as characteristic of the Cariboo-Chilcotin. These values are encapsulated within the ideal of the self-made man. All individuals are believed to have equal opportunity to advance in Canadian society; those with sufficient ambition and determination will succeed and prosper. This ideal is fully resonant with frontier histories that celebrate heroic individualism as the motor of history, that equate colonialism with progress, and that explain the collective disempowerment, marginalization, and poverty of Aboriginal peoples as a consequence of their own collective failure to recognize the superiority of the capitalist system and to adopt the values, beliefs, and goals appropriate to succeed in modern Euro-Canadian society. These beliefs provide the foundation not only for public values and identities in the Cariboo-Chilcotin but also for the dominant ideology of Canadian society in general.

One of the most important components of the frontier complex is the continuous division of the heterogeneous regional population into two ideal and mutually exclusive categories: Indian and white. The irreducibility of the Indian/white dichotomy found in frontier histories is repeated in the everyday conversations of those Euro-Canadians who engage in private rituals of solidarity by collectively denigrating and condemning Aboriginal people. This duality is highlighted in the public rituals of solidarity within the Williams Lake Stampede, where the Indian/white dichotomy exists as an archetype for the construction and celebration of regional identity. The anti-Indian racism of everyday conversations and the romantic Indian representations within the stampede festival, although they may appear to be contradictory representations (one denigrating Aboriginal people, the other valorizing them), reflect variations of a standard colonial discourse that is framed on the presumption of the inherent difference between Indian and white, between colonized and colonizer.

Racism, which I have defined as an ideology that marks Aboriginal people as inherently inferior to non-Aboriginal people by virtue of biological and/or cultural criteria, has long served in various ways to maintain the marginalized and relatively powerless position of Aboriginal people in the Cariboo-Chilcotin. Racist notions have legitimated the restrictive policies of the Indian Affairs bureaucracy that have seen Aboriginal people isolated and impoverished in reserve communities; they have underpinned the province's historic denial of Aboriginal title and the loss of Aboriginal lands to settlers and resource industries. These structural consequences of racism are matched by the everyday forms of interpersonal racism in which Aboriginal people are subjected to casual insults, demeaning remarks, and subtle or overt violence simply for being Aboriginal. These attitudes, when expressed by those controlling access to resources, may translate into the denial of rental housing, employment, educational advancement, or fair and equal treatment within the justice system.

Racism, however, cannot by itself capture the complexity of relations of power that exist between the Euro-Canadian and the Aboriginal populations. Instead, power is exercised in the ability of privileged groups to control the public definitions of identities, historical realities, and current issues and events. In fact, an equally important way in which power is exercised is not through the manipulation of dimensions of difference – by portraying Aboriginal people as inferior, as culturally exotic, or as romantic noble savages – but through the simple denial of Aboriginal existence. Euro-Canadians may exercise power by rendering Aboriginal people invisible in the public domain: by avoiding acknowledgment of Aboriginal people whom they pass on the streets, by failing to register the names and locations of area reserve communities, by filtering out knowledge of the achievements of area Aboriginal people who defy the negative stereotypes, and by rendering inaudible the attempts of Aboriginal people to draw public attention to the issues of racism and historical injustice, issues that would require a self-critical examination of the dominant assumptions that many Euro-Canadians hold of their world. These filtering processes are matched by the selective invisibility of Secwepemc, Tsilhqot'in, and Carrier people in frontier histories. This pervasive invisibility of Aboriginal peoples – or, more precisely, the ability of townspeople to control the terms and contexts in which the existence of Aboriginal peoples will be publicly acknowledged – lies at the heart of current struggles between Aboriginal and Euro-Canadian populations.

The inadequacy of racism as an analytical framework for interpreting power relations is brought to the fore in my examination of public discourses now circulating on the issue of Aboriginal land claims and treaties. Reform Party members oppose Aboriginal treaties by drawing not on racist ideologies of innate Aboriginal inferiority but on the public ideal of equality. They deny the historical and legal grounds on which Aboriginal leaders argue their difference from non-Aboriginal Canadians, and they argue for the desirability and inevitability of Aboriginal people's political and cultural assimilation into Canadian society. Some Euro-Canadians oppose Aboriginal treaties by denying the "true" Aboriginality of people – they argue that "There are no real Indians left anymore," and thus Aboriginal claims are invalid. Yet other opponents draw on a moral discourse that encodes racist notions of Aboriginal people's inferiority, whether construed as an innate laziness and incompetence or as the historical consequence of government paternalism and learned dependence. Whether Aboriginal difference is denied, rendered culturally innate, or historically determined, those Euro-Canadians opposing land claims and treaties propose a similar solution. Drawing on the popular theory of cultural evolution and on the self-made man vision of history, they argue that Aboriginal people must abandon their own cultural traditions, values, and orientations and assimilate into the capitalist economy and society.

As Patrick Macklem has shown, a similar dynamic of power operates in the Canadian legal system, where notions of Aboriginal similarity to and difference from non-Aboriginal Canadians are manipulated in order to maintain relations of inequality and Aboriginal dependence on the Canadian state.[2] These dynamics are clearly evident in recent court decisions and commissions of inquiry into Aboriginal justice.[3] I agree with Macklem's conclusion that "the law's logic of justification ... identifies and uses similarities and differences between Native and non-Native people to perpetuate hierarchical relationships between First Nations and the Canadian state."[4] But to refer to this "logic" as an expression of racism[5] because it perpetuates inequality is to distort the reality of the complex processes by which power is exercised both through the assertion of Aboriginal inferiority and through the control of public identities.

There is a danger that the analytical concept of racism (which I define as an ideology rather than as an exclusionary practice) may become "conceptually inflated," as Robert Miles argues,[6] to the point that any practice can be construed as racist. It is especially important to be cautious given the way in which racist discourses have been modified since the Second World War with the emergence of multiculturalism and pluralism as universal values in Western societies. Racist ideologies are no longer acceptable; nevertheless, equally hegemonic and exclusionary practices persist. For example, anti-immigration movements in Britain and France draw not on the undesirability of racially inferior peoples but on the danger of mixing people who adhere to different cultural practices and worldviews. Such discourses, referred to in the European context as the "new racism"[7] or as "cultural fundamentalism,"[8] have incorporated the multiculturalist notion of the inherent value and equality of all cultural groups. Anti-immigration proponents argue that, given the valid commitment that people have to their distinct cultures, the "mixing" of different cultures will inevitably result in social conflict. They argue that "it is natural for people to prefer to live amongst 'their own kind' and therefore natural for people to discriminate against those not considered to be part of that common community."[9] As Miles points out, racism is "An integral component of a wider, historical process of racialisation which is interlinked with exclusionary practices and with the expression of other forms of exclusionary ideology. In a social context structured by historical change and, in a post-colonial and post-Fascist era, by a desire to obscure intentionality, our conceptual framework warrants a greater degree of complexity and sophistication than is allowed by those who employ the concept of racism in a loose or undefined manner."[10] Given the emergence of more covert forms of exclusionary practice – which seem framed on liberal notions of cultural pluralism and, in the Canadian context, on the public value of equality – it is critical that racist ideologies and hegemonic practices be analytically distinguished; the former is only one expression of the latter.

Secwepemc, Tsilhqot'in, and Carrier people encounter aspects of the dominant culture as a regular part of their experience in Williams Lake: in their interactions with non-Aboriginal people in the public school system, in local stores and businesses, in government agencies. They encounter expressions of the dominant culture in the city newspaper, in the books filling the downtown library, in public school curriculum, in the speeches of non-Aboriginal politicians, and in the very way in which the city is geographically divided into a grid of streets bearing the names of early pioneers and politicians. Many people, whether they live on a reserve or in the city, believe that Williams Lake is not neutral territory but a place where they are treated as outsiders by an immigrant population that now holds inordinate influence over their everyday lives.

The changing political, economic, and social contexts of Canadian society in the past two decades have brought new resources for Cariboo-Chilcotin Aboriginal people to use in confronting these dominating practices. With the rise of multiculturalism in federal policy in the 1970s, and the increasing urban concerns with issues of racism, equality, and the plurality of identities and histories in the 1990s, the moral critiques of racism have been immensely strengthened. Aboriginal people are strategically manipulating the symbols of power embedded in the dominant culture – the ideals of equality, multiculturalism, and justice – in their attempts to highlight critical problems in their relationships with members of non-Aboriginal society. These moral politics have become more effective due, in part, to the intense scrutiny that local Euro-Canadians feel from urban society. Accusations of racial discrimination may be ignored when they occur in private, local contexts, but when brought to the attention of the provincial public these concerns gain much greater strength. For example, it was only when a provincial court judge spoke out against the RCMP's discriminatory treatment of suspected Aboriginal criminals, and his concerns were picked up by the provincial media, that the provincial government agreed to strike the Cariboo-Chilcotin Justice Inquiry in 1992.

Changes in government policies concerning Aboriginal treaties, Crown land management, and forestry regulations, and the increasing "subcontracting" of government responsibilities to First Nations and tribal council organizations and thus the burgeoning administrative budgets within which these organizations operate, have resulted in a growing recognition by non-Aboriginal politicians, businesspeople, and industry executives of the potential political and economic power of Cariboo-Chilcotin First Nations. The Aboriginal treaty process and the potential transfer of lands and resources to Aboriginal communities are motivating various public sectors, ranging from forest companies and local governments to the Chamber of Commerce, to enter discussions with area First Nations over their future economic relationships. Williams Lake civic leaders and business representatives are now sitting down with First Nations leaders in face-to-face meetings in Indian reserve community halls to discuss their mutual futures. These events are unprecedented in the history of Aboriginal/Euro-Canadian relations in the Cariboo-Chilcotin. They reflect not only how these relations may be driven by external – that is, nonlocal – policy directives and political-economic forces but also how these relations are shaped by the inherent contingency of the dominant culture of the region.

This contingency should be emphasized. In tracing the various dimensions of the frontier complex, my intent has not been to offer an argument of cultural determinism: that these beliefs and assumptions determine the current state of Aboriginal/non-Aboriginal relations or that elements of this complex are fixed and unchangeable. Rather, it is important to trace how certain beliefs and assumptions enjoy the status of common-sense truths and how some Euro-Canadians, in specific contexts, not only draw on these assumed truths but also engage culturally specific modes of *arriving* at truth in order to defend existing relations of power. Yet the looming possibility of transfers of land, resources, and decision making to First Nations organizations is already causing important shifts in local discourses and relations. This study, then, documents the cultural practices of colonialism in one particular historical moment in which some of the most long-standing structural features of Aboriginal/non-Aboriginal relations in the Cariboo-Chilcotin – the ownership of land and resources, the legislative and bureaucratic forms of government control over reserve communities – are now being renegotiated.

In the meantime, area Secwepemc, Tsilhqot'in, and Carrier people, from youths in public schools to formally elected band chiefs, engage with and confront the terms of the dominant culture in a variety of ways. In confronting forms of everyday racism, Aboriginal people are attempting to demonstrate their essential similarities to non-Aboriginal Canadians and their right to be treated with the same dignity and respect as other citizens. In contrast, in engaging in private joking, Aboriginal people are not directly confronting but epistemologically defusing dominant stereotypes into ambiguous illusions of meaning. This form of resistance has also been documented in everyday Aboriginal conversational practices[11] and in the work of Aboriginal artists.[12] In yet other strategies, notably displays and performances of cultural identity, Aboriginal leaders strive implicitly to overcome the barriers of racism by replacing negative notions with positive notions of Aboriginal difference. These varied modes of resistance, like dominant discourses, make use of alternating concepts of Aboriginal similarity to and difference from mainstream Euro-Canadian society.

This raises the issue of the cultural power that Aboriginal people are drawing from the Canadian public's long-standing fascination with Aboriginal cultural exoticism. In engaging in strategic essentialisms to communicate with non-Aboriginal audiences, First Nations leaders are making use of the power of the "colonial gaze." They are drawing on the symbols of power and the traditions of representation that prevail among the dominant society. These strategies could be read as a reflection of how extensively relations of power have restricted other opportunities for communication. But when viewed in the broader context, cultural reifications through symbols that could be interpreted as hegemonic stereotypes of the noble savage constitute only one aspect of a diverse repertoire of projects of cultural and political resistance.

Not all area Aboriginal people speak from identical perspectives and social positions. Secwepemc, Carrier, and Tsilhqot'in teenagers, reserve residents, single mothers raising families in town, elected chiefs, and men, women, and elders not only may experience domination differently but also may enact different forms of both resistance and accommodation to the dominant structures that impinge on their lives. This diversity has been hinted at in my discussion of the different strategies that individuals are using to communicate with non-Aboriginal audiences. Not all of these strategies are confrontational. Not all involve the politics of embarrassment. As evident in the discussions that took place during the land claims public forum, some First Nations speakers at times make use of more indirect discursive strategies in which they employ strategic equivalences: they juxtapose Aboriginal and Euro-Canadian values and apply creative metaphors to bridge the gulf in understanding that separates the two populations. When one Secwepemc leader likens treaty negotiations to labour-management talks, he offers non-Aboriginal people a way of understanding these negotiations that acknowledges their own cultural values of right-wing entrepreneurialism. This Secwepemc leader's approach reflects his personal history as a band leader, his style of conciliatory politics, and his carefully developed discursive strategy for "talking to politicians."

In this study, I have limited my discussion to a brief overview of the ways in which Cariboo-Chilcotin Aboriginal people are resisting the dominant culture of the region. This is an admittedly incomplete picture of contemporary Aboriginal life. For example, I have not explored the complexity – and particularly the ambiguities and forms of collaboration – in Aboriginal relations with non-Aboriginal society. Nor have I considered the very real internal complexities of Secwepemc, Tsilhqot'in, and Carrier life: the internal politics, the nascent class divisions, the gender politics, the generational differences, or the conflicts between those supporting and those denouncing the BC treaty process. One could consider the different views of status and non-status Indians, of those living on and off reserve, of those working within various provincial ministries administering Crown lands, and of those profitably employed in the forest industry as loggers and truckers. A number of First Nations, for example, have started their own small logging companies and have successfully applied to the Ministry of Forests for harvesting licences. In other instances, such as the Williams Lake First Nation's Northern Shuswap Wood Products, First Nations have built "value added" mills, purchasing lumber (often scrap lumber) from forest companies in the city and producing secondary manufactured products such as pallets and fruit and vegetable crates. Some new partnerships are true joint ventures, such as Ecolink, a forestry and silvicultural company co-owned by the Alkali Lake First Nation and Lignum Ltd. These new relationships, although bringing a degree of prosperity to impoverished reserve communities, also raise difficult questions about complicity with forest companies that are continuing to clearcut in Aboriginal territories and about acquiescence to the government's presumption to the ownership of Crown lands. It will be critical to trace these new developments for a complex and nuanced understanding of the shifting modes of articulation, accommodation, and resistance within Aboriginal communities themselves.[13]

To what extent is the frontier culture described here a specifically local cultural complex, and to what extent does it contain features common to other regions of Canada? Similar cultural patterns have been described in other studies of rural social relations in Canada. In previous chapters, for example, I indicated the way in which Aboriginal people in rural Saskatchewan, Manitoba, and northern Ontario have also been subjected to intense forms of interpersonal racism and the way in which the public culture of other northern resource towns is characterized by a cluster of frontier values very similar to those prevalent in the Williams Lake area.

Other anthropologists have explored the diversity and context-dependent nature of rural Euro-Canadian attitudes toward Aboriginal people. In her study of a small Labrador settler community, Evelyn Plaice finds that settler identities and attitudes toward Aboriginal people are fluid constructs continually being reformed in different social contexts of interaction.[14] At times, settlers construct self-identities based on their fundamental differences from Indians. At other times, settlers claim "old-timer" status by relating their long history of association with bush life and Aboriginal peoples. In yet other circumstances – notably to avoid being excluded from land claims settlements – settlers claim Aboriginal status by highlighting Inuit ancestry. Plaice's study reveals the intricate ways in which factors of generation, historical experience, and social context influence how settlers use the idea of Aboriginality – and, in her term, play "the Native game" – to construct identities and to advance their interests.

These variables also shape Euro-Canadian discourses about Aboriginal people in the Cariboo-Chilcotin. John Hall, in his study of Aboriginal/non-Aboriginal relations in the west Chilcotin, suggests that the long history of Aboriginal employment on ranches has created a context in which Euro-Canadian ranchers may defend Aboriginal people against the charges of laziness levelled by businesspeople who see Aboriginal people in no other context but as welfare recipients and consumers of goods and services.[15] The kinds of discourses that one hears in the rural regions of the Cariboo-Chilcotin may be quite different from those that prevail in Williams Lake, where most residents are recent arrivals to the region and have limited personal contact with Aboriginal people, interacting anonymously over cash registers and service counters and observing Aboriginal people from a distance in public places.

One of the most important aspects of the frontier complex is the construction of Euro-Canadian identity as one of benevolent paternalism. This belief in the goodwill, the benevolence, the "niceness" of Canadians finds expression not only in the historical narratives celebrating the discovery and settlement of Canada but also in the very way that many Euro-Canadians conceive of their relationships with Aboriginal people and speak about Aboriginal issues. Regardless of their personal experience with or knowledge about Aboriginal peoples and communities, rural Euro-Canadians often offer opinions about the nature of the "problem" in Aboriginal communities and about how that "problem" should be solved. This paternal attitude subtly underlies the remarks of the shop clerk who patronizingly approved of Aboriginal customers adopting Euro-Canadian standards of domestic materialism. It is more evident in the remarks of those Euro-Canadians who argue that local Aboriginal communities "aren't ready" for land claims settlements. The assumption of paternal superiority is most striking in the rhetoric of Reform Party advocates who insist, despite the obvious disagreement of First Nations leaders throughout the province, that treaty settlements are not in Aboriginal people's best interests.

These speakers engage in a specific style of discourse common among members of the general Canadian public who discuss and contemplate "the Indian problem."[16] As Noel Dyck suggests, implicit in this attitude is the notion that Aboriginal people are relatively childlike and naïve, are not well equipped to manage their own affairs and form effective strategies for the future, and should follow the advice of Euro-Canadians who have Aboriginal people's best interests at heart. These discourses have a momentum and dynamic of their own, and they exist largely independent of the thoughts, wishes, or goals of Aboriginal people. Aboriginal voices are ignored or dismissed; in the face of Aboriginal resistance, these paternal discourses only intensify. Aboriginal people whose houses are judged to be in disrepair are condemned as irresponsible and ungrateful recipients of huge amounts of "taxpayers' money"; First Nations leaders asserting ownership of traditional territories have been naïvely misled by manipulative white lawyers and liberal governments conveying false impressions of Aboriginal rights. Although different sectors of the public may hold conflicting notions about what Aboriginal people "should do" – they should leave the reserves and assimilate, they should market their cultural traditions to non-Aboriginal audiences – what remains consistent is the way in which certain assumptions of benevolent superiority have authorized various non-Aboriginal Canadians to assert views about how Aboriginal people should live and to criticize them for failing to conform to these imposed expectations.

These deep-seated notions of paternalism within Aboriginal/Euro-

Canadian relations in the Cariboo-Chilcotin are consistent with the patterns of colonialism in other regions of Canada. One of the earliest discussions of colonial paternalism is found in Robert Paine's study of Inuit-white relations in the Canadian Arctic.[17] In contrast to many regions of southern Canada, the Inuit experience of colonialism in the Arctic has not been one of sudden economic intrusion and the imposition of restrictive government legislation and institutions. Rather, as the Arctic became a strategic military region in the Cold War era and an increasingly attractive region for oil and gas resource industry expansion, it brought, for the Inuit, an "epoch of colonialism infused with concepts of social welfare."[18] Industrial expansion was facilitated through a process of "welfare colonialism": the sudden expansion of government authority and administration in the North through which the Inuit were transformed into a client population dependent on the provision of welfare, health, and educational services. In short, the institutions that came to dominate Inuit lives were not restrictive but designed on the surface to support Inuit communities and bring to them the same standards of health, housing, and education enjoyed by southern Canadians.

Paine applied the concept of "tutelage" to critically assess the nature of the colonial relationships that subsequently developed. Through the 1950s and 1960s, the Inuit were gradually drawn in from widely dispersed camps to permanent settlements. Schools, medical clinics, stores, churches, and government offices were built and then staffed by a cadre of Euro-Canadian middle-class professionals from the south: teachers, nurses, civil servants, administrators. These Euro-Canadian policy makers and service providers controlled all aspects of settlement life. They became, in essence, "tutors" to the Inuit, rationalizing the imposition of services as in the Inuit's best interests and ultimately seeking to transform Inuit cultures into the ideals of southern, middle-class, Euro-Canadian society. For the Inuit, though, the cost of accepting tutelage, whether in the form of educational, medical, or welfare provisions, was that it required them to accept the status of children who needed the ongoing guidance of Euro-Canadian bureaucrats and institutions. By the 1970s, Paine argues, the Inuit had become caught in the grip of institutional and ideological practices that reinforced their dependency and presumed need for government guidance and hegemony in the North. It is from this dense web of institutional and ideological constraints that the Inuit are now seeking to emerge through initiatives such as Inuit-controlled settlement administration, the resolution of land claims through treaties with the Canadian government in 1984 and 1993, and the creation of the Inuit-governed territory of Nunavut, replacing much of the Northwest Territories in the eastern Arctic.

Social relations in these new settlements were profoundly shaped by the paternal institutional structures and policies. In his study of settlement life in the eastern Arctic during the 1970s, Hugh Brody illustrates how colonialism operated by conditioning the attitudes, identities, and everyday interactions of Euro-Canadians and Inuit residents.[19] Euro-Canadians lived in the most comfortable homes, held the key positions, and earned the best salaries in the settlement institutions. The "white" houses were geographically separate from those of the Inuit, and strong forces influenced Euro-Canadian residents to maintain solidarity with one another and to avoid social contact with Inuit residents. Euro-Canadians were held together by a shared commitment to maintaining middle-class values, lifestyles, and class consciousness within the settlement. These commitments translated into a set of shared attitudes regarding the Inuit and their relationships with them.

Euro-Canadians held various stereotypes of Inuit personality and culture: romantic images of the traditional Inuit adapting to and thriving in the harsh northern climate were juxtaposed with nostalgia for the passing of the old ways, which, ironically, were the very traditions that Euro-Canadians were in the North to change. Yet the mandate for transforming Inuit culture was justified by underlying presumptions about the "primitiveness" of Inuit culture and the desirability of bringing to the Inuit the lifestyles and technologies equated with middle-class, southern Canadian standards of "civilization."

Euro-Canadians shared a sense of being in the North as a mission of benevolence, and this benevolence, and the underlying assumption of superiority, authorized Euro-Canadians to criticize individual Inuit, often on the basis of scant information. As Brody notes, "whites often pronounced judgements on areas of competence of which they can have only limited knowledge at best, and of which they are usually totally ignorant. These judgements provide bases for criticism and complaint against individuals with whom the whites have no daily association and, in many cases, with whom they can never talk."[20] Furthermore, these judgments rested on an individual's failure to live up to contradictory Euro-Canadian expectations: "An Inuk can be condemned from any point of view: if a young man is uneasy in the settlement, unwilling to work there or inexpert at the jobs he takes, he is characterized as 'stupid'; yet if he chooses to live on the land and tries to make a success of hunting and trapping, he is scorned for trying to be a 'real Eskimo,' or for attempting to succeed in a life that has no economic future."[21] Thus, Inuit were caught in a double bind, simultaneously criticized for their failed attempts to adopt middle-class values and behaviours and for their failed attempts to be so-called real Eskimos.

Most significantly, Euro-Canadians in the North applied the program of assimilation with little consideration for the wishes, desires, or goals of the Inuit populations. Brody concludes that Euro-Canadians "believe that they know what is best for them [the Inuit], and if the people themselves are not enthusiastic about the good things whites have to offer, that is attributed to Inuit misunderstanding or error. Inuit are continuously being urged to be grateful for what whites say Inuit need."[22] Euro-Canadians in the North "insist on regulating the way in which Inuit live and on identifying what it is that Inuit should want. These decisions are taken with minimum reference to the people's own aspirations and with scarcely any attempt to assess what local circumstances actually require."[23] These authoritarian modes of control, which, as Brody points out, are in sharp contrast to middle-class, liberal democratic commitments to individualism and freedom, were masked by the unexamined convictions of paternalism, goodwill, and superiority among those enforcing these policies.

In the arctic settlements of the 1970s, the Euro-Canadian populations were small, homogeneous, and closed communities where strong pressures toward social conformity and ideas of Inuit-white difference maintained community boundaries. These communities formed in a period of intense government intrusion into Inuit lives, and expressions of benevolent paternalism perhaps took extreme forms under these circumstances. To what extent northern Euro-Canadian attitudes toward, and relations with, Inuit populations have shifted in the 1990s remains an open question. What Brody's ethnography demonstrates is a particularly condensed expression of colonialism under the guise of benevolent paternalism that nevertheless parallels broader trends in colonial relations across different historical periods in Canada.

Noel Dyck has since elaborated the concept of "coercive tutelage" in his analysis of the development of federal Indian Affairs policy in Canada.[24] He shows that the presumptions underlying patterns of tutelage in Inuit-white relations in the Arctic – of Aboriginal inferiority, of the need for Aboriginal people to change into images acceptable to Euro-Canadians, and of the paternal benevolence of Euro-Canadians enforcing these changes – are not unique to the Arctic but have defined colonial relationships in Canada since the first Europeans arrived and persist today both within government agencies and among the general Canadian public. For over a century, Indian Affairs officials have engaged in coercive tutelage in forcibly implementing programs of directed social, cultural, and economic change in reserve communities despite persistent Aboriginal resistance. Government officials justified their coercive acts as gestures of "charitable benevolence"[25] and interpreted Aboriginal resistance as confirmation of their naïveté and need for Euro-Canadian guidance.

Even more important, these presumptions of inferiority and the need for Euro-Canadian direction are not limited to those in direct institutional relationships with Aboriginal peoples but occur among the general public as well. As Dyck points out, definitions of the "Indian problem" generally coalesce around Aboriginal people's perceived failure to adhere to Euro-Canadian values, ideals, morals, and patterns of social and economic practice. Yet what remains unrealized among the general public is the fact that the Aboriginal "problem" lies not with Aboriginal people but with the premises underlying and legitimating Euro-Canadian criticism of and interference in Aboriginal lives.[26] That assumptions of Euro-Canadian colonial benevolence extend beyond government policy and Euro-Canadian attitudes, permeating Euro-Canadian historical consciousness, frontier narratives, and diverse expressions of Canadian national identity, only reinforces the taken-for-granted nature of these colonial attitudes.

The findings of this study have important implications for understanding current debates in British Columbia regarding Aboriginal claims to land, rights, and self-government. The rhetoric of public opposition to Aboriginal treaties and rights at the provincial level involves a manipulation of the same public ideals and notions of history that prevail in rural Euro-Canadian settings. In December 1995, for example, the *Vancouver Sun* ran a prominent article on its "Opinion" page.[27] The article was written by a Simon Fraser University economist who had recently edited a volume entitled *Market Solutions for Native Poverty* published by the C.D. Howe Institute. In this excerpt from his afterword, the author provided a seemingly objective, scholarly argument opposing Aboriginal self-government and treaty settlements.

There were two basic arguments. First, explicitly drawing on the popular belief in cultural evolution now presented as anthropological theory (although, in fact, rejected by contemporary anthropologists), the writer argues that "traditional Aboriginal culture is dramatically at odds with the requirements for success in industrial society." He states, in a startling ethnocentric judgment, that "personal success in an industrial society requires that people restrict voluntary sharing of their personal income and wealth essentially to those in their (extended) family. It also requires that they invest in individual training and defer consumption via financial savings. Such activities are severely at odds with the values of most traditional cultures." Thus, Aboriginal people must abandon their cultural orientation and adopt the values of materialism, thrift, individualism, and private property if they are to overcome their current poverty and socioeconomic disadvantage. Second, drawing on the myth of the self-made man and the stereotype of the "wealthy, undeserving Indian," the writer argues that "government policies have encouraged large-scale Aboriginal unemployment and welfare dependency." Governments have been too generous in providing programs to Aboriginal peoples and in funding Aboriginal governments. In contrast, "Aboriginals living off their reserves fare better, in terms of lower welfare rates and higher earnings, than Aboriginals on reserves." The solution, he suggests, is to encourage Aboriginal people to leave the reserves and assimilate into the capitalist economy and culture.

This opinion article is consistent with the Reform Party's populist, right-wing analysis of the current difficulties that Aboriginal people in Canada face. It is also founded on a particular historical worldview that continues to explain history as the triumphant expansion of corporate capitalism driven by values of competition, materialism, thrift, and aggressiveness. This history results in the natural filtering of individuals into different social strata, where the fit survive and the unfit fall to the bottom of the social ladder. The problem of Aboriginal poverty does not implicate the structures of colonial society – the history of repression of Aboriginal populations by the legal system, by Indian Affairs policies, by the ordinary racism of non-Aboriginal Canadians – but is explained by Aboriginal people's stubborn refusal to transform themselves into European ideals and by the liberal policies of governments that only further Aboriginal dependency through transfer payments. Once again, the "Indian problem" is defined, and solutions are posed, with complete disregard to First Nations leaders who are now vociferously asserting their own concerns and interests and their own visions of their place in Canadian society. Although the views expressed in this opinion article are the subject of much public debate, it is important to recognize that they emerge from a widely shared form of frontier historical consciousness that is fully supported by key cultural assumptions in many rural and urban settings across British Columbia. These views express a progressivist version of the frontier myth, resonating with the values, attitudes, and identities found in public school textbooks, popular histories, and everyday conversations in coffeeshops across rural British Columbia.

Another example concerns the much-discussed 1991 BC Supreme Court decision in the *Delgamuukw* (Gitksan-Wet'suwet'en) Aboriginal title case. In his reasons for the judgment, Chief Justice Allan McEachern dismissed the Gitksan and Wet'suwet'en hereditary chiefs' claims to Aboriginal ownership of and jurisdiction over their traditional territories. He legitimated his ruling by making several rather blunt assertions: that the early Gitksan and Wet'suwet'en were "primitive" peoples whose cultures were inherently inferior to those of civilized European societies, that colonization has been in Aboriginal people's best interests, and that the difficulties the Gitksan and Wet'suwet'en now face are the result of their unwillingness to assimilate into mainstream society.[28]

The McEachern decision has been widely condemned by scholars and First Nations critics for being grounded in a colonial ideology, for drawing on nineteenth-century anthropological theories of cultural evolution, for privileging written documents and rejecting Aboriginal oral traditions as valid forms of historical evidence, and for being framed by a fundamentally racist view of Aboriginal peoples.[29] Significant aspects of the decision were overturned in 1993 by the BC Court of Appeal, which found that Aboriginal rights were not extinguished and thus persist in the present and that the Crown's title to the land is subject to these continuing Aboriginal "interests." In December 1997, the Supreme Court of Canada ruled that a retrial was necessary because McEachern had erred in his failure to consider First Nations oral history as historical evidence. Nevertheless, the McEachern decision remains a focus of much critical discourse regarding the role of anthropologists as expert witnesses in the courts and the way that ideology shapes the purportedly objective domain of the legal system.[30]

In the flood of critical responses to the decision, there has been some tendency to focus criticism on the judge himself rather than on the broader colonial cultural context in which he is situated. For example, McEachern has been personally criticized for being ethnocentric, myopic, illogical, and racist. These criticisms, however, distract attention from the fact that many of his propositions – about the "primitiveness" of Aboriginal cultures, about the benefits of colonialism, about the desirability of Aboriginal assimilation – reflect conventional attitudes among the Canadian public. McEachern himself argued that his conclusions reflected "common-sense" thinking.[31] His judgment was rooted not only in a nineteenth-century colonial ideology but also in the ideology of twentieth-century colonialism that is alive and well in rural British Columbia and beyond.[32]

Political scientist Paul Tennant has suggested that McEachern's judgment reflects "traditional white views" of history. "What is significant today is that an increasing number of non-Aboriginal British Columbians are willing to put the old views in historical perspective and, in so doing, to create a new understanding of British Columbia history," one framed by the principles of the moral equality of Aboriginal and non-Aboriginal cultures, the distinctiveness of Aboriginal identities, and the recognition and acceptance of the legitimacy of Aboriginal rights and claims.[33] Clearly, an increasing number of scholars and critics of Aboriginal/non-Aboriginal relations in British Columbia are committed to encouraging a new understanding of provincial history.[34] However, it is important to ask whether this movement – in either academic or popular discourse – truly represents a new vision of history or whether it is a counterhegemonic rearticulation of the frontier myth in which Aboriginal people appear in romantic terms as victims of the dark forces of colonialism. For example, many new cultural trends, such as New Age spiritualism, environmentalism, and cultural heritage tourism, are being mobilized in sympathetic support of Aboriginal issues. But in different ways these cultural trends may reformulate aspects of the colonial culture – in their exoticization and romanticization of Aboriginal "difference" – rather than move beyond the terms and symbols supplied by the frontier culture and consciousness that I have described here.

Although there may be a new understanding of history emerging in British Columbia, we must continue to ask to what degree it reflects a radical break with the colonial cultural past. What I have sought to demonstrate here is that contemporary Canadian culture, as practised in one rural BC city, is deeply imprinted by the ongoing legacy of colonialism. The polarization of public opinion around the Gustafsen Lake standoff, the public resistance to the Aboriginal treaty process, and the reluctance of the courts to fully acknowledge the legitimacy of Aboriginal title and rights cannot be simply dismissed as expressions of ignorance, racism, redneckism, or outdated colonial ideology. A proper understanding of these public crises requires an appreciation of the systematic way in which a dominant colonial culture operates in multiple dimensions of ordinary life and how public attitudes are rooted in a complex, sophisticated, and partial vision of the world that is profoundly shaped by past and present colonial experience.

# Notes

**Preface**

1 Elias (1975: i).

2 In contrast, see Crapanzano (1985), Dunk (1991), and Menzies (1994). Crapanzano, in the opening paragraph of his study of white South Africans in a small village north of Cape Town, states: "[This book] is not about the sources of economic, political, and military power or of their display; rather, it is about the discourse of people who are privileged by that power and, paradoxically, in their privilege victims of it. My concern is with social entrapment – the way in which a people's understanding of themselves, their world, their past, and their future limits their possibility" (xiii). One danger in portraying those who engage in racist discourses as victims is that it suggests an overdetermination of consciousness – an entrapment – that allows little possibility for social or cultural change.

3 Marcus and Fisher (1986: ix).

**Chapter 1: Culture and Colonialism in Rural BC**

1 One of the earliest blockades in the province was that of the Nazko and Kluskus Carrier, who attempted in 1974 to prevent the expansion of clear-cut logging by blocking the path of a bulldozer clearing a logging road into Nazko and Kluskus hunting and trapping grounds. For a review of First Nations road blockades in British Columbia since 1984, see Blomley (1996).

2 I use the term "rural" to refer to cities and towns that lie beyond the metropolitan core regions of Victoria, Vancouver, and the Lower Mainland. By other definitions, Williams Lake may not be considered rural. For example, Census Canada identifies a rural area as having a population concentration of fewer than 1,000 residents and a population density of fewer than 400 inhabitants per square kilometre. From this vantage, Williams Lake, with its population of over 10,000, would be considered an urban region. In everyday discourse, "rural" is used in the more general sense in which I use the term. It could be argued that the urban-rural divide has become one of the most important divisions within Canadian politics, evident in the rise of the Reform Party and in increasing rural opposition to initiatives such as gun control, Aboriginal self-government, distinct-society status for Quebec, and multiculturalism. There is a growing articulation of a rural identity in the Cariboo-Chilcotin, particularly in contexts in which local politicians oppose government policies on forest industry regulation, environmental protection, and Aboriginal treaties. For example, at the November 1996 Select Standing Committee on Aboriginal Affairs, one prominent regional politician publicly stated that he was advocating "rural common sense" in his opposition to the provincial government's Aboriginal treaty policy.

3 Since 1997, First Nations in the Cariboo region have been using the term Secwepemc to refer to themselves instead of the older anglicized term, Shuswap. For a number of years, Tsilhqot'in First Nations have been using the spelling Tsilhqot'in, a more linguistically accurate rendition of their name for themselves in place of the older spelling, Chilcotin.

4 Based on Statistics Canada figures for 1991 (1994: 82). Ethnic background was reported only for individuals claiming single ethnic origin, which in Williams Lake was 5,910 of the city's 10,385 residents. Of this number, 725 reported East Indian ancestry, and 490 reported Aboriginal heritage. The ranges provided here result from calculating against both the total reporting single-ethnic origin and the total population. In 1996, the city's population was 10,472, having changed little since 1991.
5 This figure does not include Aboriginal people who are not registered with one of the fifteen regional Indian bands, nor does it include non-status Indians.
6 Braroe (1975), Elias (1975), Stymeist (1975), Lithman (1984).
7 Elias (1975), Paine (1977a), Dyck (1991: 98-104).
8 The Tsilhqot'in First Nations are Alexandria ('Esdilagh), Toosey (Tl'esqox), Stone (Yunesit'in), Alexis Creek (Tŝideldel, also known as Redstone), Anaham (Tl'etinqox-T'in), and Nemiah Valley (Xeni). The southern Carrier First Nations are Lhtako (formerly Red Bluff), Nazko, Kluskus (Lhoosk'uz Dené), and Ulkatcho. The Secwepemc First Nations are Soda Creek, Williams Lake (Sugar Cane), Alkali Lake, Canoe Creek, and Canim Lake.
9 Braroe (1975), Stymeist (1975), Brody (1981), Lithman (1984), Speck (1987), Plaice (1990).
10 Asch (1995: 274).
11 Kew (1974), Dinwoodie (1996), Furniss (1996).
12 Palmer (1994), Dinwoodie (1996).
13 For a discussion and critique of this term, see McClintock (1994), Mishra and Hodge (1994), Williams and Chrisman (1994a), and Childs and Williams (1997).
14 The term "postcolonialism" is often used in academic contexts in a second sense, in which it refers to a particular form of writing and critical inquiry that takes as its subject the analysis of colonialism and colonial discourses. Following this definition, we can identify "postcolonial" literatures in Canada; indeed, this book is written in the spirit of such a critical reflection on the working of colonial discourses in one rural Canadian setting. Yet these cultural movements themselves do not fully transcend the discourses of colonialism. Academic institutions, for example, have long been implicated in the production of knowledge of the indigenous other. Academics are privileged with an authority that accrues from the theoretical discourses that we generate and the institutional settings in which we are situated. At best, academic postcolonial literatures occupy an uneasy, liminal space, not fully transcending but committed to a more critical self-awareness of the workings of colonial discourses and practices.
15 For an introduction to and summary of critical responses to Said, see Williams and Chrisman (1994b: 127-71) and Childs and Williams (1997: 97-121).
16 Thomas (1994).
17 Sider (1987), Thomas (1994: 142).
18 The way in which colonialism influences and conditions everyday social relations and attitudes between indigenous people and non-Aboriginal colonizers has been explored among the Inuit and whites in the Canadian Arctic by Paine (1977b) and Brody (1991).
19 Williams (1977, 1980), Roseberry (1991).
20 Williams (1980: 38).
21 Williams (1980).
22 Roseberry (1991: 48).
23 Scott (1985).
24 Scott (1985: 205).
25 Williams (1977: 118).
26 Dyck (1986), Cruikshank (1997).
27 Slotkin (1973, 1986, 1992). The terms "historical consciousness" and "historical epistemology" might be used interchangeably. In keeping with my use of Williams's concept of a dominant culture as a process of representation, historical epistemology is preferable. Historical consciousness is rather abstract and describes forms of awareness; historical epistemology, as a set of rules guiding the construction and representation of historical "truths," is empirically more accessible and concrete. It directs our attention to the way in which individuals actively generate representations of the past in particular social,

political, and economic contexts of interaction and conflict. I also prefer historical epistemology because it allows for the coexistence of multiple epistemologies. I am not suggesting that individuals are trapped within the frontier historical epistemology; other epistemological frameworks are available, for example, through academic studies of colonialism and postcolonialism, from which individuals may construct alternative understandings of the past. My goal here, though, is to trace the dominance of one particular historical epistemology, that associated with the myth of the frontier, in the public culture and discourse of a rural BC town.

28 I am not using the term "myth" in the structuralist sense, as being comprised of binary archetypes that have an objective existence in language independent of human will or consciousness. Instead, as Slotkin writes, "Myth and ideology are created and recreated in the midst of historical contingency, through deliberate acts of human memory, intention, and labour ... Myth has a human-historical rather than a natural or transcendent source and is continually modified by human experience and agency" (1992: 25). The frontier myth, although it exerts a conservative cultural force, is subject to continual reworking through history and – in theory at least – is capable of being transcended through critical self-reflection.

29 Fogelson (1984, 1989). Fogelson discusses the role of epitomizing events in Native North American historical narratives; these events are also features of Western narratives of history (see Cruikshank 1992).

30 For example, Trigger (1985), Hanks (1986), Abu-Lughod (1990), Comaroff and Comaroff (1991), Bhabha (1994), and Ortner (1995).

31 Slotkin (1992: 6).

32 Slotkin (1992: 5).

33 Slotkin (1992: 6).

34 To my knowledge, no other ethnographic studies have traced the expression of the frontier myth in the Canadian context. There is, of course, a large literature in Canadian history assessing the degree to which Frederick Jackson Turner's influential frontier thesis of American history is relevant in the Canadian context (see Cross 1970 for a recent review). These discussions, however, are not ethnographic applications. They look at how the specific features of the Canadian frontier environment may have shaped Canadian history but not at the way in which the *idea* of the frontier has shaped Canadian historiography – how Canadian history has been understood and represented. Indeed, Michael Cross states that the frontier ideology has had less impact on Canada, and as evidence he points to "the fact that Canada's western heroes have been not rugged individual gunmen like Wyatt Earp or Jesse James, but rather a collective law-enforcement agency, the Mounties" (3). As I argue in Chapter 3, this difference is significant, but it indicates not the absence of a frontier ideology in Canada but the presence of a frontier ideology adapted to the Canadian context.

Historians and other scholars today are applying the concerns of the new social history to analyses of Canada's past, emphasizing the plurality of social and ethnic groups interacting with one another in remote regions and the different ways in which factors of gender, class, and ethnicity shaped these experiences (e.g., Brown 1980, Van Kirk 1992). In this way, scholars are transcending the limitations of earlier historical analyses that homogenized the experiences of Aboriginal people and settlers and reproduced the rigid categories on which the frontier myth, and colonial discourses generally, were structured. Still lacking are ethnographic analyses of how the idea of the frontier shaped earlier scholarly and popular historical representations. To be clear, my assumption is that the frontier is neither a place (Limerick 1987) nor a process of encounter in a certain historical epoch (Turner 1963) but an idea imposed on particular places and processes to provide a framework of understanding. It is this process of imposing the idea of the frontier to order history and contemporary social relations in which I am interested.

35 These issues have been taken up elsewhere by Furniss (1987, 1995a, 1996), Palmer (1994), and Dinwoodie (1996). Dinwoodie's work focuses on historical consciousness among the Tsilhqot'in of Nemiah Valley.

36 See Cruikshank (1992) for an effective use of such a strategy of juxtaposition.

37 Clifford (1988: 21-54).
38 Dyck (1985: 15), Paine (1985: 214).
39 Scott (1990: 198).

**Chapter 2: The Burden of History**

1 Goldman (1953: 410-11).
2 Teit (1975: 595-6).
3 For example, Ridington (1978), Robinson and Wickwire (1989, 1992), Cruikshank et al. (1990).
4 Fladmark (1986), Rousseau (1993).
5 Fladmark (1986: 41).
6 Rousseau (1993: 168).
7 Teit (1975: 450).
8 Teit (1975: 450).
9 Teit (1975: 760-1).
10 Lane (1981: 407).
11 Tobey (1981: 416), Furniss (1993a: 5).
12 The following overview is based on Teit (1975), Tobey (1981), Lane (1981), and Furniss (1995b). In describing Carrier culture, I am referring specifically to the southern bands. The Carrier to the north and west, from present-day Prince George west to the Bulkley River, were heavily reliant on salmon as a resource, had more permanent summer villages, and had somewhat different forms of sociopolitical organization, being divided into matrilineal clans and houses represented by permanent, hereditary chiefs.
13 Goldman (1940: 334-5), Grossman (1965), Lane (1981: 407).
14 Teit (1975: 458).
15 Teit (1975: 760 n3, 786).
16 Dawson (1891: 15).
17 Richards and Rousseau (1987: 39).
18 Teit (1975: 535-7).
19 Teit (1975: 535).
20 Teit (1975: 535, 541).
21 Harrington (1967), Teit (1975: 784), Carlson (1994).
22 Mackenzie (1970: 320, 338, 342-3).
23 Teit (1975: 761,779, 784-6), Mackenzie (1970: 320, 340).
24 Mackenzie (1970: 319-20, 354-5).
25 Furniss (1993b: 25).
26 Teit (1975: 784).
27 McGillivray (1947).
28 Hudson's Bay Company Archives, Fort Alexandria Journals, 1845-8 (B.5-a-7), 18, 29 Sept. 1845.
29 McGillivray (1947).
30 McGillivray (1947: 217), Furniss (1993b: 28-9).
31 Fisher (1992: 24).
32 Harris (1997: 48).
33 Harris (1997: 31-67).
34 Teit (1975: 582-3), Furniss (1996). The tendency of extended family groups in other northern hunting societies to develop exclusive rights to specific trapping grounds in response to the European fur trade has been debated elsewhere (Speck 1915, 1927, Cooper 1939, Leacock 1954, Rogers 1963, Bishop 1970). In the case of the Secwepemc, these shifts were probably a reflection not of a one-way "evolutionary" assimilation into capitalist notions of private property but of ongoing tensions in Secwepemc societies between the autonomy of extended family groups and the solidarity of the band collective.
35 Boyd (1994), Harris (1994), Vibert (1995), Boyd (1996), Galois (1996).
36 Boyd (1994).
37 Boyd (1985), cited in Vibert (1995: 206).
38 Boyd (1994: 7,35), Fisher (1992: 45).

39 Jenness (1943: 475).
40 Morice (1978: 257), Hudson's Bay Company Archives, Fort Alexandria Journals, 1845-8 (B.5-a-7), 1855 (B.5-a-8).
41 Boyd (1994: 28).
42 Teit (1975: 463-6). In later decades, measles, scarlet fever, whooping cough, and influenza took many lives among the Secwepemc (Teit 1975: 463). By 1890, probably due primarily to disease, the overall population of the Carrier nation was reduced to fewer than a fifth of former numbers (Tobey 1981: 416).
43 Elliott (1978: 19-20).
44 Tennant (1990: 36), Fisher (1992: 152-3).
45 Tennant (1990: 26-38).
46 Skelton (1980: 39, 66).
47 As early as the 1840s, for example, the Williams Lake Secwepemc were cultivating crops of potatoes, carrots, and turnips through seeds obtained from the Hudson's Bay Company fort at Alexandria. Hudson's Bay Company Archives, Fort Alexandria Journals, 1845-8 (B.5-a-7), 24 July 1847.
48 The Soda Creek people, for example, were cultivating acres of wheat, barley, oats, potatoes, turnips, and other vegetables on the high bank adjacent to their village at the Fraser River. British Columbia Archives and Records Service (hereafter BCARS), McGuckin to Chief Commissioner of Lands and Works, 12 May 1868, Colonial Correspondence, file 1047d(1).
49 For the Canoe Creek band, see BCARS, Elliott to Colonial Secretary, 15 July 1864, C-AB 30.1J 6, letter no. 297. See also Fisher (1992: 107). For the Soda Creek Band, see BCARS, McGuckin to Chief Commissioner of Lands and Works, 12 May 1868; Saunders to Trutch, 17 Sept. 1868; and Trutch to Colonial Secretary, 28 Sept. 1868, all in Colonial Correspondence, file 1564. For the Williams Lake band, see BCARS, Nind to Acting Colonial Secretary, 4 May 1861, Colonial Correspondence, Letterbook (Alexandria), GR216, vol. 9, 99-100; C.J. Grandidier to Superintendent General of Indian Affairs, Ottawa, 20 Jan. 1880, RG10, vol. 3680, file 12,395-1.
50 References to the "old" reserves at Alexandria, Alkali Lake, Dog Creek, and Canoe Creek can be found in the letters of Reserve Commissioner Peter O'Reilly to the Superintendent General of Indian Affairs, Annual Report of the Department of Indian Affairs for the Year 1881 (Canada 1882: 183, 188, 191, 193). For the Soda Creek band, see note 49, above.
51 Fisher (1992: 160-1).
52 Apparently, there was only one instance of an Aboriginal person in the district applying to preempt land in such a manner. Jim Soulest, of the Williams Lake Secwepemc, was granted special permission in July 1868 to preempt 160 acres of land on Williams Lake about six miles from the village (Canada 1882: 178).
53 BCARS, An Ordinance Further to Define the Law Regulating the Acquisition of Land in British Columbia, 31 Mar. 1866. Preemption rights were restricted to British male subjects eighteen years or older.
54 Fisher (1992: 166-7).
55 BCARS, C.J. Grandidier to Superintendent General of Indian Affairs, Ottawa, 20 Jan. 1880, RG10, vol. 3680, file 12,395-1.
56 Canada (1885: 106-7).
57 Canada (1882: 177-94). In 1884, the Indian agent reported: "From the total absence of salmon, and the failure of the berry crop this summer, it is certain that there will be a great scarcity of food in all the reserves of this agency during the coming winter ... These Indians are most anxious to maintain themselves by farming, which they all perfectly understand. Their former resources of a livelihood – hunting, trapping and gold mining – are almost exhausted, and in a few years will be totally so" (Canada 1885: 115).
58 BCARS, C.J. Grandidier to Superintendent General of Indian Affairs, Ottawa, 20 Jan. 1880, RG10, vol. 3680, file 12,395-1.
59 BCARS, Chief William to Victoria Colonist, 7 Nov. 1879.
60 BCARS, "An Astonishing State of Things at Williams Lake," 7 Nov. 1879; "the Williams Lake Indians Again," 6 Dec. 1879; "the Distressed Williams Lake Indians," 6 Dec. 1879; "the Condition of the Indians," 20 Jan. 1880, all in the Victoria *Daily Colonist*. Also see

BCARS, James McGuckin to Indian Superintendent Lenihan, 15 Apr. 1878, RG10, vol. 3680, file 12,395-1; William Laing-Meason, J.P., to Gilbert Malcolm Sproat, 21 Apr. 1879, RG10, vol. 3680, file 12,395-1; James McGuckin to Indian Superintendent Lenihan, 22 Nov. 1879, RG10, vol. 3680, file 12,395-1; C.J. Grandidier to Superintendent General of Indian Affairs, Ottawa, RG10, vol. 3680, file 12,395-1; F.W. Foster to I.W. Powell, 28 June 1880, RG10, vol. 3681, file 12,395-2.

61 Tennant (1990: 46).
62 Tennant (1990: 44, 47), Fisher (1992: 176-7).
63 Fisher (1992: 181).
64 British Columbia (1987: 153).
65 Teit (1975: 458).
66 BCARS, C.J. Grandidier to Superintendent General of Indian Affairs, Ottawa, 20 Jan. 1880, RG10, vol. 3680, file 12,395-1.
67 BCARS, Nind to Acting Colonial Secretary, 4 May 1861, Colonial Correspondence, Letterbook (Alexandria), GR216, vol. 9, 99-100.
68 BCARS, Acting Colonial Secretary to Nind, 10 June 1861, C AB 30.1 J 3, 329-31.
69 Canada (1882: 177-96).
70 Canada (1882: 178); BCARS, Smithe to Vankoughnet, 12 Apr. 1884, RG10, vol. 3583, file 1092; Chiefs Barnard and Thomas to Minister of Indian Affairs, 20 Dec. 1888, RG10, vol. 3583, file 1092; Pinchbeck to Powell, 2 June 1888, RG10, vol. 3583, file 1092.
71 Canada (1885: 115).
72 Canada (1882: 181).
73 BCARS, O'Reilly to Chief Commissioner of Lands and Works, 20 Sept. 1895, RG10, vol. 1279, 70.
74 Canada (1888: 150).
75 Canada (1888: 148-54), Canada (1893: 255-6).
76 Tennant (1990: 87).
77 BCARS, Memorial to Sir Wilfrid Laurier, Premier of the Dominion of Canada, from the Chiefs of the Secwepemc, Okanagan, and Couteau Tribes of British Columbia, Kamloops, BC, 25 Aug. 1910.
78 Tennant (1990: 88).
79 Tennant (1990: 101).
80 Cited in Tennant (1990: 111).
81 Indian Act, *Revised Statutes of Canada*, 1927, Chapter 98, Section 141.
82 Tobias (1983).
83 Tobias (1983: 44-6).
84 Canada (1888: 115).
85 Canada (1885: 115).
86 Canada (1885: 106, 107, 110).
87 Canada (1885: 105), Murphy (1894: 317).
88 Canada (1888: 148).
89 Furniss (1995a).
90 For example, BCARS, C.J. Grandidier to Superintendent General of Indian Affairs, Ottawa, 20 Jan. 1880, RG10, vol. 3680, file 12,395-1; James McGuckin to Indian Superintendent Lenihan, 22 Nov. 1879, RG10, vol. 3680, file 12,395-1; McGuckin to Chief Commissioner of Lands and Works, 12 May 1868, Colonial Correspondence, file 1564.
91 Furniss (1995a).
92 Furniss (1995c).
93 Furniss (1995c).
94 Furniss (1995c).
95 Hawthorn (1966: 260, 262).
96 Stangoe (1994: 10-12).
97 Skelton (1980: 68).
98 Bonner, Bliss, and Litterick (1995).
99 BCARS, Canada Census, 1901, Province of British Columbia, District of Yale and Cariboo, Williams Lake Subdivision, reel B-11275.

100 Teit (1975: 464).
101 Skelton (1980: 205), Stangoe (1994: 20, 34).
102 Skelton (1980: 205-6).
103 Weir (1964).
104 Thomson (1990).
105 Weir (1964: 100).
106 Sloan (1956).
107 Weir (1964: 65).
108 Marchak (1983: 49).
109 Marchak (1983: 50).
110 Marchak (1983: 40).
111 Commission on Resources and the Environment, Appendix 1, 15.
112 Commission on Resources and the Environment, Appendix 1, 15.
113 Hawthorn, Belshaw, and Jamieson (1960: 144), Weir (1964: 103). Weir reported that in 1950 Indians comprised 70 percent of temporary ranch help in the Chilcotin and 50 percent in the Cariboo. Most of this labour was for haying contracts, but it was being made redundant by mechanization.
114 Hawthorn, Belshaw, and Jamieson (1960: 144).
115 Hawthorn (1966: 312-38).
116 For example, "Saviours of the Shuswaps," *Reader's Digest* Nov. 1986: 84-8. The history of the community's fight against alcoholism has been depicted in the video documentary *The Honor of All*, which has been shown widely in First Nations communities across Canada and the United States and has served as an inspiration for other communities tackling similar social problems.
117 In 1973, the Supreme Court of Canada ruled in the *Calder* case that the Nisga'a held title over their lands when the first colonial government was established in 1858, a fact that the province had long denied. The court came close to recognizing that the Nisga'a still held title, three judges ruling in favour, three against.
118 British Columbia Court of Appeal (1993).
119 Supreme Court of Canada (1997: 6).
120 Supreme Court of Canada (1997: 109).
121 Savage and Associates (1993).
122 Savage and Associates (1993).

**Chapter 3: The Landscape of Public History**

1 Williams (1977: 116).
2 Hobsbawm and Ranger (1983).
3 By "public history," I mean the representation of history in public places: museums, galleries, festivals, parks, public schools, and so on. My use of the term is similar to the way in which Karp and Lavine (1991), Karp, Kreamer, and Lavine (1992), and others have used the term "public culture." I define "popular history" more generally as histories produced in nonacademic settings for nonacademic audiences.
4 Trigger (1985), Walker (1971).
5 Walker (1971).
6 Barman, Hébert, and McCaskill (1987), Mazurek (1987), Barman and Battiste (1995).
7 Trigger (1985: 4).
8 Trigger (1985, 1986).
9 Collins and Sheffe (1979).
10 Bowers and Garrod (1987).
11 Collins and Sheffe (1979: 95).
12 Collins and Sheffe (1979: 245).
13 Collins and Sheffe (1979: 134).
14 Bowers and Garrod (1987: 161).
15 Bowers and Garrod (1987: 171).
16 Collins and Sheffe (1979: 134).
17 Bowers and Garrod (1987: 111).

18 Prucha (1986: 179-80).
19 Bowers and Garrod (1987: 126-8).
20 Bowers and Garrod (1987: 127).
21 Bowers and Garrod (1987: 187).
22 Bowers and Garrod (1987: 187).
23 Bowers and Garrod (1987: 187).
24 Bowers and Garrod (1987: 188).
25 Bowers and Garrod (1987: 190).
26 Bowers and Garrod (1987: 190).
27 Braroe (1975), Stymeist (1975), Dunk (1991).
28 Francis (1992).
29 Walker (1983: 346).
30 British Columbia (1995: 16).
31 *Outlaws and Lawmen of Western Canada* (1983, 1987).
32 BC Provincial Police Veteran's Association (1991).
33 Clark (1986, 1989, 1993).
34 Denny (1994).
35 Berton (1978, 1982).
36 Berton (1982: 31).
37 Berton (1982: 28-9).
38 Berton (1982: 30).
39 Smith (1980), Pritchard (1992).
40 Trigger (1986: 321).
41 McKelvie (1985).
42 Rothenberger (1978).
43 Glavin's *Nemiah: The Unconquered Country* (1992), presenting Tsilhqot'in elders' narratives of the events surrounding the confrontation, is an exception.
44 In an effort to acknowledge these discrepant historical experiences and perspectives, the Cariboo-Chilcotin Justice Inquiry (Sarich 1993) recommended that these men be given an official pardon and that a monument be erected to honour their efforts to protect Tsilhqot'in territories.
45 *Cariboo Gold Rush* (1987).
46 Cruikshank (1992).
47 Fisher (1992: 69-70).
48 Fisher (1992: 71).
49 Fisher (1992: 70).
50 Marriott (1966), Lavington (1982), Collier (1991), Hobson (1993).
51 Collier (1991), Hobson (1993).
52 Collier (1991: 3).
53 Atwood (1972).
54 Collier (1991: 127).
55 Collier (1991: 139).
56 Collier (1991: 104).
57 Collier (1991: 108).
58 Collier (1991: 111-12).
59 Hobson (1993: 16).
60 Hobson (1993: 9).
61 Hobson (1993: 9).
62 Hobson (1993: 165-73).
63 For example, in 1912 a Carrier family at Trout Lake in Nazko country was running a herd of sixteen cattle and had built a thirty-kilometre sleigh road through the bush to take their cattle to market (Canada 1913: 259). In 1915 at Ulkatcho, two brothers, Old Cahoose and Capoose, owned almost 200 horses; one brother had recently sold his stock of sixty cattle. The two had set up trading stores in the region and had built a sixty-kilometre road to haul freight into and out of their territory; this road eventually facilitated opening up the country for non-Aboriginal settlement (BCARS, Evidence Heard Before

the Royal Commission on Indian Affairs for the Province of BC, Bella Coola Agency, Meeting with the Ulkatcho Band, Victoria, 3 August 1915, 132-40).

64 One Ulkatcho man, Capoose, had dealt with this dilemma by asking a local white settler to "lend" his name and preempt the land on which Capoose was living and on which he had built a house, barns, and several miles of fencing. The settler did so but then refused to sell the deed to Capoose. Capoose raised this issue with the commissioners during the 1912-6 Royal Commission on Indian Affairs; the commission refused to intervene in the matter (BCARS, Evidence Heard Before the Royal Commission on Indian Affairs for the Province of BC, Bella Coola Agency, Meeting with the Ulkatcho Band, Victoria, 3 August 1915, 132-40).
65 Goldman (1953).
66 Bonner, Bliss, and Litterick (1995).
67 Bonner, Bliss, and Litterick (1995: 8).
68 Bonner, Bliss, and Litterick (1995: 10, 12, 15, 275).
69 Bonner, Bliss, and Litterick (1995: 12, 112, 113, 136).
70 Speare (1973), Tatla Lake School Project (1986-93), Boyd (1989, 1990a, 1990b), Coffey et al. (1990), Birchwater (1991, 1993), Glavin (1992), Furniss (1993a, 1993b), Mack (1993, 1994).
71 Birchwater (1993).
72 Birchwater (1993: vii).
73 Kohl (1990), Hale and Barman (1991).
74 Bennett (1995: 112). There is one notable exception. A display on the "Cariboo's First Japanese Family" discusses the extensive racial discrimination that this family suffered during the Second World War. Given the powerful forces that bear down on city museums to represent history as harmonious and progressive, this display constitutes a significant movement into areas of history in which there are usually considerable silences. In contrast, there is virtually no reference to the racial discrimination that Aboriginal people historically experienced, and continue to experience, in the city.
75 Bommes and Wright (1982), Alonso (1988), Bodnar (1992), Cohen (1994).

**Chapter 4: Mobilizing History**

1 Canada (1994: 2073-4).
2 Vidich (1990).
3 Vidich (1990: 18).
4 In the context of the American media, Vidich (1990) defines this idealized public morality as a watered-down version of nineteenth-century small-town populist norms.
5 See Watkins (1990).
6 Commission on Resources and the Environment (1994: Appendix 3. 10).
7 Vidich and Bensman (1968), Stymeist (1975), Nadel (1983), Dunk (1991).
8 Neering (1991), McLean (1992).
9 Farber (1983), Errington (1987), Lavenda (1992).
10 Vidich (1990: 17).
11 McLean (1992).
12 Williams (1973).
13 Nadel-Klein (1995).
14 Fabian (1983).
15 Rosaldo (1989: 69).
16 Marchak (1988).
17 Dunk (1991).
18 Clearly, these values are associated in general with the rise of industrial capitalism and, as Weber (1958) argued, with the rise of ascetic Protestantism, which transformed the individual's pursuit of wealth through continuous labour into a sacred duty.
19 Bakke (1940a, 1940b).
20 Nadel-Klein (1991), in her ethnography of a rural fishing village in Scotland, describes how various parties – outside filmmakers and playwrights, old-time villagers, and upper-class residents – construct different versions of local identity, portraying villagers as

romantic and tradition bound, as backward and unprogressive, or as marginalized and struggling against external state-corporate powers. Expressions of "localism," Nadel-Klein argues, are constructed in specific political and economic contexts and serve as weapons of political struggle. Similar complexities in the construction of localism – identities tied to place – can undoubtedly be found in the Cariboo-Chilcotin. In the following pages, I trace only two contexts in which such identities arise.

21 "Mooney Wants Refund," *Tribune* [Williams Lake], 28 May 1992: A10.

22 "Mooney Loses House to Bulldozer," *Tribune* [Williams Lake], 5 Dec. 1991: A2.

23 Paine (1985: 190-1).

24 Armitage and Kennedy (1989).

25 See Broady (1975), Nadel (1983), Landsman (1987: 108), and Nadel-Klein (1995).

26 "Let's Bomb Mooney," *Tribune* [Williams Lake], 5 Dec. 1991: A6.

27 For example, St. Pierre (1984, 1985).

28 "Gook Is Correct, Bulldozing Cruel," *Tribune* [Williams Lake], 4 Feb. 1992: A5.

29 "Fire the Top CRD Brass for Decision," *Cariboo Observer* [Quesnel], 11 Dec. 1991: A5, 14.

30 The public responses of CRD officials were extremely weak in the face of such powerful symbolic rhetoric. The CRD chairman fell back on the image of paternal government: the regional district, he said, was responsible for ensuring the safety of the public. It was merely protecting itself – and thus "saving" taxpayers money – from a potential civil lawsuit should an occupant or tenant be hurt. "CRD Enforcing the Law in Rick Mooney Case – Reeves," *Cariboo Observer* [Quesnel], 30 Oct. 1991: A5; "Mooney Loses House to Bulldozer," *Tribune* [Williams Lake], 5 Dec. 1991: A2.

31 Slotkin (1992: 6).

32 Slotkin (1992: 23).

33 Slotkin (1992: 151).

34 Loo (1994).

35 Innis (1962), Marchak (1983).

36 "Wells's Sharpest Thorn Awaits His Day in Court," *Vancouver Sun*, 15 Sept. 1993: A15.

37 "Then Again, Some Don't: Arcand of the IWA Explains How to Break the Back of CORE," *Vancouver Sun*, 8 Apr. 1994: A19; "How to Wreck the CORE Process, IWA Style," *Tribune* [Williams Lake], 21 Apr. 1994: A4.

38 "Premier Fails to Provide Forestry Workers with Assurance He Will Reject Land-Use Plan," *Vancouver Sun*, 22 Mar. 1994: A3.

39 "15,000 Forest Workers Drown Out Premier," *Vancouver Sun*, 22 Mar. 1994: A1.

40 The following quotations are from pamphlets, newsletters, and advertising material contained in an informational package supplied to me by the Cariboo Communities Coalition (Cariboo Communities Coalition, 1995).

41 Dominy (1993, 1995).

42 Griffiths (1996), Read (1996: 52-74).

43 Nadel-Klein (1991, 1995).

44 Dominy (1995).

45 Dominy (1995: 363).

46 Dominy (1995: 369).

47 For example, a Williams Lake *Advocate* advertisement (3 Aug. 1994) argued that 98 percent of job losses in the forest industry were due to mechanization; only 2 percent were due to the establishment of parks. "Mechanized sawmills are laying off workers and consuming more and more wood – their appetites are insatiable" the ad read. A *Tribune* ad (14 July 1994) stated: "The [Cariboo Communities Coalition] campaign is backed by groups financed by big forest companies. These are the same companies that have been laying off workers and replacing them with machines. They are racing to cut as much wood as they can before the saw logs disappear."

48 This conflict was finally resolved in October 1994 when the Cariboo Communities Coalition, the Cariboo Chilcotin Conservation Council, and the provincial government negotiated an agreement over a new land-use plan. Park lands were designated, and other regions were cleared for future logging activity. A year later, the chief forester announced that the five-year annual allowable cut for the Williams Lake region would remain

unchanged from the pre-CORE levels, suggesting that the CORE report, now passed into legislation, had little impact on harvest levels. Debates continue in Williams Lake over the implementation of the CORE plan, over the provisions for protected areas, and over the sustainability of current harvest levels.

49 "Worried about Recent Hatred," *Tribune* [Williams Lake], 4 Aug. 1994: A5.

50 Goldie (1989).

**Chapter 5: Indians, Whites, and Common-Sense Racism**

1 Scott (1990: 198).

2 Dunk (1991: 107).

3 Stymeist (1975: 75-6)

4 At times, Aboriginal people are also blamed for other aspects of the poor public image of Williams Lake. In 1995, for example, a report by the provincial medical health officer found that the Cariboo-Chilcotin was one of the least healthy regions of the province. As the Cariboo-Chilcotin medical health officer explained to the Williams Lake *Tribune*, health was judged by rates of premature death, which were linked to a variety of factors, notably socioeconomic conditions. The mayor of Williams Lake responded that the low rating of the Cariboo-Chilcotin was a statistical artifact. "There is a very high youth native mortality rate which throws the figures off," he was quoted as stating. Whether or not this is true is a matter for debate. What is significant is that, in drawing a distinction between Aboriginal and non-Aboriginal health status, the mayor implicitly excluded Aboriginal people from the definition of "our community." Rather than responding with concern for the conditions of life among certain regional residents, the mayor dismissed and externalized the problem. "Cobb Disputes Health Statistics," *Tribune* [Williams Lake], 21 Mar. 1995: A2.

5 My own review of six months of court reports in the Williams Lake *Tribune* did not support this generalization. Based on my familiarity with Aboriginal surnames in the region, I concluded that about 53 percent of the people named were probably Aboriginal, a number very close to that in the attorney general's records, as I discuss below.

6 "Williams Lake Crime Rate Dismays Mayor," *Vancouver Sun*, 26 Oct. 1991: A19.

7 Hamilton and Sinclair (1991a: 85).

8 Hamilton and Sinclair (1991a: 109-10).

9 Hamilton and Sinclair (1991a: 107).

10 Sarich (1993: 11).

11 Braroe (1975: 4-5, 87-120), Stymeist (1975: 75-6), Dunk (1991: 109-14).

12 Francis (1992).

13 These comments are inaccurate in many respects. For example, many Aboriginal homes have productive vegetable gardens, and many Aboriginal men have successfully completed carpentry apprenticeships. Most homes on reserves are now constructed using Aboriginal labour. The Dene Development Corporation is owned by four area First Nations; it both trains Aboriginal people in the construction trades and operates a successful business building homes on reserves.

14 Dunk (1991).

15 Dyck (1991).

16 Goldie (1989).

17 Memmi (1965).

18 "Deposit, Please," *Tribune* [Williams Lake], 2 Feb. 1993: A4.

19 Schutz (1971).

20 Schutz (1971: 11-13).

21 Kennedy (1997).

22 Fanon (1970: 10).

23 This failure to link degrees of whiteness with skin colour is in sharp contrast to rural social relations in Australia, where Aboriginal people use the term "yellafella" to denote Aboriginal people of mixed background, a term that mediates the other commonly heard terms, "blackfella" and "whitefella." In contrast to Canada, in Australia there has long been a much more heightened public notion of Aboriginality as a racial rather than an

ethnic construct, and the association of Aboriginality with degrees of blood quantum has been central in government and public discourses for over a century (Weaver 1984).

24 Braroe (1975: 184).
25 Miles (1989: 79).
26 Hall (1978: 26), cited in Miles (1989: 82).
27 Thomas (1994: 171).
28 Braroe (1975), Stymeist (1975), Lithman (1984).
29 Braroe (1975: 3-4).
30 Stymeist (1975: 6).
31 Schwimmer (1972), Braroe (1975).
32 Scott (1991: 198).
33 Fanon (1963), Memmi (1965).
34 Braroe (1975: 42).
35 Braroe (1975: 42-3, 105-7), Stymeist (1975: 68-9).
36 Gleadow (1992).
37 Gleadow (1992: 5).
38 See Dunk (1991: 108-9, 114), Hamilton and Sinclair (1991b: 52).
39 Acoose (1995).
40 Hickman, Poitras, and Evans (1989), Alberta Task Force (1991), Hamilton and Sinclair (1991a, b), Sarich (1993).
41 Transcripts, Cariboo-Chilcotin Justice Inquiry, Nenqai Yaheltig Law Centre, Anaham Reserve.
42 For example, the substantive issues of RCMP abuse of authority and use of excessive force, and the differential treatment of Aboriginal people by agents of the provincial court system, went virtually unreported in the city newspaper, despite receiving prominent coverage in the *Vancouver Sun*.
43 Braroe (1975: 105-7), Stymeist (1975: 68-9).
44 One T-shirt had inscribed on it "Gustafsen Lake, '95," and pictured an Indian status card imprinted with the Monopoly board game phrase "Get out of jail free."
45 "Judge Hears of Difficulties with Mall Guard," *Vancouver Sun*, 8 Jan. 1993: B5. See also Sarich (1993: 30).
46 *Tribune* [Williams Lake], 28 Feb. 1995: A5.
47 Braroe (1975: 42-3, 105-7), Stymeist (1975: 70).
48 Braroe (1975: 115-18).
49 Hawthorn, Jamieson, and Belshaw (1960: 65).
50 Memmi (1965).
51 See Lithman (1984) for a discussion of this point in rural Manitoba.
52 Scott (1990: 206).
53 Schwimmer (1972), Braroe (1975).
54 Lurie (1971).
55 Certainly, too, there are contexts in which Aboriginal people exploit these stereotypes, just as there are instances in which Euro-Canadians challenge them. For example, romantic images of the noble savage are strategically promoted by the Soda Creek First Nation, which, initially in partnership with a German couple, recently constructed a "heritage village" on reserve land overlooking the Fraser River. The Soda Creek First Nation now offers international tourists the opportunity to experience authentic Secwepemc culture and traditions.
56 Friendship Centers are found in many regional cities across Canada. They provide short-term housing, services, and a gathering place for transient or urban Aboriginal people.
57 Errington and Gewertz (1994).
58 Errington and Gewertz (1994: 106).
59 Errington and Gewertz (1994: 106).
60 Basso (1979: 37).
61 Dunk (1991).
62 Menzies (1994: 778).
63 Menzies (1994: 784).
64 Foucault (1980: 39).

**Chapter 6: Encountering Histories**

1 Treaty negotiations initially proceeded rapidly, but since 1996 they have slowed down significantly. Some First Nations leaders believe that the province is deliberately stalling negotiations.

2 The Reform Party's influence is not limited to the Cariboo-Chilcotin. In the 1993 federal election, the Reform Party won fifty-two seats, replacing the previous Progressive Conservative MPs when their party fell to its crushing defeat. The vast majority of those seats were in Alberta and British Columbia. In British Columbia, the Reform Party swept the province, electing candidates in twenty-four of the province's thirty-two ridings (Eagles et al. 1995). The Reform Party has consistently opposed the settlement of Aboriginal land claims not only in British Columbia, most recently the Nisga'a agreement in principle, but also in the western Arctic and Yukon.

3 Grand Council of the Crees (1995).

4 Alfred (1995).

5 Tanner (1993).

6 Secwepemc First Nations also strongly resisted the participation of the province and third-party interests (municipal governments) at the negotiating table but chose to proceed nevertheless.

7 Smith (1995).

8 The BC Court of Appeal dismissed the Gitksan and Wet'suwe'ten's claim to ownership and jurisdiction but found that Aboriginal rights with respect to the land continue today and that the Crown's title to the land is subject to these continuing Aboriginal "interests." The court ruled that the nature of these interests could only be determined through negotiated treaty settlements or through subsequent court cases (British Columbia Court of Appeal 1993: 68-9). In 1997 the Supreme Court of Canada ordered a retrial of the case. It concluded that Judge McEachern erred in his failure to consider First Nations oral history as an important source of historical evidence. The Supreme Court also provided further legal definition of the nature and scope of Aboriginal title and rights. Aboriginal title includes the right to "exclusive use and occupation of the land"; Aboriginal rights are not limited to traditional activities but can include contemporary cultural practices that are not "integral to distinctive Aboriginal cultures." This interpretation opens the door for consideration of a broad range of contemporary activities to be construed as Aboriginal rights. The decision also clarified which evidence is required to show proof of Aboriginal title, stating that occupation (rather than the centrality of the land to the culture) is sufficient to prove Aboriginal title, which persists as long as a group has held a "substantial connection" to the land, even if the occupation has been discontinuous (Supreme Court of Canada, 1997).

9 In sharp contrast are the ideologies against assimilation now emerging in postcolonial contexts in Europe in response to increased Third World immigration. The political rhetoric of right-wing groups opposing immigration is framed not by the assumption of the inevitability of assimilation but by the opposite: the incompatibility of different cultures and the "natural" tendency of cultural groups to avoid communication and contact and to maintain separate cultural traditions. Immigration thus threatens a nation's presumed homogeneous integrity and "inevitably" leads to violence (Stolcke 1995).

10 Murphy and Steward (1956), Steward (1960).

11 For example, Asch (1982), Feit (1982).

12 A similar group has emerged in Ontario, calling itself ON FIRE: the Ontario Federation for Individual Rights and Equality. For an analysis of ON FIRE's anti-land claims rhetoric, see Valentine (1997).

13 "Only One Law for Canadian People," *Tribune* [Williams Lake], 1 Aug. 1995: A5.

14 Merlan (1995: 71).

15 Merlan (1995: 72).

16 Sharp (1990: 194).

17 Sharp (1990: 194-5).

18 For a discussion of this issue in the Canadian context see Asch (1981); in Australia, Peterson and Sanders (1998); in New Zealand, Sharp (1990).

19 See Kymlicka (1995) for an introduction to the accommodation of minority collective rights within liberal democracies.
20 Bayefski and Eberts (1985: 599-607).
21 Asch (1981: 82-3).
22 Asch (1981: 84).
23 Bayefsky (1985), Weiler and Elliot (1986), Beckton (1987), Hudson (1987), Sanders (1987).
24 Gold (1986: 88).
25 Sharp (1990: 22).
26 Sharp (1990: 21).
27 Asch (1981: 74-5).
28 In very different contexts, Aboriginal people too may discuss and debate Indian identity based on the degree of Indian "blood," as I have described in Chapter 5.
29 *Tribune* [Williams Lake], 24 Nov. 1994: A5.
30 *Tribune* [Williams Lake], 31 Mar. 1994: A5.
31 *Tribune* [Williams Lake], 19 Dec. 1995: A5.
32 The real names of the first and third First Nations speakers I quote here are used with consent.
33 Dyck (1986). Chief Charleyboy, in fact, used a different strategy to reach non-Aboriginal audiences during a public meeting in the city in December 1996. The meeting had been called by the RCMP to discuss the epidemic of vehicle thefts in Williams Lake and to elicit public feedback on how this problem could be addressed. The RCMP believed that the thefts were being carried out by a group of forty to fifty teenagers, most of whom were from one of the Tsilhqot'in reserves. Although the moderator insisted that the meeting had been called not to blame any particular groups but to discuss solutions, the spectre of the "Indian criminal" stereotype hovered over the room. Chief Charleyboy used the occasion to lobby for support for his initiative to create a Tsilhqot'in-controlled and -run youth detention centre. In arguing that the Young Offenders Act was "a joke," and that a Tsilhqot'in-run youth detention centre would "save taxpayers money," his appeal resonated with some of the key rhetorical slogans and political concerns of the local Euro-Canadian right-wing public. Charleyboy ultimately received overwhelming support for his proposal.
34 The efforts of Aboriginal leaders to develop specific discursive styles for negotiating with government officials is also described by Beckett (1985) for Torres Strait Islanders, whose representatives must "know how to talk to white people" (104).
35 Kaplan and Kelly (1994: 129).
36 Henry and Tator (1994).
37 Henry and Tator (1994: 1).

**Chapter 7: Re-creating the Wild West**

1 When I speak of Indian participation, I mean the participation of Aboriginal people in forms emphasizing their cultural identity and heritage.
2 Spivak (1990: 11-12).
3 Graham (1991: 25).
4 Slatta (1990: 148-54).
5 Flieger (1991: 34-5).
6 Russell (1970: 14).
7 Slotkin (1992).
8 Slotkin (1992: 68).
9 Hinsley (1991).
10 Russell (1970: 64, 69).
11 Gray (1985).
12 LeCompte (1985).
13 Pettipas (1994: 147-8).
14 Burgess (1992).
15 Whyte (1985).

16 Regular (1986), Pettipas (1994).
17 Cited in Pettipas (1994: 149).
18 Pettipas (1994: 149, 163).
19 Graham (1991: 25).
20 1926 Stampede Program, personal collection of Mrs. Irene Stangoe, Williams Lake.
21 1924 Stampede Program, personal collection of Mrs. Irene Stangoe, Williams Lake.
22 Stoeltje (1988), LeCompte (1993).
23 Richard Slotkin refers to the overwhelming growth in popularity of Hollywood westerns in the post-Second World War period as the "golden age of the Western" (1992: 347).
24 Powers (1988).
25 "A Success Is Recorded," *Tribune* [Williams Lake], 15 June 1950: 2.
26 For a discussion of the role of powwows in cultural revitalization and politics among other Native North Americans, see, for example, Howard (1955, 1976), Corrigan (1970), Dyck (1979, 1983), Lerch (1992), and Kracht (1994).
27 Green (1988).
28 Stoeltje (1981), Lawrence (1982), Errington (1990).
29 Farber (1983), Lawrence (1987).
30 Farber (1983), Lavenda (1983), Errington (1987).
31 Dirks (1994), Myers (1994), Holland and Skinner (1995), Cruikshank (1997); also see Grimes (1976) for an early example.
32 Farber (1983), Lavenda (1983, 1992), Smith (1984).
33 LeCompte (1985, 1993).
34 Lawrence (1982: 7).
35 *Lahal* is a traditional gambling game.
36 Pan-Indian-style powwows have been held in Secwepemc communities since the early 1980s and in Tsilhqot'in communities since 1991. Indian princess competitions have been held in the Cariboo-Chilcotin only since the early 1990s. By 1994, these competitions were held in conjunction with powwows in two Secwepemc and two Tsilhqot'in reserve communities. A pageant was also held during the annual First Nations Awareness Days, organized by a First Nations educator with the Cariboo-Chilcotin School District. The Miss Chief Anaham Princess is chosen at the annual Chief Anaham Powwow, held each spring since 1991 at the Anaham Tsilhqot'in reserve. Contestants are judged on a combination of poise, speech, powwow regalia, and dancing ability.
37 Warner (1959).
38 One woman whom I spoke with from the Anaham First Nation float, when I asked why her group had entered the parade, expressed this risk: "It's like we're finally getting brave enough to do these kind of things." She hoped that, by portraying Tsilhqot'in culture and people in a positive light, the Euro-Canadian public would "get to know us a bit better" and that the racial tensions encountered by Aboriginal children in the school system might be diminished.
39 This was my observation in both the 1994 and 1995 stampede parades.
40 Green (1975), Montrose (1991).
41 Green (1975).
42 This comment should be contrasted with the ability of Aboriginal people in the Cariboo-Chilcotin to organize funeral feasts for over 100 people on a mere three or four days' notice.
43 See Dyck (1991).
44 Lavenda (1983, 1988), Manning (1983).
45 Grimes (1976), Cruikshank (1997).
46 Wolfe (1991: 198).
47 Carrier (1992: 198).
48 Spivak (1990), Coombes (1994), Parry (1994), Thomas (1994).

**Chapter 8: The Frontier Complex**

1 Prucha (1986).
2 Macklem (1993).

3 Culhane (1998: 261), Furniss (in press).
4 Macklem (1993: 13).
5 Macklem (1993: 12).
6 Miles (1989: 51).
7 Barker (1981), Miles (1989: 62), Balibar (1991).
8 Stolcke (1995).
9 Miles (1989: 63).
10 Miles (1989: 98).
11 Deloria (1969).
12 Ryan (1992).
13 See Abu-Lughod (1990), Ortner (1995), and Brown (1996) for similar comments on the silences in current resistance studies.
14 Plaice (1990).
15 Hall (1980: 186).
16 Dyck (1991: 11-23).
17 Paine (1977b).
18 Paine (1977a: 12).
19 Brody (1991).
20 Brody (1991: 98-9).
21 Brody (1991: 99).
22 Brody (1991: 113).
23 Brody (1991: 114).
24 Dyck (1991).
25 Dyck (1991: 26).
26 Dyck (1991: 2-3, 11-15).
27 "Anthropology's Terrible Triumph," *Vancouver Sun,* 21 Dec. 1995: A17.
28 McEachern (1991: 13, 25, 31, 128-9, 250, 252, 299-301).
29 For example, Cassidy (1992), Miller (1992), Waldram, Berringer, and Warry (1992), Daly and Mills (1993), Mills (1994, 1994-5, 1996), Culhane (1998).
30 In addition to the references cited above, see also Cove (1996) and Paine (1996).
31 McEachern (1991: 284).
32 Elsewhere I have discussed in more detail how the frontier myth makes its appearance both in the BC Supreme Court's Delgamuukw decision and in the report of the Cariboo-Chilcotin Justice Inquiry, which took a much more sympathetic stance to First Nations and to Aboriginal title and rights (Furniss, in press).
33 Tennant (1992: 80-1).
34 Although one of my goals here has been to encourage a new way of looking at BC history, or historiography more precisely, I am not presuming that my analysis is completely free from these colonial influences. I am instead suggesting the importance of an ongoing commitment to self-reflexivity in all academic work focusing on First Nations and colonialism in Canada.

# References


Abu-Lughod, Lila. 1990. The Romance of Resistance: Tracing Transformations of Power through Bedouin Women. *American Ethnologist* 17(1): 41-55.

Acoose, Janice. 1995. *Iskwewak: Kah' Ki Yaw Ni Wahkomakanak. Neither Indian Princesses nor Easy Squaws.* Toronto: Women's Press.

Alberta Task Force on the Criminal Justice System. 1991. *Justice on Trial: Report of the Task Force on the Criminal Justice System and Its Impact on the Indian and Métis People of Alberta.* Edmonton: Alberta Task Force.

Alfred, Gerald R. 1995. *Heeding the Voices of Our Ancestors: Kahnawake Mohawk Politics and the Rise of Native Nationalism.* Don Mills, ON: Oxford University Press.

Alonso, Ana Maria. 1988. The Effects of Truth: Re-Presentations of the Past and the Imagining of Community. *Journal of Historical Sociology* 1(1): 33-57.

Armitage, Peter, and John C. Kennedy. 1989. Redbaiting and Racism on Our Frontier: Military Expansion in Labrador and Quebec. *Canadian Review of Sociology and Anthropology* 26(5): 798-817.

Asch, Michael. 1982. Dene Self-Determination and the Study of Hunter-Gatherers in the Modern World. In Eleanor Leacock and Richard Lee, eds., *Politics and History in Band Societies*, 347-71. Cambridge: Cambridge University Press.

–. 1984. *Home and Native Land: Aboriginal Rights and the Canadian Constitution.* Toronto: Methuen.

–. 1995. The Slavey Indians. The Relevance of Ethnohistory to Development. In R. Bruce Morrison and C. Roderick Wilson, eds., *Native Peoples: The Canadian Experience*, 260-85. 2nd ed. Toronto: McClelland and Stewart.

Atwood, Margaret. 1972. *Survival: A Thematic Guide to Canadian Literature.* Toronto: Anansi.

Bakke, E. Wight. 1940a. *The Unemployed Worker.* New Haven: Yale University Press.

–. 1940b. *Citizens without Work.* New Haven: Yale University Press.

Balibar, Etienne. 1991. Is There a "Neo-Racism"? In Etienne Balibar and Immanuel Wallerstein, eds., *Race, Nation, Class: Ambiguous Identities*, 17-28. London: Verso.

Barker, M. 1981. *The New Racism.* London: Junction.

Barman, Jean, and Marie Battiste, eds. 1995. *First Nations Education in Canada: The Circle Unfolds.* Vancouver: UBC Press.

Barman, Jean, Yvonne Hébert, and Don McCaskill, eds. 1987. *Indian Education in Canada, Volume 2: The Challenge.* Vancouver: UBC Press.

Basso, Keith H. 1979. *Portraits of "the Whiteman": Linguistic Play and Cultural Symbols among the Western Apache.* Cambridge: Cambridge University Press.

Bayefsky, Anne. 1985. Defining Equality Rights. In Anne Bayefsky and Mary Eberts, eds., *Equality Rights and the Canadian Charter of Freedoms*, 1-79. Toronto: Carswell.

Bayefsky, Anne, and Mary Eberts, eds. 1985. *Equality Rights and the Canadian Charter of Rights and Freedoms.* Toronto: Carswell.

Beckett, Jeremy. 1985. "Knowing How to Talk to White People": Torres Strait Islanders and the Politics of Representation. In Noel Dyck, ed., *Indigenous Peoples and the Nation-State: Fourth World Politics in Canada, Australia, and Norway*, 95-112. St. John's: Institute of Social and Economic Research, Memorial University.

Beckton, Clare. 1987. Section 27 and Section 15 of the Charter. In *Multiculturalism and the Charter: A Legal Perspective*, Canadian Human Rights Foundation, ed., 1-13. Vancouver: Carswell.

Bennett, Tony. 1995. *The Birth of the Museum: History, Theory, Politics*. London: Routledge.

Berton, Pierre. 1978. *The Wild Frontier: More Tales from the Remarkable Past*. Toronto: McClelland and Stewart.

–. 1982. *Why We Act Like Canadians: A Personal Exploration of Our National Character*. Toronto: McClelland and Stewart.

Bhabha, Homi. 1994. *The Location of Culture*. New York: Routledge.

Birchwater, Sage. 1991. *'Ulkatchot'en: The People of Ulkatcho*. Anahim Lake: Ulkatcho Indian Band.

–. 1993. *Ulkatcho Stories of the Grease Trail*. Anahim Lake: Ulkatcho Indian Band.

Bishop, Charles A. 1970. The Emergence of Hunting Territories among the Northern Ojibwa. *Ethnology* 9(1): 1-15.

Blomley, Nicholas. 1996. "Shut the Province Down": First Nations Blockades in British Columbia, 1984-1995. *BC Studies* 111: 5-35.

Bodnar, John. 1992. *Remaking America: Public Memory, Commemoration, and Patriotism in the Twentieth Century*. Princeton: Princeton University Press.

Bommes, Michael, and Patrick Wright. 1982. "Charms of Residence": The Public and the Past. In Richard Johnson et al., eds., *Making Histories: Studies in History-Writing and Politics*, 254-301. London: Hutchinson.

Bonner, Vera, Irene E. Bliss, and Hazel Henry Litterick. 1995. *Chilcotin: Preserving Pioneer Memories*. Surrey, BC: Heritage House.

Bowers, Vivien, and Stan Garrod. 1987. *Our Land: Building the West*. Toronto: Gage Educational Publishing.

Boyd, Laura. 1989. *My Home Forever*. Quesnel: Quesnel School District.

–. 1990a. *'Atsoo and I/Si'nk'ez 'Atsoo*. Quesnel: Quesnel School District.

–. 1990b. *For Someone Special*. Quesnel: Quesnel School District.

Boyd, Robert. 1994. Smallpox in the Pacific Northwest. *BC Studies* 101: 5-35.

–. 1996. Commentary on Early Contact-Era Smallpox in the Pacific Northwest. *Ethnohistory* 43(2): 307-28.

Braroe, Niels Winther. 1975. *Indian and White: Self-Image and Interaction in a Canadian Plains Community*. Stanford: Stanford University Press.

British Columbia Court of Appeal. 1993. *Delgamuukw* v. *Her Majesty the Queen*. Vancouver: Vancouver Registry.

British Columbia. 1987 (1875). *Papers Connected to the Indian Land Question, 1850-1875*. Victoria: Queen's Printer.

–. 1995. *BC First Nations Studies 12, Integrated Resource Package*. Victoria: Queen's Printer.

British Columbia Police Veteran's Association. 1991. *Off Patrol: Memories of B.C. Provincial Policemen*. Surrey, BC: Heritage House.

Broady, Maurice. 1975. The Drumbuie Inquiry: David and Goliath in Scottish Rural Development. *Community Development Journal* 10(2): 79-88.

Brody, Hugh. 1981. *Maps and Dreams*. New York: Pantheon.

–. 1991. *The People's Land: Inuit, Whites, and the Eastern Arctic*. Vancouver: Douglas and McIntyre.

Brown, Jennifer. 1980. *Strangers in Blood: Fur Trade Company Families in Indian Country*. Vancouver: UBC Press.

Brown, Michael. 1996. On Resisting Resistance. *American Anthropologist* 98(4): 729-35.

Burgess, Marilyn. 1992. "Dark Devils in the Saddle": A Discursive Analysis of Tourist and Entertainment Formations Constituting Western Canadian Regional Identity. PhD dissertation, Department of Communications, Concordia University, Montreal.

Cail, Robert E. 1974. *Land, Man, and the Law: The Disposal of Crown Lands in British Columbia, 1871-1913*. Vancouver: UBC Press.

Canada. 1882. Annual Report of the Department of Indian Affairs, 1881. Sessional Papers (No. 14), 44 Victoria, A.1881, Ottawa.

–. 1885. Annual Report of the Department of Indian Affairs, 1884. Sessional Papers (No. 3), 48 Victoria, A.1885, Ottawa.

–. 1888. Annual Report of the Department of Indian Affairs, 1887. Sessional Papers (No. 15), 51 Victoria, A.1888, Ottawa.

–. 1893. Annual Report of the Department of Indian Affairs, 1892. Sessional Papers (No. 14), 56 Victoria, A.1893, Ottawa.

–. 1913. Annual Report of the Department of Indian Affairs, 1911. Sessional Papers (No. 27), 3 George V, A.1913, Ottawa.

Cariboo Communities Coalition. 1995. *Making of the "Made in the Cariboo Solution": A Summary of the Proceedings Between the Cariboo Communities Coalition and the Government of British Columbia.* Williams Lake: Cariboo Communities Coalition.

*Cariboo Gold Rush.* 1987. Surrey, BC: Heritage House.

Carlson, Roy L. 1994. Trade and Exchange in Prehistoric British Columbia. In Timothy Baugh and Jonathon Ericson, eds., *Prehistoric Exchange Systems in North America,* 307-61. New York: Plenum.

Carrier, James. 1992. Occidentalism: The World Turned Upside-Down. *American Ethnologist* 19(2): 195-212.

Cassidy, Frank, ed. 1992. *Aboriginal Title in British Columbia:* Delgamuukw *v.* the Queen. Montreal: Institute for Research on Public Policy.

Childs, Peter, and Patrick Williams, eds. 1997. *An Introduction to Post-Colonial Theory.* Toronto: Prentice-Hall.

Clark, Cecil. 1986. *B.C. Provincial Police Stories: Mystery and Murder from the Files of Western Canada's First Lawmen.* Surrey, BC: Heritage House.

–. 1989. *B.C. Provincial Police Stories: More True Crime Cases from the Files of Western Canada's First Police Force.* Surrey, BC: Heritage House.

–. 1993. *B.C. Provincial Police Stories.* Surrey, BC: Heritage House.

Clifford, James. 1988. *The Predicament of Culture.* Cambridge: Harvard University Press.

Coffey, J., E. Goldstrom, G. Gottfriedson, R. Matthew, and P. Walton. 1990. *Shuswap History: The First 100 Years of Contact.* Kamloops: Secwepemc Cultural Education Society.

Cohen, David. 1994. *The Combing of History.* Chicago: University of Chicago Press.

Collier, Eric. 1991 (1959). *Three against the Wilderness.* Toronto: General Paperbacks.

Collins, Paul, and Norman Sheffe. 1979. *Exploration Canada.* Toronto: Oxford University Press.

Comaroff, Jean, and John Comaroff. 1991. *Of Revelation and Revolution: Christianity, Colonialism, and Consciousness in South Africa.* Chicago: University of Chicago Press.

Commission on Resources and the Environment. 1994. *Cariboo-Chilcotin Land Use Plan.* Victoria: Queen's Printer

Coombes, Annie. 1994. The Recalcitrant Object: Culture, Contact, and the Question of Hybridity. In Francis Barker, Peter Hulme, and Margaret Iversen, eds., *Colonial Discourse/Postcolonial Theory,* 89-114. Manchester: University of Manchester Press.

Cooper, John M. 1939. Is the Algonquian Family Hunting Ground System Pre-Columbian? *American Anthropologist* 41(1): 66-90.

Corrigan, Samuel W. 1970. The Plains Indian Powwow: Cultural Integration in Manitoba and Saskatchewan. *Anthropologica* 12: 253-77.

Cove, John. 1996. Playing the Devil's Advocate: Anthropology in Delgamuukw. *POLAR: Political and Legal Anthropology Review* 19(2): 53-8.

Crapanzano, Vincent. 1985. *Waiting: The Whites of South Africa.* New York: Random House.

Cross, Michael, ed. 1970. *The Frontier Thesis and the Canadas: The Debate on the Impact of the Environment.* Toronto: Copp Clark.

Cruikshank, Julie. 1992. Images of Society in Klondike Gold Rush Narratives: Skookum Jim and the Discovery of Gold. *Ethnohistory* 39(1): 20-39.

–. 1997. Negotiating with Narrative: Establishing Cultural Identity at the Yukon International Storytelling Festival. *American Anthropologist* 99(1): 56-69.

Cruikshank, Julie, with Angela Sidney, Kitty Smith, and Annie Ned. 1990. *Life Lived Like a Story: Life Stories of Three Yukon Elders*. Vancouver: UBC Press.

Culhane, Dara. 1998. *The Pleasure of the Crown: Anthropology, Law, and First Nations*. Vancouver: Talon Books.

Daly, Richard, and Antonia Mills. 1993. Ethics and Objectivity. *American Anthropology Newsletter* 34(8): 1.

Dawson, George M. 1891. Notes on the Shuswap Peoples of British Columbia. *Transactions of the Royal Society of Canada* (sec. 2): 3-44.

Deloria Jr., Vine. 1969. *Custer Died for Your Sins: An Indian Manifesto*. London: Collier-Macmillan.

Denny, Sir Cecil E. 1994. *March of the Mounties*. Surrey, BC: Heritage House.

Dinwoodie, David. 1996. Reserve Memories: Historical Consciousness on the Nemiah Valley Indian Reserve. PhD dissertation, Department of Anthropology, University of Chicago.

Dirks, Nicholas B. 1994. Ritual and Resistance: Subversion as a Social Fact. In Nicholas B. Dirks, Geoff Eley, and Sherry B. Ortner, eds., *Culture/Power/History*, 483-503. Princeton: Princeton University Press.

Dominy, Michelle. 1993. "Lives Were Always, Here": The Inhabited Landscape of the New Zealand High Country. *Anthropological Forum* 6(4): 567-85.

–. 1995. White Settler Assertions of Native Status. *American Ethnologist* 22(2): 358-74.

Dunk, Thomas W. 1991. *It's a Working Man's Town: Male Working-Class Culture in Northwestern Ontario*. Kingston: McGill-Queen's University Press.

Dyck, Noel. 1979. Powwow and the Expression of Community in Western Canada. *Ethnos* 44(1-2): 78-98.

–. 1983. Political Powwow: The Rise and Fall of an Urban Native Festival. In Frank Manning, ed., *The Celebration of Society: Perspectives on Contemporary Cultural Performance*, 165-84. Bowling Green University: Popular Press.

–. 1985. Aboriginal Peoples and the Nation-States: An Introduction to the Analytical Issues. In Noel Dyck, ed., *Indigenous Peoples and the Nation-State: Fourth World Politics in Canada, Australia, and Norway*, 1-26. St. John's: Institute of Social and Economic Research, Memorial University.

–. 1986. Negotiating the Indian "Problem." *Culture* 6(1): 31-41.

–. 1991. *What Is the Indian "Problem"? Tutelage and Resistance in Canadian Indian Administration*. St. John's: Institute of Social and Economic Research, Memorial University.

Eagles, Munroe, James P. Bickerton, Alain-G. Gagnon, and Patrick J. Smith. 1995. *The Almanac of Canadian Politics*. 2nd ed. Toronto: Oxford University Press.

Elias, Peter Douglas. 1975. *Metropolis and Hinterland in Northern Manitoba*. Winnipeg: Manitoba Museum of Man and Nature.

Elliott, Gordon R. 1978. *Barkerville, Quesnel, and the Cariboo Gold Rush*. Vancouver: Douglas and McIntyre.

Errington, Frederick. 1987. Reflexivity Deflected: The Festival of Nations as an American Cultural Performance. *American Ethnologist* 14(4): 654-67.

–. 1990. The Rock Creek Rodeo: Excess and Constraint in Men's Lives. *American Ethnologist* 17(4): 628-45.

Errington, Frederick, and Deborah Gewertz. From Darkness to Light in the George Brown Jubilee: The Invention of Nontradition and the Inscription of a National History in East New Britain. *American Ethnologist* 21(1): 104-22.

Fabian, Johannes. 1983. *Time and the Other: How Anthropology Makes Its Object*. New York: Columbia University Press.

Fanon, Frantz. 1963. *The Wretched of the Earth*. New York: Grove Press.

–. 1970. *Black Skin, White Masks*. St. Albans, Hertfordshire: Paladin.

Farber, Carole. 1983. High, Healthy, and Happy: Ontario Mythology on Parade. In Frank Manning, ed., *The Celebration of Society: Perspectives on Contemporary Cultural Performance*, 33-50. Bowling Green University: Popular Press.

Feit, Harvey. 1982. The Future of Hunters within Nation-States: Anthropology and the James Bay Cree. In Eleanor Leacock and Richard Lee, eds., *Politics and History in Band Societies*, 373-411. Cambridge: Cambridge University Press.

Fisher, Robin. 1992. *Contact and Conflict: Indian-European Relations in British Columbia, 1774-1890*. 2nd ed. Vancouver: UBC Press.

Fladmark, Knut. 1986. *British Columbia Prehistory.* Ottawa: National Museums of Canada.

Flieger, Jo Curtis, as told to J.G. Harcourt Huckle. 1991. *Dreams Come True for Cowboys, Too!* Tucson: Westernlore Press.

Fogelson, Raymond. 1984. Who Were the Ani-Kutani? An Excursion into Cherokee Historical Thought. *Ethnohistory* 31(4): 255-63.

–. 1989. The Ethnohistory of Events and Non-Events. *Ethnohistory* 36(2): 133-47.

Foucault, Michel. 1980. *Power-Knowledge: Selected Interviews and Other Writings, 1972-1977*. Colin Gordon, ed. and trans. New York: Pantheon.

Francis, Daniel. 1992. *The Imaginary Indian: The Image of the Indian in Canadian Culture.* Vancouver: Arsenal Pulp Press.

Furniss, Elizabeth. 1987. A Sobriety Movement among the Shuswap Indians of Alkali Lake. MA Thesis, Department of Anthropology and Sociology, University of British Columbia, Vancouver.

–. 1993a. *Dakelh Keyoh: The Southern Carrier in Earlier Times*. Quesnel: Quesnel School District.

–. 1993b. *Changing Ways: Southern Carrier History, 1793-1940*. Quesnel: Quesnel School District.

–. 1995a. Resistance, Coercion, and Revitalization: The Shuswap Encounter with Roman Catholic Missionaries, 1860-1900. *Ethnohistory* 42(2): 231-63.

–. 1995b. The Carrier Indians and the Politics of History. In R. Bruce Morrison and C. Roderick Wilson, eds., *Native Peoples: The Canadian Experience,* 508-46. 2nd ed. Toronto: McClelland and Stewart.

–. 1995c. *Victims of Benevolence: The Dark Legacy of the Williams Lake Residential School.* Vancouver: Arsenal Pulp Press.

–. 1996. Clans, Families, and Bands: Nineteenth- and Twentieth-Century Sociopolitical Organization in the Northern Plateau of North America. Paper presented to the American Society for Ethnohistory, 4-6 Nov., Portland.

– In press. Indians, Odysseys, and Vast Empty Lands: The Myth of the Frontier in the Canadian Justice System. *Anthropologica* 41(2).

Galois, R.M. 1996. Measles, 1847-1859: The First Modern Epidemic in British Columbia. *BC Studies* 109: 31-43.

Glavin, Terry. 1992. *Nemiah: The Unconquered Country.* Vancouver: New Star.

Gleadow, Norman. 1992. A Native Education Needs Assessment for School District No. 27 (Cariboo-Chilcotin). Manuscript.

Gold, Marc. 1986. Moral and Political Theories of Equality Rights Adjudication. In Joseph Weiler and Robin Elliot, eds., *Litigating the Values of a Nation: The Canadian Charter of Rights and Freedoms,* 85-104. Toronto: Carswell.

Goldie, Terry. 1989. *Fear and Temptation: The Image of the Indigene in Canadian, Australian, and New Zealand Literatures.* Montreal: McGill-Queen's University Press.

Goldman, Irving. 1940. The Algatcho Carrier of British Columbia. In Ralph Linton, ed., *Acculturation in Seven American Indian Tribes,* 333-86. New York: D. Appleton-Century.

–. 1953. The Algatcho Carrier of British Columbia. Manuscript. Royal British Columbia Museum, Victoria.

Graham, Bill, and Joyce Graham. 1991. Those Cariboo Stampedes! In Art Downs, ed., *Pioneer Days in British Columbia, Volume 1,* 24-27. Surrey, BC: Heritage House.

Grand Council of the Crees. 1995. *Sovereign Injustice: Forcible Inclusion of the James Bay Crees and Cree Territory into a Sovereign Quebec.* Nemaska, PQ: Grand Council of the Crees.

Gray, James. 1985. *A Brand of Its Own: The 100 Year History of the Calgary Exhibition and Stampede.* Saskatoon: Western Producer Prairie Books.

Green, Rayna D. 1975. The Pocahontas Perplex: The Image of the Indian Woman in American Culture. *Massachusetts Review* 16: 698-714.

–. 1988. The Tribe Called Wannabee: Playing Indian in America and Europe. *Folklore* 99(1): 30-55.

Griffiths, Tom. 1996. *Hunters and Collectors: The Antiquarian Imagination in Australia.* Cambridge: Cambridge University Press.

Grimes, Ronald. 1976. *Symbol and Conquest: Public Ritual and Drama in Santa Fe, New Mexico.* Ithaca: Cornell University Press.

Grossman, Daniel. 1965. The Nature of Descent Groups of Some Tribes in the Interior of Northwestern North America. *Anthropologica,* n.s., 7: 249-62.

Hale, Linda L., and Jean Barman. 1991. *British Columbia Local Histories: A Bibliography.* Victoria: Heritage Trust.

Hall, John L. 1980. Ethnic Tensions and Economics: Indian-White Interaction in a British Columbia Ranching Community. *Canadian Journal of Anthropology* 1: 179-90.

Hamilton, A.C., and C.M. Sinclair, Commissioners. 1991a. *Report of the Aboriginal Justice Inquiry of Manitoba, Volume 1: The Justice System and Aboriginal People.* Winnipeg.

–. 1991b. *Report of the Aboriginal Justice Inquiry of Manitoba, Volume 2: The Deaths of Helen Betty Osborne and John Joseph Harper.* Winnipeg.

Hanks, William F. 1986. Authenticity and Ambivalence in the Text: A Colonial Maya Case. *American Ethnologist* 13(4): 721-44.

Harrington, Robert F. 1967. Eulachon and the Grease Trails of British Columbia. *Canadian Geographic Journal,* Jan. 1967: 28-31.

Harris, Cole. 1994. Voices of Disaster: Smallpox around the Strait of Georgia in 1782. *Ethnohistory* 41(4): 591-626.

–. 1997. *The Resettlement of British Columbia: Essays on Colonialism and Geographical Change.* Vancouver: UBC Press.

Hawthorn, H.B. 1966. *A Survey of the Contemporary Indians of Canada, Volume 1.* Ottawa: Indian Affairs Branch.

Hawthorn, H.B., C.S. Belshaw, and S.M. Jamieson. 1960. *The Indians of British Columbia: A Study of Contemporary Social Adjustment.* Toronto: University of Toronto Press.

Henry, Francis, and Carol Tator. 1994. The Ideology of Racism – "Democratic Racism." *Canadian Ethnic Studies* 26(2): 1-14.

Hickman, Chief Justice T. Alexander, Associate Chief Justice Lawrence A. Poitras, and the Honorable Mr. Gregory T. Evans, Commissioners. 1989. *Royal Commission on the Donald Marshall Jr. Prosecution.* Nova Scotia: Province of Nova Scotia.

Hinsley, Curtis M. 1991. The World as Marketplace: Commodification of the Exotic at the World's Columbian Exposition, Chicago, 1893. In Ivan Karp and Steven Lavine, eds., *Exhibiting Cultures: The Poetics and Politics of Museum Display,* 344-65. Washington, DC: Smithsonian.

Hobsbawm, Eric, and Terence Ranger, eds. 1983. *The Invention of Tradition.* Cambridge: Cambridge University Press.

Hobson Jr., Richmond P. 1993 (1951). *Grass beyond the Mountains.* Toronto: McClelland and Stewart.

Holland, Dorothy C., and Debra G. Skinner. 1995. Contested Ritual, Contested Femininities: (Re)Forming Self and Society in a Nepali Women's Festival. *American Ethnologist* 22(2): 279-305.

Howard, James H. 1955. Pan-Indian Culture of Oklahoma. *Scientific Monthly* 81: 215-20.

–. 1976. The Plains Gourd Dance as a Revitalization Movement. *American Ethnologist* 3(2): 243-59.

Hudson, Michael. 1987. Multiculturalism, Government Policy, and Constitutional Enshrinement: A Comparative Study. In Canadian Human Rights Foundation, ed., *Multiculturalism and the Charter: A Legal Perspective,* 59-122. Vancouver: Carswell.

Innis, Harold. 1962. *The Fur Trade in Canada.* Rev. ed. Toronto: University of Toronto Press.

Jenness, Diamond. 1943. *The Carrier Indians of the Bulkley River: Their Social and Religious Life.* Washington, DC: Smithsonian.

Kaplan, Martha, and John D. Kelly. 1994. Rethinking Resistance: Dialogics of "Disaffection" in Colonial Fiji. *American Ethnologist* 21(1): 123-51.

Karp, Ivan, Christine Mullen Kreamer, and Steven D. Lavine. 1992. *Museums and Communities: The Politics of Public Culture.* Washington, DC: Smithsonian.

Karp, Ivan, and Steven D. Lavine. 1990. *Exhibiting Cultures: The Poetics and Politics of Museum Display*. Washington, DC: Smithsonian.

Kennedy, John. 1997. Labrador Métis Ethnogenesis. *Ethnos* 3-4: 5-23.

Kew, J.E. Michael. 1974. Nazko and Kluskus: Social Conditions and Prospects for the Future. In *Report on the Nazko and Kluskus Bands from the Nazko Kluskus Study Team*. Special Collections Division, Main Library, University of British Columbia, Vancouver.

Kohl, Seena B. 1990. Writing Popular History: Contrasting Approaches from Rural Mississippi and Rural Canada. In Benita J. Howell, ed., *Cultural Heritage Conservation in the American South,* 42-53. Athens: University of Georgia Press.

Kracht, Benjamin R. 1994. Kiowa Powwows: Continuity in Ritual Practice. *American Indian Quarterly* 18(3): 321-48.

Kymlicka, Will. 1995. *Multicultural Citizenship: A Liberal Theory of Minority Rights*. Oxford: Oxford University Press.

Landsman, Gail. 1987. Indian Activism and the Press: Coverage of the Conflict at Ganienkeh. *Anthropological Quarterly* 60(3): 101-13.

Lane, Robert B. 1981. Chilcotin. In June Helm, ed., *Handbook of North American Indians, Volume 6: The Subarctic,* 402-12. Washington, DC: Smithsonian.

Lavenda, Robert H. 1983. Family and Corporation: Celebration in Central Minnesota. In Frank Manning, ed., *The Celebration of Society: Perspectives on Contemporary Cultural Performance,* 51-64. Bowling Green University: Popular Press.

–. 1988. Minnesota Queen Pageants: Play, Fun, and Dead Seriousness. *Journal of American Folklore* 101(400): 168-75.

–. 1992. Festivals and the Creation of Public Culture: Whose Voice(s)? In Ivan Karp, Christine Mullen Kreamer, and Steven D. Lavine, eds., *Museums and Communities: The Politics of Public Culture,* 76-104. Washinton: Smithsonian.

Lavington, H. Dude. 1982. *The Nine Lives of a Cowboy*. Victoria: Sono Nis Press.

Lawrence, Denise L. 1987. Rules of Misuse: Notes on the Doo Dah Parade in Pasadena. In Alessandro Falassi, ed., *Time out of Time: Essays on the Festival,* 123-36. Albuquerque: University of New Mexico Press.

Lawrence, Elizabeth Atwood. 1982. *Rodeo: An Anthropologist Looks at the Wild and the Tame*. Knoxville: University of Tennessee Press.

Leacock, Eleanor. 1954. *The Montagnais "Hunting Territory" and the Fur Trade*. Memoirs of the American Anthropological Association, no. 78. Menasha, WI.

LeCompte, Mary Lou. 1985. Wild West Frontier Days, Roundups, and Stampedes: Rodeo before There Was Rodeo. *Canadian Journal of History of Sport* 16(2): 54-67.

–. 1993. *Cowgirls of the Rodeo: Pioneer Professional Athletes*. Chicago: University of Illinois Press.

Lerch, Patricia B. 1992. Pageantry, Parade, and Indian Dancing: The Staging of Identity among the Waccamaw Sioux. *Museum Anthropology* 16(2): 27-34.

Limerick, Patricia. 1987. *The Legacy of Conquest: The Unbroken Past of the American West*. New York: Norton.

Lithman, Yngve Georg. 1984. *The Community Apart: A Case Study of a Canadian Indian Reserve Community*. Winnipeg: University of Manitoba Press.

Loo, Tina. 1994. *Making Law, Order, and Authority in British Columbia, 1821-1871*. Toronto: University of Toronto Press.

Lurie, Nancy. 1971. The World's Oldest On-Going Protest Demonstration: North American Indian Drinking Patterns. *Pacific Historical Review* 40: 311-32.

Mack, Clayton. 1994. *Bella Coola Man*. Madeira Park, BC: Harbour.

–. 1993. *Grizzlies and White Guys*. Madeira Park, BC: Harbour.

Mackenzie, Alexander. 1970. *The Journals and Letters of Sir Alexander Mackenzie*. W. Kaye Lamb, ed. Hakluyt Society, Extra Series 41. Cambridge: Cambridge University Press.

Macklem, Patrick. 1993. Ethnonationalism, Aboriginal Identities, and the Law. In Michael D. Levin, ed., *Ethnicity and Aboriginality: Case Studies in Ethnonationalism,* 9-28. Toronto: University of Toronto Press.

Manning, Frank. 1983. Cosmos and Chaos: Celebration in the Modern World. In Frank Manning, ed., *The Celebration of Society: Perspectives on Contemporary Cultural Performance,* 3-30. Bowling Green University: Popular Press.

Marchak, M. Patricia. 1983. *Green Gold: The Forest Industry in British Columbia.* Vancouver: UBC Press.
–. 1988. *Ideological Perspectives on Canada.* 3rd ed. Toronto: McGraw-Hill Ryerson.
Marcus, George E., and Michael J. Fisher. 1986. *Anthropology as Cultural Critique.* Chicago: University of Chicago Press.
Marriott, Harry. 1966. *Cariboo Cowboy.* Sidney, BC: Gray's Publishing.
Mazurek, Kas. 1987. Multiculturalism, Education, and the Ideology of Meritocracy. In Terry Wotherspoon, ed., *The Political Economy of Canadian Schooling,* 141-63. Agincourt, ON: Methuen.
McClintock, Anne. 1994. The Angel of Progress: Pitfalls of the Term "Post-colonialism." In Patrick Williams and Laura Chrisman, eds., *Colonial Discourse and Post-Colonial Theory: A Reader,* 276-90. New York: Columbia University Press.
McEachern, Chief Justice Allan. 1991. Reasons for Judgment, *Delgamuukw* v. *A.G.* Vancouver: Vancouver Court Registry.
McGillivray, Joseph. 1947. Report of Fort Alexandria Western Caledonia Columbia River District Outfit 1827. In E.E. Rich, ed., *Part of a Dispatch from George Simpson, Esquire, Governor of Ruperts Land, to the Governor and Committee of the Hudson's Bay Company,* 188-221. Toronto: Champlain Society.
McKelvie, B.A. 1985. *Tales of Conflict: Indian-White Murders and Massacres in Pioneer British Columbia.* Surrey, BC: Heritage House.
McLean, Stuart. 1992. *Welcome Home: Travels in Smalltown Canada.* Toronto: Viking.
Memmi, Albert. 1965. *Colonizer and Colonized.* New York: Orion Press.
Menzies, Charles. 1994. Stories from Home: First Nations, Land Claims, and Euro-Canadians. *American Ethnologist* 21(4): 776-91.
Merlan, Francesca. 1995. The Regimentation of Customary Practice: From Northern Territory Land Claims to Mabo. *Australian Journal of Anthropology* 60(1,2): 64-82.
Miller, Bruce, ed. 1992. *Anthropology and History in the Courts.* Special issue of *BC Studies* 95.
Miles, Robert. 1989. *Racism.* London: Routledge.
Mills, Antonia. 1994. *Eagle Down Is Our Law: Witsuwit'en Law, Feasts, and Land Claims.* Vancouver: UBC Press.
–. 1994-5. Cultural Contrasts: The British Columbia Court's Evaluation of the Gitksan-Wet'suwet'en and Their Own Sense of Self and Self-Worth as Revealed in Cases of Reported Reincarnation. *BC Studies* 104: 149-72.
–. 1996. Problems on Establishing Authority in Testifying on Behalf of the Witsuwit'en. *POLAR: Political and Legal Anthropology Review* 19(2): 39-51.
Mishra, Vijay, and Bob Hodge. 1994. What Is Post(-)colonialism? In P. Williams and L. Chrisman, eds., *Colonial Discourse and Post-Colonial Theory: A Reader,* 276-90. New York: Columbia University Press.
Montrose, Louise. 1991. The Work of Gender in the Discourse of Discovery. *Representations* 33: 1-41.
Morice, Adrian G. 1978. *The History of the Northern Interior of British Columbia.* Smithers: Interior Stationery.
Murphy, James. 1894. A Modern Indian Chief. *Missionary Record of the Oblates of Mary Immaculate* 4: 312-19.
Murphy, Robert, and Julian Steward. 1956. Tappers and Trappers: Parallel Processes in Acculturation. *Economic Development and Cultural Change* 4: 393-408.
Myers, Fred R. 1994. Culture-Making: Performing Aboriginality at the Asia Society Gallery. *American Ethnologist* 21(4): 679-99.
Nadel, Jane Hurwitz. 1983. Houston's Little Sisters: A Cross-Cultural Perspective on Off-shore Oil. *Human Organization* 42(2): 167-72.
Nadel-Klein, Jane. 1991. Reweaving the Fringe: Localism, Tradition, and Representation in British Ethnography. *American Ethnologist* 18(3): 500-17.
–. 1995. Occidentalism as a Cottage Industry: Representing the Autochthonous "Other" in British and Irish Rural Studies. In James Carrier, ed., *Occidentalism: Images of the West,* 109-34. Oxford: Clarendon.

Neering, Rosemary. 1991. *Down the Road: Journeys to Small-Town British Columbia*. Vancouver: Whitecap.

Ortner, Sherry B. 1995. Resistance and the Problem of Ethnographic Refusal. *Comparative Studies in Society and History* 37(1): 173-93.

*Outlaws and Lawmen of Western Canada*. 1983. Vols. 1 and 2. Surrey, BC: Heritage House.

*Outlaws and Lawmen of Western Canada*. 1987. Vol. 3. Surrey, BC: Heritage House.

Paine, Robert. 1977a. The Path to Welfare Colonialism. In Robert Paine, ed., *The White Arctic: Anthropological Essays in Tutelage and Ethnicity*, 7-28. St. John's: Institute of Social and Economic Research, Memorial University.

–, ed. 1977b. *The White Arctic: Anthropological Essays in Tutelage and Ethnicity*. St. John's: Institute of Social and Economic Research, Memorial University.

–. 1985. Ethnodrama and the "Fourth World": The Saami Action Group in Norway, 1979-1981. In Noel Dyck, ed., *Indigenous Peoples and the Nation-State: Fourth World Politics in Canada, Australia, and Norway*, 190-235. St. John's: Institute of Social and Economic Research, Memorial University.

–. 1996. In Chief Justice McEachern's Shoes: Anthropology's Ineffectiveness in Court. *POLAR: Political and Legal Anthropology Review* 19(2): 59-70.

Palmer, Andie Diane. 1994. Maps of Experience: Shuswap Narratives of Place. PhD diss., Department of Anthropology, University of Washington, Seattle.

Parry, Benita. 1994. Resistance Theory/Theorizing Resistance; or, Two Cheers for Nativism. In Francis Barker, Peter Hulme, and Margaret Iversen, eds., *Colonial Discourse/Postcolonial Theory*, 172-96. Manchester: University of Manchester Press.

Peterson, Nicholas, and Will Sanders, eds. 1998. *Citizenship and Indigenous Australians: Changing Conceptions and Possibilities*. Cambridge: Cambridge University Press.

Pettipas, Katherine. 1994. *Severing the Ties That Bind: Government Repression of Indigenous Religious Ceremonies on the Prairies*. Winnipeg: University of Manitoba Press.

Plaice, Evelyn. 1990. *The Native Game*. St. John's: Institute of Social and Economic Research, Memorial University.

Powers, William K. 1988. The Indian Hobbyist Movement in North America. In Wilcomb E. Washburn, ed., *Handbook of North American Indians, Volume 4: History of Indian-White Relations*, 557-61. Washington, DC: Smithsonian.

Pritchard, Allan. 1992. The Shapes of History in British Columbia Writing. *BC Studies* 93: 48-69.

Prucha, Francis Paul. 1986. *The Great Father: The United States Government and the American Indians*. Abr. ed. Lincoln: University of Nebraska Press.

Read, Peter. 1996. *Returning to Nothing: The Meaning of Lost Places*. Cambridge: Cambridge University Press.

Regular, Keith. 1986. On Public Display. *Alberta History* 34(1): 1-10.

Richards, Thomas H., and Michael Rousseau. 1987. *Late Prehistoric Cultural Horizons on the Canadian Plateau*. Department of Archaeology, Simon Fraser University, Publication 16. Burnaby: Simon Fraser University.

Ridington, Robin. 1978. *Swan People: A Study of the Dunne-za Prophet Dance*. Ottawa: National Museums of Canada.

Robinson, Harry, and Wendy Wickwire. 1989. *Write It on Your Heart: The Epic World of an Okanagan Storyteller*. Penticton, BC: Theytus Books.

–. 1992. *Nature Power: In the Spirit of an Okanagan Storyteller*. Wendy Wickwire, comp. and ed. Vancouver: Douglas and McIntyre.

Rogers, Edward S. 1963. *The Hunting Group-Hunting Territory Complex among the Mistassini Indians*. Anthropological Series 63, National Museum of Canada Bulletin 195. Ottawa: National Museums of Canada.

Rosaldo, Renato. 1989. *Culture and Truth: The Remaking of Social Analysis*. Boston: Beacon Press.

Roseberry, William. 1991. *Anthropologies and Histories*. New Brunswick, NJ: Rutgers University Press.

Rothenberger, Mel. 1978. *The Chilcotin War*. Langley, BC: Mr. Paperback.

Rousseau, Mike. 1993. Early Prehistoric Occupation of South-Central British Columbia: A Review of Evidence and Recommendations for Future Research. *BC Studies* 99: 140-83.

Russell, Don. 1970. *The Wild West: or, A history of the Wild West shows, being an account of the prestigious, peregrinatory pageants pretentiously presented before the citizens of the Republic, the crowned heads of Europe, and multitudes of awe-struck men, women, and children around the globe, which created a wonderfully imaginative and unrealistic image of the American West.* Fort Worth: Amon Carter Museum of Western Art.
Ryan, Allan J. 1992. Postmodern Parody: A Political Strategy in Contemporary Canadian Native Art. *Art Journal* 51(3): 59-65.
Said, Edward. 1978. *Orientalism.* New York: Pantheon.
–. 1994. *Culture and Imperialism.* New York: Vintage.
Sanders, Douglas. 1987. Article 27 and the Aboriginal Peoples of Canada. In Canadian Human Rights Federation, ed., *Multiculturalism and the Charter: A Legal Perspective,* 155-66. Vancouver: Carswell.
Sarich, Commissioner Anthony. 1993. *Report on the Cariboo-Chilcotin Justice Inquiry.* Victoria: Queen's Printer.
Savage and Associates. 1993. *Cariboo Forest Sector Employment Trends Project.* Victoria: Ministry of Economic Development, Small Business and Trade.
Schutz, Alfred. 1971. *Collected Papers, Volume 1: The Problem of Social Reality.* Maurice Natanson, ed. The Hague: Martinus Nijhoff.
Schwimmer, Erik G. 1972. Symbolic Competition. *Anthropologica,* n.s., 14(2): 117-55.
Scott, James. 1985. *Weapons of the Weak: Everyday Forms of Peasant Resistance.* New Haven: Yale University Press.
–. 1990. *Domination and the Arts of Resistance: Hidden Transcripts.* New Haven: Yale University Press.
Sharp, Andrew. 1990. *Justice and the Maori: Maori Claims in New Zealand Political Argument in the 1980s.* New York: Oxford University Press.
Sider, Gerald. 1987. When Parrots Learn to Talk, and Why They Can't: Domination, Deception, and Self-Deception in Indian-White Relations. *Comparative Studies in Society and History* 29(1): 3-23.
Skelton, Robin. 1980. *They Call It the Cariboo.* Victoria: Sono Nis Press.
Slatta, Richard W. 1990. *Cowboys of the Americas.* New Haven: Yale University Press.
Sloan, Gordon McG. 1957. *Report of the Commissioner, Gordon McG. Sloan, Relating to the Forest Resources of British Columbia, 1956.* Victoria.
Slotkin, Richard. 1973. *Regeneration through Violence: The Mythology of the American Frontier, 1600-1860.* Middletown, CT: Wesleyan University Press.
–. 1986. *The Fatal Environment: The Myth of the Frontier in the Age of Industrialization.* New York: Atheneum.
–. 1992. *Gunfighter Nation: The Myth of the Frontier in Twentieth-Century America.* New York: Atheneum.
Smith, Allan. 1980. The Writing of British Columbia History. *BC Studies* 45: 73-102.
Smith, Melvin H. 1995. *Our Home or Native Land?* Victoria: Crown Publishers.
Smith, Sheldon. 1984. The Re-establishment of Community: The Emerging Festival System of the American West. *Journal of American Culture* 7: 91-100.
Speare, Jean E., ed. 1973. *The Days of Augusta.* Vancouver: J.J. Douglas.
Speck, Dara Culhane. 1987. *An Error in Judgement: The Politics of Medical Care in an Indian/White Community.* Vancouver: Talon.
Speck, Frank. 1915. The Family Hunting Band as the Basis of Algonkian Social Organization. *American Anthropologist* 2: 289-305.
–. 1927. Family Hunting Territories of the Lake St. John Montagnais and Neighboring Bands. *Anthropos* 22: 387-403.
Spivak, Gayatri Chakravorty. 1990. *The Post-Colonial Critic: Interviews, Strategies, and Dialogues.* Sara Harasym, ed. London: Routledge.
St. Pierre, Paul. 1984. *Breaking Smith's Quarter Horse.* Vancouver: Douglas and McIntyre.
–. 1985. *Smith and Other Events.* Vancouver: Douglas and McIntyre.
Stangoe, Irene. 1994. *Cariboo-Chilcotin: Pioneer People and Places.* Surrey, BC: Heritage House.
Statistics Canada. 1994. Profile of Census Divisions and Subdivisions in British Columbia

– Part B. *Census of Canada,* Catalogue 95-385. Ottawa: Industry, Science and Technology Canada.

Steward, Julian. 1960. Carrier Acculturation: A Direct Historical Approach. In Stanley Diamond, ed., *Culture in History: Essays in Honor of Paul Radin,* 732-44. New York: Columbia University Press.

Stoeltje, Beverly. 1981. Cowboys and Clowns: Rodeo Specialists and the Ideology of Work and Play. In Richard Bauman and Roger Abrahams, eds., *"And Other Neighborly Names": Social Process and Cultural Image in Texas Folklore,* 123-51. Austin: University of Texas Press.

–. 1988. Gender Representations in Performance: The Cowgirl and the Hostess. *Journal of Folklore Research* 25: 219-41.

Stolcke, Verena. 1995. Talking Culture: New Boundaries, New Rhetorics of Exclusion in Europe. *Current Anthropology* 36(1): 1-13.

Stymeist, David H. 1975. *Ethnics and Indians: Social Relations in a Northwestern Ontario Town.* Toronto: Peter Martin.

Supreme Court of Canada. 1997. Reasons for Judgement, *Delgamuukw* v. *British Columbia.* File 23799. Ottawa.

Tanner, Adrian. 1993. History and Culture in the Generation of Ethnic Nationalism. In Michael D. Levin, ed., *Ethnicity and Aboriginality,* 75-96. Toronto: University of Toronto Press.

Tatla Lake School Heritage Project. 1986-93. *Hoofprints in History.* 7 vols. Tatla Lake: Tatla Lake Elementary Junior Secondary School.

Teit, James. 1975 (1909). *The Shuswap.* The Jesup North Pacific Expedition, Volume 2, Part 7. New York: Academic Press.

Tennant, Paul. 1990. *Aboriginal Peoples and Politics: The Indian Land Question in British Columbia, 1849-1989.* Vancouver: UBC Press.

–. 1992. The Place of *Delgamuukw* in British Columbia History and Politics – and Vice Versa. In Frank Cassidy, ed., *Aboriginal Title in British Columbia:* Delgamuukw *v.* The Queen, 73-91. Montreal: Institute for Research on Public Policy.

Thomas, Nicholas. 1994. *Colonialism's Culture: Anthropology, Travel, and Government.* Princeton: Princeton University Press.

Thomson, Duane. 1990. Cayuses and Shorthorns: The Ranching Industry in the Southern Interior of British Columbia in the Nineteenth Century. Paper presented to the BC Studies Conference. Special Collections Division, Main Library, University of British Columbia, Vancouver.

Tobey, Margaret. 1981. The Carrier. In June Helm, ed., *Handbook of North American Indians, Volume 6: The Subarctic,* 413-32. Washington, DC: Smithsonian.

Tobias, John. 1983. Protection, Civilization, Assimilation: An Outline History of Canada's Indian Policy. In Ian Getty and Antoine Lussier, eds., *As Long as the Sun Shines and Water Flows: A Reader in Canadian Native Studies,* 39-55. Vancouver: UBC Press.

Trigger, Bruce G. 1985. *Natives and Newcomers: Canada's Heroic Age Reconsidered.* Montreal: McGill-Queen's University Press.

–. 1986. The Historian's Indian: Native Americans in Historical Writing from Charlevoix to the Present. *Canadian Historical Review* 67(3): 315-42.

Turner, Frederick Jackson. 1963 (1893). *The Significance of the Frontier in American History.* Harold P. Simonson, ed. New York: Frederick Ungar.

Valentine, Lisa Philips. 1997. Constructing a Public Enemy: The Reconstruction of First Nations Claims by Cottagers. Paper presented to the annual meeting of the American Anthropological Association, Washington, DC.

van Kirk, Sylvia. 1992. A Vital Presence: Women in the Cariboo Gold Rush, 1862-1875. In Gillian Creese and Veronica Strong-Boag, eds., *British Columbia Reconsidered: Essays on Women,* 21-37. Vancouver: UBC Press.

Vibert, Elizabeth. 1995. "The Natives Were Strong to Live": Reinterpreting Early Nineteenth-Century Prophetic Movements in the Columbia Plateau. *Ethnohistory* 42(2): 197-229.

Vidich, Arthur J. 1990. American Democracy in the Late Twentieth Century: Political Rhetorics and Mass Media. *International Journal of Politics, Culture, and Society* 4(1): 5-29.

Vidich, Arthur J., and Joseph Bensman. 1968. *Small Town in Mass Society.* Princeton: Princeton University Press.

Waldram, James B., Pat Berringer, and Wayne Warry. 1992. "Nasty, Brutish, and Short": Anthropology and the Gitksan-Wet'suwet'en Decision. *Canadian Journal of Native Studies* 12(2): 310-16.

Walker, James W. 1971. The Indian in Canadian Historical Writing. *Historical Papers/Communications Historiques* (1971): 21-47.

–. 1983. The Indian in Canadian Historical Writing, 1972-1982. In Ian Getty and Antoine Lussier, eds., *As Long as the Sun Shines and Water Flows: A Reader in Canadian Native Studies,* 340-57. Vancouver: UBC Press.

Warner, W. Lloyd. 1959. *The Living and the Dead: A Study of the Symbolic Life of the Americans.* Yankee City Series 5. New Haven: Yale University Press.

Watkins, Barbara. 1990. Marginalization and Self-Sufficiency: The Lives of Women in Williams Lake, British Columbia. MA thesis, Vermont College, Norwich University.

Weaver, Sally. 1984. Struggles of the Nation-State to Define Aboriginal Ethnicity: Canada and Australia. In Gerald L. Gold, ed., *Minorities and Mother Country Imagery,* 182-210. St. John's: Institute of Social and Economic Research, Memorial University.

Weber, Max. 1958. *The Protestant Ethic and the Spirit of Capitalism.* New York: Charles Scribner's Sons.

Weiler, Joseph, and Robin Elliot, eds. 1986. *Litigating the Values of a Nation: The Canadian Charter of Rights and Freedoms.* Toronto: Carswell.

Weir, Thomas R. 1964. *Ranching in the Southern Interior Plateau of British Columbia.* Memoir 4, Geographical Branch, Mines and Technical Surveys. Ottawa: Queen's Printer.

Whyte, Jon. 1985. *Indians in the Rockies.* Banff: Altitude Publishing.

Williams, Patrick, and Laura Chrisman. 1994a. Colonial Discourse and Post-Colonial Theory: An Introduction. In P. Williams and L. Chrisman, eds., *Colonial Discourse and Post-Colonial Theory: A Reader,* 1-20. New York: Columbia University Press.

–, eds. 1994b. *Colonial Discourse and Post-Colonial Theory: A Reader.* New York: Columbia University Press.

Williams, Raymond. 1973. The Country and the City. London: Chatto and Windus.

–. 1977. *Marxism and Literature.* Oxford: Oxford University Press.

–. 1980. *Problems in Materialism and Culture: Selected Essays.* London: Verso.

Wolfe, Patrick. 1991. On Being Woken Up: The Dreamtime in Anthropology and in Australian Settler Culture. *Comparative Studies in Society and History* 33(2): 197-224.

# Index

Set in Stone by Brenda and Neil West, BN Typographics West

Printed and bound in Canada by Friesens

Copy editor: Dallas Harrison

Proofreader: Joanne Richardson

Cartographer: Eric Leinberger

**Visit the UBC Press Web site at**

**www.ubcpress.ubc.ca**

**for information and detailed descriptions of other UBC Press books**

**Ask for UBC Press books in your bookstore or contact us at**

Toll-free fax: 1-800-668-0821
Toll-free number: 1-UPRESS-WEST
E-mail: info@ubcpress.ubc.ca

## The Resettlement of British Columbia

### Essays on Colonialism and Geographical Change

Cole Harris

An engaging, provocative introduction to the early history of the province ... Full of wonderful insights and candid observations, it offers a nuanced look at the history of Canada's Pacific province.
*Western Historical Quarterly*

Students interested in methodological approach and theory will be fascinated by Harris's approach ... rich visual presentation, and the profound insights in this beautifully crafted collection of essays.
*Canadian Historical Review*

## Beyond the City Limits

### Rural History in British Columbia

R.W. Sandwell

This book expands our understanding of what "rural" was and what it meant in the history of British Columbia. R.W. Sandwell draws together a distinguished group of contributors who bring expertise, methodologies, and theoretical perspectives taken from social and political history, environmental studies, cultural geography, and anthropology. Their wide-ranging and provocative essays challenge the dominant urban-based and overwhelmingly capitalist interpretation of the province's history.